PRAISE FOR *A SELFISH PLAN TO CHANGE THE WORLD*

"Dillon channels the heart-cry of a generation who want to live lives of meaning and hope, but don't know how. With an artist's craft, he draws the reader in through stories of everyday people who have found a way to live their soul dream. He invites us to consider how in giving we will gain, and to join a global tribe of doers, not talkers."

—JACQUELLINE FULLER, PRESIDENT OF GOOGLE.ORG
AND GOOGLE FOUNDATION

"We children of the '70s know nothing is more punk rock than standing up for the disenfranchised. The seeds of rebellion are planted in a search for meaning. What drives the chords and the snare beats is a desire to matter. Dillion illustrates through his vivid storytelling how so many have discovered their inner punk rocker in working for change, and provides a guide for all generations to look inside . . . and find a riot of our own."

—KELLY FLYNN, CREATOR AND EXECUTIVE PRODUCER OF CNN HEROES

"Energizing. Infecting. Exciting. We're all made for something bigger than ourselves. But, over time, comparison and comfort dull our dreams of leaving the world better than what we're born into. With the voice of a poet and seasoned sage, Justin Dillon reminds us that world change isn't just for the experts or the experienced; it's born from ordinary people whose gifts and passions collide with injustice and combust into unstoppable action. *A Selfish Plan to Change the World* is a helpful road map to a rising generation of change-makers."

—LOUIE GIGLIO, PASTOR OF PASSION CITY CHURCH
AND AUTHOR OF *GOLIATH MUST FALL*

"Having a desire to be part of solutions that heal this broken world is essential, but insufficient. We need wisdom and guidance. Justin offers both, weaving helpful perspective and brilliant insight inside of story. If you want to help change the world, this book is a great place to start."

—WM. PAUL YOUNG, *NEW YORK TIMES*
BESTSELLING AUTHOR OF *THE SHACK*

"How does the denizen of a very small world (a little slice of the California music scene) *decide* to, and then, *change* the whole big world? Justin Dillon explains how this happens, but not because he is some sort of special hero. If anything, Justin is exemplary in his ordinariness. Like Everyman, like the Pilgrim who made Progress, he confronted hard truths about the world and himself, and came out the same but very different. *A Selfish Plan to Change the World* is more than his path, it's what we *all* have to decide about who we are and what we're going to do with our lives. No preaching, no ego, no whining, no knocking you over the head with guilt or sadness, just an inspiring and clear path to a life of meaning—for all of us. And Justin, he's just a guy . . . but what a guy!"

—KEVIN BALES, COFOUNDER OF FREE THE SLAVES

"Writing from the front lines of activism, Justin Dillon challenges and inspires us to each fight for change. His dream is for a generation to find their riot and change the world."

—LUIS CDEBACA, AMBASSADOR AT LARGE TO MONITOR AND COMBAT TRAFFICKING IN PERSONS (OBAMA ADMINISTRATION)

"Justin is proof that anybody can change the world. I would read this even if I wasn't Justin's friend."

—LEIF COORLIM, EXECUTIVE EDITOR AT CNN INTERNATIONAL

"If you ever felt that your planned path lacked meaning, Justin shows you how to follow your purpose, explore an uncharted path, and live your dream while doing good for others. Powerful."

—ALEX ATZBERGER, PRESIDENT OF SAP ARIBA

"Justin's extraordinary book and work represent a new way to look at things. He offers to all of us the opportunity to effectively make changes and live with purpose."

—FEDERICA MARCHIONNI, EXECUTIVE BUSINESS LEADER

A SELFISH PLAN TO CHANGE THE WORLD

A SELFISH PLAN TO CHANGE THE WORLD

FINDING BIG PURPOSE IN BIG PROBLEMS

JUSTIN DILLON

NELSON
BOOKS

An Imprint of Thomas Nelson

Published in Nashville, Tennessee, by Nelson Books, an imprint of Thomas Nelson. Nelson Books and Thomas Nelson are registered trademarks of HarperCollins Christian Publishing, Inc.

Published in association with Foundry Literary and Media, www.foundrymedia.com.

Thomas Nelson titles may be purchased in bulk for educational, business, fund-raising, or sales promotional use. For information, please e-mail SpecialMarkets@ ThomasNelson.com.

ISBN 978-0-7180-8457-8 (eBook)

Library of Congress Cataloging-in-Publication Data

ISBN 978-0-7180-8453-0

Library of Congress Control Number: 2017933497

Printed in the United States of America

17 18 19 20 21   LSC   10 9 8 7 6 5 4 3 2 1

This book is dedicated to Danelle and Valentine.
You are my sun and moon.

CONTENTS

CONTENTS

INTRODUCTION

The word *selfish* and the phrase *change the world* don't immediately appear to belong together. *Selfish* sounds like self-dealing and indifference. *Change the world* sounds like self-denial and martyrdom. I once thought that if I ever wanted to change the world, I would have to become a malaria-infected social worker in Ethiopia. I operated from a zero-sum perspective in which the time and talent I might invest to improve the lives of others would somehow register as a loss in my personal account. Changing the world was the work of selfless and sacrificial people, not someone like me who is mostly ambitious for things that benefit me. I thought giving myself to the problems of others would somehow keep me from achieving the things I wanted in life. This perspective is completely wrong. Changing the world is one of the most selfish things you can do.

The S-word often comes up when we talk about changing the world. *Should* is one of the worst words in the English language. No one likes to hear it. Whenever I do, I tense up and automatically want to do the exact opposite. *You should go to the gym. You should try and relax. You shouldn't get involved in things you don't understand. You shouldn't stand so close to the edge of the electric eel tank.* I don't like to be told what to do. Almost no one does. So I'm not going to "should" on you in this book. Instead, I'm going to let you in on something I know you can benefit from. I'm going to show you the front door to meaning and purpose.

We tend to look at all problems through two lenses: salience and proximity. By salience, I mean the relative importance of the problem, such as the difference between receiving a two-percent latte when you ordered an almond-milk latte and losing your job. Two problems with a sizeable difference in importance. By proximity, I mean the distance of the problem from you, as seen in the difference in your feelings about your job loss and the situation of an enslaved Cambodian man forced to fish for the prawns on your lunch salad. Two problems, one close and one seemingly distant. These two lenses that we all use, saliency and proximity, allow us to prioritize problems and enable us to be functional and productive. We take care of the most salient and proximate problems first, and then, if we have anything left over, we try to address the less important and distant problems. This is a reasonable way to live, but it misses one very important detail: it's nearly impossible to find purpose in life while avoiding the problems of others.

I learned this truth the hard way. I was in the middle of a music career and possessed a very clear idea about how my life should go when I first started hearing about the distant (proximity) and infuriating (salience) problems of those trapped inside modern-day slavery. Once I learned about this injustice and then saw it for myself, I became convinced that these problems were somehow both highly salient and highly proximate to my life. I knew I had to do something, so I took a chance by allowing a problem that I've never had to face personally, weave itself into my life.

I wanted to give more than money. I wanted to give some of myself—not all of myself, just some. So I created a way to contribute who I am to the problem—which I talk about later in the book. This reconfiguration of salience and proximity about other people's problems has created chapters in my own story that I never could have written myself. My life has taken on more meaning and purpose than I could have ever imagined. While my motive was to help others, the experience helped me immeasurably. I didn't have to become someone else to help another person; I simply needed to offer myself to the problems of others. Changing the world is not an act of selflessness; it's the opposite.

Think of this book as a self-help-others manual. It's about finding who you are and how far you can go with your own story. You will learn how the fabric of your everyday life can bring value to someone else's. We've been taught to separate doing good and doing life into different accounting ledgers. We've been handed life plans that say when the doing life ledger somehow reaches its financial goal, then we can "give back" to the doing good ledger. These life plans will bankrupt your soul because the doing life ledger is rarely, if ever, complete. More important, we don't need to stop what we are doing now—unless it's illegal or immoral—to make a real difference in the world. We don't need to do something spectacular or historic to change the world in some way. Who you are, where you are, what you do, and who you know are everything you need to change the world. It's your very selfishness that the world desperately needs right now.

We are repurposing the word selfish to mean doing something good for ourselves and for our world. I have seen firsthand how we can leverage the story of our lives to improve the lives of others. I would have never had the opportunity to fight slavery if I weren't a musician first. I didn't have to let go of the things I am passionate about in order to do something good for others. A selfish plan to change the world means that the things you are already passionate about and good at can be used to improve the world while also providing a richer story for your own life. This is not a special opportunity for a select few. A divine ordering exists over each of our lives that points toward meaning and purpose. Selfish is just another way of saying the world needs who you are, not just what you can donate.

We tend to think changing the world is the job of other people with lives very different from ours: charity workers, government workers, wealthy philanthropists, famous celebrities, and religious leaders. And while the impact of professional and influential world-changers cannot be understated, the challenges humanity faces today cannot be handled by "professionals" alone. We face a new era, where change must be open-sourced and where the extraordinary gets birthed from the ordinary. Anyone who has ever changed the world started without any idea of how to do it. The world needs you, just as you are, more than you know.

This book is meant to help you begin acting on whatever it is you want to see changed, giving you the tools to do good, be good, and feel good. Each chapter places you in a scene where you can look around and learn through the experience of others. We'll take a journey from a punk rock concert in Dublin to a do-gooder prom in New York, from a fishing boat in Ghana to an Indiana Jones–like mine in India, with several other stops along the way. You will meet ordinary individuals who have stepped up to change the world and in the process built a wealth of meaning and purpose in their own lives. A hip-hop artist. A software salesman. A missionary wife. A war refugee. A warlord. A school teacher. A surgeon. A housewife. A singer with a speech impediment. By the end you will understand how to leverage all that you have, and all that you don't yet realize you have, for others.

I've set up the book in three parts. In part 1 we see why we need a plan to change the world. We'll learn why our lives are designed for meaning and how helping others is our path toward it. In part 2 we learn what's preventing us from changing the world and finding meaning. Finally, in part 3, we will walk through the initial steps to take in order to change the world and find meaning. These steps aren't linear, but they are required. This self-help-others manual is designed to help you build a selfish plan to change a world that desperately needs your wit, your charm, your ideas, your determination, your sense of humor, your network, your backstory, your skills, your perspective, your disappointments, your mistakes, your smile, yourself. Are you ready?

PART 1

WHY CHANGE THE WORLD

CHAPTER 1

FIND YOUR RIOT

OCTOBER 21, 1977
DUBLIN, IRELAND
EXAMINATION HALL, TRINITY COLLEGE

"THANK YOU, GOOD NIGHT."

The Bishops walk offstage drenched in the sweat and saliva of the raging *boyos* in the front row. The band knows that the manic applause roaring behind them isn't so much an affirmation of their performance, but rather the unbridled anticipation for the headliners coming up next. The Bishops just plowed through a set of songs reminiscent of their influences, such as the Beatles and Dr. Feelgood. But tonight this city, this venue, and this audience aren't interested in looking backward.

The twelve hundred or so acne-laden concertgoers have come to rage inside the sonic advent of a new era that matches the ire and restlessness of their day-to-day Dublin lives. The testosterone-powered crowd entertained themselves by launching salvos of goobers—or phlegmy spit—pelting the Bishops throughout their set. The Bishops knew that this was not the show to fight back, so they received the incoming DNA samples with labored dignity. The goober-launchers now make a few meager requests for an encore, but the Bishops push on to their dressing room as the houselights come up. This isn't the night for an encore. Rock-and-roll honor code forbids such a pitiful grab from an opening band. Everyone is here for one reason: to see

Britain's hottest new band perform their first concert in Ireland. What no one here tonight can possibly know is just how much this concert will change their lives—and the world.

Trinity College's Examination Hall is not the ideal venue for a show like this. For hundreds of years the university has earned a reputation as one of the few academic institutions to uphold the value of free speech, making it a *symbolically* fitting venue for this show. But this antiquated hall has some serious sonic limitations. Its statues of dour academic achievers, its lavish Georgian design, and its cathedral-high ceilings make it more suited for Gregorian chants than for a rock concert full of war-painted teenagers out for a fiercely good time. The owners of the football stadium across town wouldn't book this show for fear of violent mobs, and the show in Belfast last night was canceled hours before the doors were to open due to similar concerns.

The stage is a simple temporary platform installed about a foot off the ground so the performers can look directly into the eyes of their audience. And what an audience it is. The youth of Dublin represented here tonight look to be in the middle of a style renaissance. It will be hard to find soft-rock handlebar mustaches and Jim Morrison coifs tonight. Standard issue consists of tight leather jackets, military boots, striped T-shirts with perfectly torn holes down the sides, all complemented by King Tut–inspired mascara. Examination Hall was designed for students to take tests, but tonight the hall will be tested by the students.

The headliners have just arrived backstage and are taking their sweet time preparing for their performance. Despite having formed only a year ago, they have already mastered the art of anticipation—something performers wield like puppeteers over their audiences. Great performers don't give their audience what they want. They give them what they need, when they need it. They build an imaginary world through their songs and take listeners to it with their performance. Isn't that why we go to concerts? We want to visit another world. We turn our bodies and emotions over to globe-trotting troubadours, trusting them to transport us from our *here* to some other *there*. Tonight is no different, and the headliners backstage know it. The roadies have finished setting up all the instruments and checking the microphones. The houselights dim. It's showtime.

A cacophony of screaming teenage voices bounces off the sculpted ceilings while triumphant arcs of goobers, reminiscent of the fountains at Versailles, launch across the hall. Nicky, Paul, Mick, and Joe swagger onstage as the first punk rock band to play Ireland. The large backdrop behind the drum kit bears an image of bobbies (British police) swinging clubs at a race riot in London, an image that looks all too familiar to this audience. This band is leading a new movement that's sweeping across the globe. Their movement challenges status quos with distorted guitars, reveals class inequalities at 101 beats per minute, and advocates for minorities through the poetry of biting lyrics. Tonight, Ireland is finally being introduced to the only band that matters. Ladies and gentlemen, put your hands together for the Clash.

It's 1977, and Ireland is an ancient land wrestling with its national identity—again. For seven hundred years the Emerald Isle had been part of the United Kingdom, until in 1920 a revolution resulted in independence for southern Ireland, now called the Republic of Ireland. Northern Ireland remained within the British Empire. As with all territorial wars, religious divisions played a role. The Irish were now left to deal with not only a dividing line across their land, but ideological divisions between the majority Roman Catholics and the minority Protestants.

Due in part to economic downturns in Northern Ireland in the late 1960s, a period of intense violence began, commonly called "the Troubles." Northern Ireland was split between the Nationalists (Roman Catholics), who considered themselves truly Irish, and the Unionists (Protestants), who identified as British. Their capital city, Belfast, was ground zero for their differences. Paramilitary groups on both sides armed themselves, creating unspeakable terror for average citizens. Car bombs, gang warfare, and targeted assassinations were what Northerners called Tuesday. Add to this the presence of the British military, with their failed attempts to remain neutral while keeping the peace, and you have a tinderbox of sectarian conflict. Over the twenty-eight-year run of the Troubles, thirty-five hundred lives were lost and countless others were injured.

Dublin is about eighty-eight miles south of Belfast, but by 1977, the effects of the violence have already shaped many of the young adults here in Examination Hall. Violence can work its way into your skin like the salt air blowing off the Irish Sea. The lack of jobs for this emerging workforce only adds to the compression building inside Irish youth looking for an outlet. Punk rock couldn't have come at a better time. It carries with it a tactile response to the daily socioeconomic challenges the young people in Examination Hall are facing. It's a call to arms for a generation who never got their summer of love. It's the Rosetta Stone used to interpret the aching questions of a new generation. Punk rock is like a new religion, and the singer walking up to the microphone right now is its mercurial cult leader.

Wearing a military-style shirt bearing spray-stenciled words like *war* and *vandalism*, Joe Strummer leans into the microphone, surveys the crowd, and shouts, "Let's have some fun tonight!" Then he screams toward the sculpted ceiling, "London's burning!" Nicky responds on the snare drum, *rat-tat-tat-tat-tat*. "London's burning!" *Rat-tat-tat-tat-tat*. And the band explodes into their angst-ridden anthem "London's Burning." The crowd erupts into a raucous response. It's reasonable to assume that some teenagers here tonight are interpreting the song a bit more personally as "Dublin's Burning."

Somewhere inside Examination Hall, away from the human-blender mosh pits, stage diving, and goober crossfire, stand four teenagers indexing everything their eyes and ears can take in. Four middle-class white boys who came as fans are about to become followers. A year before, one of the boys posted a flyer at his high school, asking if anyone wanted to start a band. The other three joined and the foursome immediately started rehearsals. They knew they needed an iconic band name. Something epic but intimate. Easy to say but laced with meaning. Naming a band is like naming a child: you want to capture some future character trait early in the hope that it will develop over time. After donning a few ill-fitting names, they eventually landed on the Hype. It was technical and raw, and it captured their rock-star ambitions.

As the four boys watch the Clash, at a somewhat safe distance, they feel as if they are witnessing the birth of a movement for which the barrier to entry is low. You don't have to be Jimmy Page; you just need to rage. You don't have to be Ringo Starr; you just have to believe you're a star. You don't have to be Simon and Garfunkel; you just . . . you get the idea. The sounds of unchained melodies and train-shuffle snare drum hits roll over the four lads like fog over the Cliffs of Moher. But this isn't a safe come-as-you-are-love-is-all-you-need type of movement. There's no clearly illuminated exit sign in the back. Once you decide to walk into the purifying fire of this punk movement, there is only one way out—forward. You are either the solution or the problem.

The game has officially been changed for these four lads. Rock and roll is no longer just about melody and rhythm and girls. It's a vibrant hazing ritual of enlightenment. It's no longer about installing hot tubs on private jets and throwing televisions out the window of your Hollywood Boulevard penthouse suite. It's about letting the dissonance of life arrest you, disturb you, and emanate back out of you with beauty, volume, truth, and justice.

The Hype see in Joe Strummer a next-level rock star. There is no barrier between him and his audience. He is as much a savant as any artist of any medium. Dalí. Hitchcock. Nina Simone. Bowie. Sacred and profane. Transparent and enigmatic. Inside this explosive performer is a man trying to intimately connect with humanity. In fact, it's been said that if you want to get into the Clash's dressing room after a show, just knock on the window and they will kindly let you in, maybe even offer you a drink. Joe is manic while singing, but in between songs he dons a shepherding demeanor with the audience . . . that is, unless someone in the audience tries to hurt someone. That's when the punk comes out of the rocker. Joe has a reputation for stopping concerts when he sees someone getting hurt. He can rage against the system while standing in the gap for the oppressed. He's a natural advocate.

The Clash is a white band writing white songs about black issues. To Joe, black issues are his issues. The black people on the receiving end of the bobbies' sticks are his friends and his community. In fact, everyone in Examination Hall tonight is his community, just like the multiethnic vagabonds he house-squatted with on the south side of London, or the students at the boarding school where his parents dropped him off, or the street children he grew up with in Turkey, Egypt, and Mexico. Joe is keenly aware of his white privilege, and he is always looking to leverage it for others without privilege.

As much as it has tried, the seventies hasn't yet produced its Elvis or Beatles like the fifties and sixties had. This decade has served up everything from mustache yacht rock to disco, all without a point of view about what is happening in the world. The world is hungry for a point of view from its artists. From Belfast to the Bronx, white to black, punk to rap, young people are looking for new music that can contextualize their socioeconomic limitations and transport them elsewhere. The members of the Hype, and everyone else here tonight, have been hungry for something authentic, opinionated, and worthy of emulation. Tonight they have found it in the Clash.

The band breaks into their first single, "White Riot," and the crowd goes wild. Joe moves across the stage like Elmer Gantry at a revival tent meeting: *"White riot, I want to riot, White riot, a riot of my own."* The audience heeds his call and releases their own riot, increasing the circumference of the mosh pit and the rapidity of stage dives. But his emphatic message to this mostly white audience isn't simply to rage at a show, but to find a riot they can own for themselves. The violent image behind him of bobbies swinging their clubs at a race riot makes it clear that the black community has their riot. They have no choice but to riot. But middle-class whites don't have a cause to riot for. Joe is telling them to live for something bigger. Don't let the world tell you how to operate. Challenge the status quo with truth and justice for everyone. Find your riot or become another thick bloke.

The moment Joe screams, *"Are you going backwards, or are you going forwards?"* a lightning bolt runs up the teenage spines of the Hype. This white riot playing out in front of them feels like a pentecostal worship service in black Harlem. It's out of control, yet altogether holy. Sacred and profane. Turn or burn. The pounding of the drums, the hands in the air, the reckless abandon all point to something bigger than themselves. They are called to the carpet by a punk rocker screaming prophetic messages into a distorted microphone. Music is no longer a career choice. It's bigger than their rock dreams. It's a calling. From here on, there is no Plan B or going backward for these boys. They are ready to go forward.

Joe is using his talent to riot for a world he wants to see. This riot is in his blood. It pumps his heart. It's a fire in his bones. He can't live without it. He's been releasing this riot like a virus into the atmospheres of basement nightclubs, television studios, football arenas, and now Examination Hall. Tonight the members of the Hype, Larry, Adam, David, and Paul, have contracted this airborne riot virus, which will guide them for decades to come. The riot inside of these Dublin teenagers will go on to change the atmosphere of every school auditorium, dive bar, festival, theater, television show, arena, and stadium they will ever play. It will take them to places few bands have ever gone, but first they will need to change their name to U2.

I SMELL CHAOS

One morning around 5:00 a.m., my son, three years old at the time, was keeping my wife and me awake with his constant pleading from his room. He was going through a sadistic phase of waking up at dark o'clock, expecting us to share his joy of a new day—before it was technically day. I suggested that my wife go sleep downstairs while I brought our little boy into bed with me. I had the delusional hope that he might fall back asleep.

He was quiet for a few minutes, allowing me just enough time to glide into the early stages of REM, when I heard his little voice whisper through the tunnel of slumber: "Dada?!"

"Yes, son," I replied with my eyes closed.

"Dada?" was his response.

"What do you want, son?" I said, still not opening my eyes.

"Dada?!"

It's important to note here that I had been teaching my son to look people in the eyes when talking to them, and now those lessons had come to punish me. "Dada?" I turned over on my pillow to see his cute little very-awake face staring me right in the eyes. Now, certain he had made eye contact, he delivered his important message: "Dada, I smell chaos." Thinking I might still be asleep, I asked him to repeat himself. "I smell chaos," he said, only this time he raised his little hazelnut eyebrows up and down like Charlie Chaplin to punctuate his declaration.

"You smell chaos?" I repeated back as a question.

"Yes," he said with a smile. Clearly satisfied, he then closed his eyes and went back to sleep.

This might sound like just another cute story of a three-year-old with a sleeping disorder, but hearing my son tell me that he smelled chaos was an alarm clock to my soul. Did this little sleep-hater understand what he was saying? Chaos? Where did he learn that word, and why was he saying that he smelled it? We were well beyond potty-training. Was it possible he knew what was going on?

My life was, in fact, full of chaos at the time. I had recently come off of an eighteen-month film tour and had begun leading an organization focused on ending slavery. I was tired, worn-out, and desperate for something certain, something predictable, and something that just worked a little easier. Fighting for the rights of others is profoundly chaotic, ambiguous, and void of certainty. This chaos had taken a toll on me, and I felt that I was failing my work and my family. And yet here a sweet little voice on a pillow, a literal place of rest, was telling me in the darkest hour of the night that it was okay to rest amid the storm of chaos. I was being given permission to keep walking despite the darkness because the light was going to come out soon.

I didn't always live with chaos. Like many, I was raised to pursue a life of certainty. As a parent myself, I understand that no loving father or mother wants a life of chaos or uncertainty for their children. My parents had paid a high price for the certainty and stability they gave me as a child. Both of them had gone through chaotic experiences in their lives, and they understandably did all they could to protect me from chaos. They created a safe environment, which came with a carefully written script for my life. Paint inside the lines of specific moral codes, finish college, get a job, find a wife, populate the earth, and go to church on the weekends. I'm not saying that's a bad script. It was just missing a few important lines. Actually, it was missing an entire second act.

Second acts in stories are where the protagonists find out who they really are because they face a trial in order to defeat an adversary. Second acts are, by their very nature, void of certainty and full of chaos. A life without a little chaos sounded dull and meaningless. I was learning in school and church about heroes who lived memorable and meaningful lives, specifically because they embraced chaos and took risks of sacrificial love. *Where is adventure without chaos?* I thought. Something in the back of my young, fragile, eggshell brain told me there was more to life than following a script that led to certainty.

On a brisk autumn night, I went to see U2 perform at the Oakland Coliseum. It was my first big concert, and it felt like going to church, a United Nations Security Council meeting, a dive bar, and an international trade policy class all at the same time. We sang along to songs about the Troubles in Ireland, apartheid in South Africa, the drug wars in Central America, and civil rights in the United States. There was something special about this band. U2 had changed the music game by being good at their craft while doing good for the world, and looking good while doing it. Somehow they were the biggest band in the world—a world that they were actively making better. U2's art and riot were indistinguishable from each other. They made compassion as cool as Telecasters. Maybe cooler.

When I saw them, I was around the same age they were when Joe Strummer unleashed his riot upon them. A hybrid of the virus Joe launched into the atmosphere of Examination Hall in Dublin in 1977 spread across all of us in the Oakland Coliseum. This sonic, airborne riot virus entered through my ears and coursed throughout my body, looking for a soul to host within. In that moment I felt something I'd never felt before. It was a feeling that no church, rally, film, concert, or speech had ever made me feel. For the first time in my life, I wanted to be a better person—not just better for me, but better for others too. I felt my life had a purpose, as if the world needed something from me. I didn't know what my purpose was, but I knew it was real. I imagine that was what the Hype felt listening to the Clash that autumn night in Dublin. I was infected, and my life's purpose became finding my riot and infecting the world with it.

Writing and performing music soon became my life, and I believed it could change the world. I still do. I loved being inside of songs. It was like being inside of a diving bell as it drops deep into the ocean. Songs were like a world within another world, and they took me to new depths where I discovered new forms of life. I wrote songs about racism, injustice, war, and pretty much anything else U2 was singing about. You always mimic your influences at first. Eventually I found my own sound and began to receive offers to perform in San Francisco's dingy nightclubs. Clubs led to record deals and eventually touring the world. I had found my life path and was living out my rock dream, but I had yet to find my riot.

THE ANSWER IS IN THE QUESTION

Several years later, I was recording some songs at a studio in Los Angeles with my friend Jacquire, an incredible sound engineer. He was using this gorgeous vintage mixing console that Led Zeppelin had used to make a few of their records. There is no language to express how exciting it is to work on the same mixing console as some of your heroes. All I could think about was how my vocals were touching the same circuitry as Robert Plant's vocals.[1] I finished recording one of my vocal tracks, and Jacquire started to mix the song together. So I took a break in the lobby.

On the coffee table was a newspaper article with the headline "Girls for Sale," featuring a picture of a young Cambodian girl in tattered clothing staring into the camera. The article contained stories about some very poor families living in remote regions of Cambodia and Thailand who were visited by labor agents from big cities such as Phnom Penh. The agents promised poor families the opportunity to send their young daughters to work in the big city. They said the girls would work at noodle shops or hair salons, earning enough money to send back to their families every month. Deciding to allow your child to leave home with someone you don't know, to go to a place you've never been, and work at a job you don't understand, is a choice most of us simply cannot comprehend. Upon arrival, girls were thrown into brothels, gang-raped into submission, and forced to service more than a dozen men a day. The brothel owners would get them addicted to drugs, making them easier to control and better for business.

As I read this in the recording studio lobby, I could feel my heart rising into my throat. I considered myself pretty well versed in human rights issues. I had visited concentration camps, studied the civil rights movement, and watched the Rwandan genocide unfold on CNN—this hidden horror seemed like a continuation of those horrific chapters in history. My mind raced with questions: How was this possible in the twenty-first century, and how was this the first time I was reading about it? Why weren't the police throwing these criminals in prison? Why wasn't someone rescuing these girls? Why wasn't the United Nations stepping in? How could sex tourists from America get away with rape?

Naturally, we want quick, easy answers to questions like these, but there is no simple solution to child rape and slavery—just as there is no simple answer to the systemic poverty that contributes to these horrific events. When it comes to complex problems, the only available answer lies within the question itself.

The answer was simple: *If young girls being sold into brothels bothers me this much, then what am I going to do to stop it? What can I do to put traffickers in jail? What can I do to get these girls out? What can I do to expose the sex tourists?*

When we begin to ask ourselves the *how* and *what* questions, our rational side tries to calm us down. We tell our megaphone-toting passionate side to get down off the table and listen to reason. The rational choice is to avoid the chaos of others, to say that it's someone else's responsibility to fix it. Yet this kind of reasoning is a very slippery slope. Rational choices to avoid the chaos of others creates a space for murderous despots to rise to power and for pimps to sell children for sex with impunity. Some of the worst travesties in history occurred because it wasn't rational for someone on the outside to engage with the chaos of others. Rational choices keep us from protecting someone else because they don't look like us, live near us, or directly affect our daily lives. Rational choices will talk us out of our riot. Those who ask, "What can I do?" usually end up being part of the answer.

So I was faced with my own question in that Los Angeles recording studio. Would I let the chaos of these girls and millions of others like them affect my life, or would I believe that it was someone else's mess to fix? Would I go forward or go backward? Sometimes the very thing that makes you mad and makes you cry is also the very thing to make you feel a fire in your bones and full of purpose. Being shocked, mad, or sad doesn't accomplish anything. Feelings may blast your rocket off the ground, but they won't get you into orbit. I had sung songs about injustice and played gaggles of charity concerts, but this was different. Could this be my riot? Was this part of the virus I contracted at Oakland Coliseum years before? The only answer was in the question. The only way to know was to move forward into the chaos.

FINDING YOUR RIOT

You might be thinking the word *riot* is a little over-the-top. It sounds scary and violent, so why would anyone want to find one? *Riot* conjures images of violent clashes in the streets with a mob launching Molotov cocktails on one side and police in gas masks on the other. I understand the word *riot* sounds downright dangerous and perhaps unlawful. I've been around a few riots, and they are definitely chaotic. The riot inside you doesn't look like any of these images. Your riot isn't violent or destructive, but it does have one thing in common with traditional riots: Your riot is a place inside of you where you stand up and say that something is wrong. It's where you turn your indignation into action. Simply put, finding your riot is how you find your purpose.

There is no secret map that can lead you to your riot, but I have learned two questions to ask that might guide you along the way. The first question is: "What do I believe is broken with the world?" That question might sound like a fool's errand, given all the challenges in the world, but try to focus on what *you* think isn't working. Is there something broken in our world that makes you angry? Sad? What makes you cry when you see or hear about it? I'm not referring to what's wrong with your job or an annoying family member with weird political views. What specifically bothers you about how the world is working? When you are all alone, without the noise of other people's opinions bombarding you, is there something you wish were different? When you scan your social media feed, does anything look broken to you? Do you ever find yourself saying things like, "It's not fair that men at my work are getting paid more than women doing the same job," or "I just saw a black teenager get stopped and frisked by a police officer for no reason," or "Why are there so many twenty-four-hour massage parlors in my neighborhood?" or "I wish someone would protect the innocent refugee children fleeing the genocide and drowning in the Mediterranean"? That frustration is your riot. When you say, "I wish someone would just fix it," there's a good chance that person is you.

Expressionist painter Paul Klee noted, "Art does not reproduce the visible; rather, it makes visible."[2] To find your riot, you first need to identify what you believe is broken in the world. Artists naturally wrestle with dissonance, be it unrequited love or social injustice, and they repurpose the dissonance into a painting, a film, or a song that everyone can see, feel, and interact with. All that Larry, Adam, the Edge, and Bono had to do to find their riot was look around and start writing about what they saw—the violence that plagued their country, tearing apart cities and families. They found their riot by allowing the chaos to affect them. What's not right with the world around you? It doesn't have to be overseas. It can be right outside your door. For U2, it was the violence and fracturing of their country. For me it was human trafficking. For you it might be something else.

ARE YOU GOING FORWARD?

A second question to ask yourself is, "Am I going forward with my life?" Joe's voice that October night in Dublin was like that of a biblical prophet screaming outside the high walls of a guarded and well-fed city, warning them that destruction was certain if they kept going backward in their safe and self-serving ways. The opening band that night in 1977 was going backward musically, following the trodden path of their musical influences instead of blazing new sonic trails. The Bishops were playing it safe. Sometimes that's how life feels, each year a warmed-over repeat from the previous year: *Don't go off script. Pursue certainty.*

Going forward with your life means doing something different, even risky, to benefit someone other than yourself. Are you operating off the same risk-averse script year after year? Going forward with your life requires walking into uncertainty. This doesn't mean that you need to get your malaria shots and move to central Africa, but it does mean disrupting some old cycles in your life. The spirit is often willing, but the flesh is weak.

Going forward with your life means letting go of some certainty. Your life will start to look a little different from those around you because most of us are looking for certainty. It might help to remember that there was no data within the music industry of the early 1980s that said a young Irish band could achieve rock-demigod status by singing about the chaos and injustice in the world. On the day U2's first single, "I Will Follow," was released, the number-one song in America was "I Love a Rainy Night" by Eddie Rabbitt. (And who doesn't love a little huggin' on a rainy night?) That song sounded nothing like U2's riot music. If they wanted to play the safe card and go for the more certain route, they would have sounded like Eddie Rabbitt. U2 took a risk by pushing their single "I Will Follow" to radio, a song about the void in the heart of a young boy whose mother had died. Radio stations and pop culture were not asking for U2's riot, but they got it anyway. We now know that the radio stations and the world actually did want songs about real life and loss, but it took a risky young Irish band to deliver them. Are you ready for your life to look a little different? Are you ready to take the unpaved and uncertain path toward a bigger narrative? Are you ready to risk certainty for a second act?

RIOT AND REWARD

We know where their story went after that seminal night in Examination Hall. U2 became one of the biggest bands in the world, with their venerable lead singer becoming one of the loudest voices for justice in the twenty-first century. What's forgotten amid success stories like theirs, or that of anyone who pursued their riot, is the seemingly small but very risky decisions that are made before there is ever a hint of reward.

Media, religion, advertisers, and politicians are busy selling us the elixir of overnight success, where no risk is required to find purpose in our lives. Belief in overnight success is like believing in the lottery: We think, *Maybe it will work out that way for me!* We want our lives to have purpose and meaning, but we are hesitant to risk our time, talent, and identity unless we see some guarantee of reward. Taking a risk on your riot never guarantees reward—which is why it's a risk! But never taking risks for others guarantees we'll *never* reap rewards, either for us or for others. Remember, the pathway to rock stardom in the early eighties did not include writing songs about Belfast bombings or performing concerts to end the imprisonment of some guy named Mandela in South Africa. In the early 1980s, most Americans probably had no idea that South Africa was a country and not a region of Africa. Yet an Irish band with dreams of being the greatest band in the world sang about people and places no one had ever heard of. They chose risk over certainty. The reward for going backward is certainty, and maybe some hugs on rainy nights. The reward of going forward and taking a risk on your riot is a life of purpose and meaning.

The three life commodities I hear all my friends say they need more of is time, money, and power. We believe any problem we face can be solved with one or more of these precious commodities. Sometimes people tell me how inspired they are by how I've devoted my life to my riot, and that maybe one day when they have more time, money, and power they will do the same. Time, money, and power are non-renewable resources. Once you use that resource, it's gone, and you need more. You currently have all the resources you need to act on your riot. I'll prove this to you over the course of this book, but for now it's important to know that if we all wait until it's safe to change the world, we never will.

PASSING THE RIOT VIRUS

What Joe Strummer asked in Examination Hall—and what was also asked of me at Oakland Coliseum—is a question I now ask you. What is your riot? What is your cause? Are you going forward with your life, or are you going backward? Do you chase certainty and avoid chaos? For centuries poets and prophets—some of whom we'll meet in this book— have been asking societies these questions. They would all tell us that we are missing out on a full life when we only consume the confections of certainty, because certainty is never certain. We were made for the sweet and salty of life, for comfort and risk, for dissonance and resolve. If all we seek is a safe path for our lives without allowing for the chaos of others, we live a half-life.

So ask yourself again: What makes me cry? What stories break my heart? Sit with that for a minute. What would I like to change in the world to benefit others? They could be people in your community or a community you've never been to. The answer to that question is your riot, and the purpose of this book is to help you launch your riot into the world. You will never know how powerful and purposeful you are until you push forward into the chaos of others.

Something important happened to me after reading that newspaper article in Los Angeles. Jacquire eventually called me back into the studio to record my vocals for the next song. I wasn't sure if I could manage a performance with all those stories now short-circuiting my heart and mind. I stood behind Jacquire, once again admiring the vintage mixing console. I was imagining all the riot and passion that had passed through its power tubes and resistors throughout the years. What were these musical heroes of mine thinking about when they stepped up to the microphone? What kind of riot were they trying to get out of themselves and into the world? Without stopping what he was doing, Jacquire mentioned how much he loved working on this mixing console. As I walked toward my microphone, I asked him who else had recorded on this mixing board. Without looking up he gave the best possible answer. The Clash.

CHAPTER 2

I HAVE A SOUL DREAM

September 24, 2012
New York City
Sheraton Ballroom

THERE WAS THIS DREAM I HAD WHEN I WAS TWENTY-ONE THAT I'VE NEVER been able to shake. I never understood what it meant, until right now.

I was walking down the outdoor breezeway connecting the mid-century buildings of my Northern California high school. To my left was a patch of dead nuclear-winter grass about the size of a basketball court. To my right were long rows of lockers. Between me and the lockers, just beyond my peripheral vision, was a group of VIPs (very important people) in formal business attire, led by one very important leader. The leader and I were walking at a brisk pace and talking intensely with each other. Our eyes were transfixed on a bewildering scene to our left, so I couldn't make out the VIP's identity. There, on the dead patch of grass, hundreds of children were kneeling with their hands tied behind their backs and their mouths gagged with dirty rags. They sat as still as the ancient Chinese Terra-cotta Army, compliant and controlled by someone we could not see. They were forbidden from acknowledging us.

Our pace and conversation quickened as we walked alongside this placid sea of desperation. We reached the end of the breezeway and turned left to get a better look at the children. As if on cue, the sea of doe-eyed children lifted their heads and looked right at us. Their only available form of communication was a widening of their eyes, a silent plea for help. In this moment all of the oxygen was sucked out of the dream. The VIP leader and I were incapable of speech. A cocktail of emotions roiled inside me: anger with a splash of ineptitude poured over a chilled block of vengeance. We were looking at hundreds, maybe thousands, of children trapped under the control of an insidious captor, invisible to the world, with no voice. In a fit of righteous indignation I turned to the VIP delegation, forgoing all decorum, and addressed their leader directly: "What are *we* going to do about this?"

Our eyes locked for a half second, but a half second was all we needed. In that moment, a solidarity was galvanized. Our missions were united. Without words we committed to protect these children and fight their captor. As I held the unwavering gaze of this *very important leader*, I kept thinking to myself, *I know these eyes. I know these eyes. I know . . .* And then I woke up. I *did* know those eyes. Everyone knew those eyes. That's what makes the dream so significant. None of it has ever made sense, until right now.

This cinematic dream has followed me around like a feral cat for most of my life, always scratching at the back door of my attention. The dream felt like a coded message wrapped in complete nonsense. I can still see the eyes of those kids and that leader as vividly as the day I dreamed them. I reached out for help from therapists, mentors, and close friends in hopes of an explanation. The best explanation given was that the dream could be one of three things. One, it could be pure nonsense, with my brain crossing wires and mixing up data points . . . but it felt too real to be nonsense. Two, it could be something that happened in the past . . . but I'd never witnessed anything like it. Three, it could be something that would happen in the future. This also seemed implausible, if only because of the cast of VIPs.

I resigned myself to believing that the dream would never be understood, but it never went away. Carrying this dream around for twenty years has taught me something. I've come to believe that dreams like this have the power to shape lives. Our dreams come from a place inside that is ancient and powerful. Just as some say you don't choose who you fall in love with, I say you don't choose your dreams. They choose you.

I HAVE A DREAM . . . OR TWO

Dreams shape our future, archive our past, and inform our present. Luis Buñuel once wrote, "Give me two hours a day of activity, and I'll take the other twenty-two in dreams."[1] When I was twenty-one years old I had two big dreams in my life. There was the literal dream I just told you about, and my aspirational dream of a career in music. As I've mentioned, I had converted to the church of rock and roll at a tender age, and from then on religiously performed in its smoky temples. This aspirational dream was my *rock dream*: a goal I imagined for myself and worked hard to make come true. I believe we all have rock dreams of some sort. Your rock dream may not include a white sequined unitard and releasing doves from behind the drums, but I'm sure it is aspirational just the same.[2] Our rock dreams are the who-do-I-want-to-be-when-I-grow-up dreams or the what-will-my-life-look-like-someday dreams. Rock dreams are goals we set about the kind of work we want to do, or the type of family we want to have, or the types of achievements we want to hit. At twenty-one, rock dreams are the promises we make to ourselves to build a life of fulfillment and meaning.

Now, a dream about helping poor, kidnapped children with the aid of a major public figure is an entirely different kind of dream. I didn't choose that dream; it chose me. I call this type of dream a *soul dream*. We all have soul dreams in one form or another. I've heard people refer to their soul dreams as callings, visions, destinies, gut instincts, and dozens of other descriptions. Put simply, your soul dream is the purpose of your life. It represents a design for your life that you did not construct for yourself. It includes chapters in your life that you can't write for yourself. It's timeless and was written over your life before you were born. It just so happened that my soul dream revealed itself in an actual dream, but that's not always the case. Soul dreams reveal themselves differently to each of us, at different times in our lives, if we are willing to listen.

So, two dreams. One dream I formed for myself, and the other formed me. What I didn't know at twenty-one was that this soul dream knew more about the trajectory of my life than I could have ever imagined or planned. It knew the story of my life, complete with a proper second act. I know it sounds crazy, but today, after two decades, I finally know what this soul dream meant all along.

It might help for me to explain where I am right now. I'm seated at an elegant round table in a beautiful hotel ballroom in New York City. Seated next to me is a CNN correspondent. Next to him are a few State Department officials, including my partner against crime, Alison Kiehl Friedman, a woman who protects girls' rights in Liberia, and an assortment of very intelligent and accomplished individuals—movers and shakers at the highest levels. Dozens of other beautiful, white-clothed tables with impressive people around them fill the ballroom. Baby-blue mood lighting paints stripes across the walls, and there's a formal stage flanked by giant screens projecting inspirational images of someone in Africa drinking clean water for the first time in their lives. Everyone you bump into here is doing something good for the world in one way or another. It looks like a prom for do-gooders.

As at any prom, power dynamics are at play. Here, the power dynamic shifts between people with ideas, people with money, and people with power. You can see this dynamic when people from charity organizations (ideas) talk with the world's leading philanthropists (money) who are interested in collaborating with national leaders (power). They speak with one another in a way that resembles an awkward slow dance to a Justin Bieber ballad, each party trying to lead while trying not to step on the others' toes. Then there are the people at the back of the room. Along the back wall stands a pyramid of reporters and journalists pointing dozens of long-lens cameras at the stage. Let's call them the wallflowers. Around the entire perimeter of the ballroom are guys in blue suits with American flag pins and in-ear walkie-talkie pieces. These are the prom's chaperones, constantly scanning the ballroom for aberrant behavior.

The agony and the ecstasy of every prom is based on who you get to dance with. In similar fashion, almost everybody here wants to *dance* with someone. That woman over there? She became the first female head of state in Africa only a few years after a brutal civil war ravaged her country. She may want to dance with someone from the International Monetary Fund. That guy on the opposite side of the room? He created a banking system for some of the poorest people on the planet. He may want to dance with someone working in finance. The gentleman standing by the door has been building health clinics in rural Haiti for years and is close to eradicating tuberculosis. There's a former fashion icon who now promotes maternal health in the developing world. There's the CEO/founder of the largest online retailer in the world. That woman sitting in the front row once worked for Apple and is now the queen of Jordan. She has made protecting women and girls her primary focus. There was a singer from Ireland running around earlier, but he had to run off to a gig. Other heads of state, CEOs, and celebrities fill every corner of the room, plus a few billionaires sprinkled about for good measure. Everyone here is looking to dance with that special someone.

Right now all of us have our eyes on the guy coming onto the stage: the master of ceremonies, President Bill Clinton. This is his room per se. You might even say it's his prom. Every year he hosts this gathering, the Clinton Global Initiative, where he pulls together some of the world's most influential leaders, CEOs, celebrities, and global luminaries to learn from one another and publicly announce commitments to make the world a little cleaner, safer, and stronger. Commitments range from a big company committing to install solar panels on their warehouse retail stores to a charity organization committing to teach one hundred thousand girls to read in West Africa.

This may be a former Democratic Party president's prom, but in a partisan sense, the room is "purple"—full of both blue Democrats and red Republicans who've come together to try and protect people and planet. They know that our ever-changing world requires commitment from both sides of the political spectrum. They also know it takes charities, businesses, cultural leaders, national leaders, and rogue innovators working in concert to create a whole greater than the sum of its parts.

PARITY IN PURPOSE

It would be easy for one to feel insignificant or intimidated in a room full of people like this. Most of the guests here are people you and I might read about in the media, but I don't see anyone here resting on their political power, wealth, Hollywood stars, or Nobel Peace Prizes. There is something unique going on here that creates a sort of uniformity. The people in this room are here to be a part of something that money, power, and ideas alone cannot achieve—dismantling the popular belief that money and power are the ultimate ends. In this room, money and power are just the means to a better end for others. There is something very specific that binds everyone together in this room. Everyone here has a need for a purpose. You would think the people here do not need anything from anyone, but that's patently untrue. Everyone in this ballroom needs their life to matter, to have a purpose greater than their own accomplishments (or rock dreams). The need to contribute to a larger narrative, to find purpose, is a universal vulnerability. The need for purpose is the great social equalizer transcending status and income, creating a powerful and useful social parity.

Some of us—and by *us* I mean all 7.5 billion of us on Earth—are less concerned with finding purpose than just finding something to eat or a safe place to live. The rest of us—and by *us* I mean those who have enough discretionary time and income to buy and read books—are still trying to understand how we fit into a narrative that includes 7.5 billion people. We ask ourselves existential questions such as: Where do I fit in? Am I good enough? What is my true purpose? Am I worthy of being loved? Am I fulfilled by my work? Am I operating at my top potential? Will my rock dreams be enough, or should I be chasing another kind of dream? The deep need for meaning and purpose in our lives is one of the greatest forces for change in the history of humankind. The need, if acted on, can change the world. Meaning isn't measured in resources, but resourcefulness.

THE KEYNOTE ADDRESS

Two days before this ballroom gathering, America marked the 150th anniversary of the signing of the Emancipation Proclamation, initiating the legal end of slavery in this country. The proclamation was a calculated move by a three-steps-ahead-of-you genius, Abraham Lincoln, and it marked a turn in America toward the still-unfinished work of living up to the best version of itself—as described in the country's mission statement, the preamble to the Constitution. The proclamation was a line drawn by a first-term president whose re-election was far from certain, an extravagant expenditure of political power with absolutely no guarantee of a returned favor from a Congress full of me-first-and-gimme-gimme partisan politics. Most important, it marked a legal end to the worst kind of treatment a body and soul can face. Slavery in America entailed the 100 percent commodification of a human being. That individual was not his or her own person but rather the property of someone else. It's hard to imagine such a condition existing today in America, or anywhere else.

Every conference has its keynote speaker, but it's rare that you get two presidents on the same stage. The keynote speaker this morning is none other than the forty-fourth president of the United States, which explains the pyramid of cameras held by the *wallflowers* in the back and the Secret Service *chaperones* around the ballroom's perimeter. You would think with six weeks left in his re-election campaign President Obama would be bringing out a ringer of a stump speech.

With huge influencers and massive campaign funders in the room, along with every major news outlet, this speech should be designed to score political points. His Republican opponent, Governor Mitt Romney, just gave a speech, and frankly, he knocked it out of the park. But President Obama will do something off the political playbook. Way off. Today, President Obama is going to talk about slavery.

Nothing wakes up a room full of globally influential figures like talking in detail about the world's oldest form of oppression. The significance of America's first African American president still in his first term talking about slavery, 150 years after another first-term president signed the Emancipation Proclamation, will not be lost on anyone here today. This will be the longest speech on slavery by a sitting president since Lincoln. Only he won't be talking about the transatlantic slavery we've all read about in our history books. He'll be talking about twenty-first-century slavery, which affects more than forty million men, women, and children who are forced to work without pay and endure unspeakable violence. This illicit trade and exploitation of humanity is the fastest-growing crime on the planet. I do not use the word *slavery* lightly. Just speaking it aloud evokes visceral reactions as it harks back to one of the most painful chapters in our country's history. But once you put on the proper lens, you can see it everywhere, and there's no denying its pernicious nature.

So, the questions you might be asking are: Why is Justin there? What country did he run? What disease did he cure? My résumé, such as it is, doesn't qualify me to be here at all. I didn't go to an Ivy League university. I didn't complete an internship with Mother Teresa. I didn't start the company that released a mind-blowing app that disrupted an established industry. It's fair to say that I am utterly unqualified to be here, and yet, strangely, I'm authorized to be here. That's what I want to talk to you about. I want you to understand why I'm here. My journey, such as it is, proves that you don't need to be qualified to change the world, because you are already authorized.

But wait. Let's pause and listen to what the president is saying:

When a man, desperate for work, finds himself in a factory or on a fishing boat or in a field, working, toiling, for little or no pay, and beaten if he tries to escape—that is slavery. When a woman is locked in a sweatshop, or trapped in a home as a domestic servant, alone and abused and incapable of leaving—that's slavery.[3]

What President Obama is doing right now is defining modern slavery. This is very important because many people don't want to use the word *slavery*, opting instead for a more politically correct term, such as *human trafficking*. This happens a lot when societies sanitize their more difficult chapters. Calling this abhorrent practice by its name frames the problem and ignites the urgency needed to alert everyone in this room, and around the world, to the problem.

Every citizen can take action: by learning more; by going to the website that we helped create—SlaveryFootprint.org; by speaking up and insisting that . . . the products we buy are made free of forced labor.

Okay, that's it. The website he just mentioned, SlaveryFootprint.org, is why I'm here today. My organization, Made in a Free World, created Slavery Footprint, and it was one year ago today that we launched it here at the Clinton Global Initiative. Slavery Footprint asks everyday consumers from around the world a simple question: "How many slaves work for you?" That's not a question you get asked every day. As you push into the website, you experience an animated lifestyle survey about the products required to operate your life. Behind every product (coffee cup, bicycle, hair dryer, and more) is a unique calculation of the number of slaves required to produce it. I've been blown away by the response over the last year. Our goal was to reach 150,000 people within a year. We passed that goal the first week. It turned out to be a pretty special platform, impacting consumers in every country in the world, and it has become a tipping point in the effort to eradicate slavery.[4] The path to this room, and to making Slavery Footprint, is a story unto itself.

DEMOCRATIZING PARTICIPATION

In her book *Walking on Water*, Madeleine L'Engle describes how the purpose of an artist is to create a cosmos in the chaos of this world. Every so often the broken parts of our beautiful world find their way to our lives, and we get to choose whether to let the chaos in and turn it into a cosmos—a place of peace and grace—or let it pass us by.[5] As an artist, I've always seen my role as someone who tries to create a cosmos in the chaos. A good song, film, dance, or painting can take something painful and transform it into something deeply moving. My journey of trying to make cosmos from chaos is the backstory of why I'm here in this ballroom today. This story is proof that anyone can change the world. Anyone can create a cosmos from the chaos. This is the story of my soul dream.

After I learned about modern slavery in that Los Angeles recording studio, I felt obligated to do something about it. I found my riot, but I wanted to do more than write songs about it. I wanted to help turn the chaos of slavery into a cosmos. So I called a couple of charity organizations and offered my help. Understandably, they asked me to raise money for them, which I did. But I wanted to do more than fund-raise. My riot was pushing me to apply all of who I am, not just my donations. It was clear to me that ending slavery would require a massive movement of people who aren't professional world-changers but who, like me, want to participate in the cosmos of freedom. I call this movement the *democratization of participation*. My goal has been to make it easy for anyone to participate in building a free world. In my mind this was another way I could play out my role as an artist. I could help build a cosmos through building ways for everyone to participate in building a free world.

So I decided to direct a rockumentary film (that's not a typo) called *Call + Response* and release it into theaters. It featured interviews with *New York Times* journalist Nicholas Kristof (the journalist who wrote that article I read), political figures such as Secretary of State

Madeleine Albright, influential entertainers such as Ashley Judd, and a philosopher named Dr. Cornel West. Their interviews were woven together with undercover footage of child brothel raids, and layered with powerful performances from musical artists such as Moby, Cold War Kids, Matisyahu, and Natasha Bedingfield. It ended up getting a lot of media exposure and brought the issue of modern slavery to millions of people who had never heard of it. But that wasn't all. I wanted to give everyone who saw the film a way to act, so I began to look at how supply chains work.

Part of the film's focus was on the power of individual consumers, and the likelihood that we are all consuming products made with slavery. My team and I decided the best way to deputize masses of consumers was to create a website where they can write to their favorite brands, asking if they were aware of slavery in supply chains. We decided the first email should be sent to my favorite CEO, Steve Jobs of Apple. My team found his email address and heard somewhere that he doesn't allow his assistants to respond to his emails, so we fired one off from our website. The email asked Steve if he was aware of a mineral called tantalum that exists in all iPhones. Tantalum is in most electronics products, and much of the world's tantalum was at risk of being mined with forced labor in the Democratic Republic of Congo. We hit send and didn't think much more about it. Four hours later we got an email back that read, "I had no idea. I'll look into it. Steve—Sent from my iPhone." High fives were thrown. Would Steve Jobs actually look into it? We didn't know, but we knew we were onto something.[6] This simple website proved to us that anyone can participate in ending slavery simply through the power of consumerism. We had found a way to democratize participation.

A few months later I learned that a high-ranking official in the Obama administration had written an Op-Ed mentioning our website as something all citizens should visit. It wasn't long before I got a call from Alison Kiehl Friedman at the State Department with a proposal to partner on something out of the box for them. They wanted to see if someone in the private sector could create a website about modern-day slavery similar to Carbon Footprint. This online platform would give consumers a "slavery score" based on their purchasing habits. The only hitch was that I'm not an activist. I don't like bummer calculators that make you feel bad about yourself without giving you a way to act on your grief. Knowing you're contributing to a problem but having no idea how to fix it makes you feel even worse. I like to create solutions and participation—cosmos from chaos. I asked if I could have full creative control and ownership, and they agreed. So, with their help, and an incredible team, we built Slavery Footprint. Working with the State Department turned out to be a wonderful and productive partnership, and part of why I am in this ballroom today.

So here's where that soul dream comes in. As I listen to the president endorsing SlaveryFootprint.org and think about all the work I did with the State Department—it hits me. Remember that VIP leader with the entourage from my soul dream? That VIP is here today. Remember how we committed to work together to protect children trapped without a voice? Now I know what it all meant. It all makes so much sense now. It all connects back to that VIP leader and entourage. Of course we would be walking alongside children who are trapped. Of course they would appeal to us with their eyes to speak for them. And of course I would find a way to help them with this leader because that VIP leader in my dream from twenty years ago was Hillary Clinton.

We made a commitment in my dream long before she led the State Department and long before I knew what modern slavery was. It makes sense now that her entourage in my dream represented the State Department. Together we created Slavery Footprint, which has become one of the most influential human rights platforms ever created. It has helped to make slavery a priority for governments, businesses, schools, and religious organizations. It has been instrumental in passing laws protecting children, women, and men in slavery. Together, we made the lives of the children in my dream real, their plight public, and their voices heard around the world. Thousands of kids have been saved because of it. We brought some cosmos to the chaos of slavery. That dream became my soul dream. My purpose, calling out to me from my soul, existed long before I could understand what it meant.

DON'T LET YOUR DREAMS BECOME DREAMS

A friend of mine has a sign in his office that says, DON'T LET YOUR DREAMS BECOME DREAMS. It's a valuable warning. The dreams we have, whether lucid or from the soul, are ours to either pursue or neglect. A full life requires us to pursue our rock dreams (ambitions) and our soul dreams (purpose), because they are two sides of the same coin. If we don't, our dreams become wispy memories inside a mental trunk full of "almosts" and "wish I hads."

I've talked a lot about my rock dreams and how all of us have them in one form or another. But here's a question: What do you do when you pursue your rock dreams and they don't turn out? What happens when you work for that job promotion, study for that degree, train for that career, or hope for that relationship, and it doesn't work out the way you wanted? Despite all the great experiences and opportunities I had in music, despite working on my craft for much longer than the requisite ten thousand hours, my rock dream didn't ever fully come to fruition. I spent years on the road and in recording studios creating music that I'm proud of to this day, but my work never reached the level of exposure I imagined when I was sixteen. Popular wisdom today teaches us to go after our dreams with wild abandon, but it doesn't offer a usable map for failure. "Social media Darwinism" tells us we need a drip line of constant affirmation to survive, convincing us to only share our successes and camera-ready sides. Where do we put our failures and bad angles? Rock dreams don't always turn into what we want, but even failed rock dreams possess the potential to become something much bigger.

To make sense of my disappointment, I opened up my memory tapes from that first concert I attended at Oakland Coliseum. I've replayed that moment, and the feeling it gave me, countless times. On that brisk autumn night, I walked away from a safe and scripted life toward a life of purpose. I was determined to create things for others that made them feel the way I do, because that's what artists do. They move paint on a canvas, chisel shape out of rock, capture light onto film, and construct notes into melodies all in the hope that their audience might feel something they feel. As I replay the tapes from that night in Oakland all the way up to today, I see something bigger than a failed rock dream. I see how a rock dream led to a soul dream—a dream that was written over my life long before I picked up a guitar. Our rock dreams, regardless of their success, make our soul dreams possible. Our ambitions are woven with our purpose.

First I made songs, then concerts, then films, then a television show, then events, and then online human rights platforms. The same thread runs through each of these creations. My rock dream taught me how to make things for others to use, making them feel what I feel. The songwriting informed the filmmaking, and so forth. If I had not pursued my rock dream, I would have never fulfilled my soul dream. I would have never been authorized for a ballroom like this. Somehow in the pursuit of my rock dream I found what the world needed from me. I want you to know that the world needs something from you as well. The desires, ambitions, and interests that make up your rock dream, whatever it is, can play a huge role in fulfilling your purpose. All that we want for our own lives can be leveraged for the lives of others.

You too will learn just how much both kinds of dreams matter, and just how much the world needs you. I believe something divine, something bigger than myself, placed that soul dream into my twenty-one-year-old self as a message to be revealed two decades later. It's the message that I share with you as well: Your life has so much more potential and purpose than your self-constructed rock dreams. There is a bigger narrative yet to be uncovered in your life, and it can take you to unexpected experiences and unscripted places. It will authorize entry into places you never imagined you could go.

You will meet people in this book who started down the path of their rock dreams and ended up in an unexpected and fulfilling place, all because they looked for and acted on their riot. You may not have a literal dream at twenty-one that follows you around for two decades, but you do have a soul dream that is written over your life unlike any other. That soul dream is your purpose. It's what the world needs from you. Your ambitions and your purpose make up a whole far greater than the sum of their parts. Don't make the mistake of believing that the only way to find purpose is to do something you don't enjoy. I would never have experienced something as cool as listening to the president endorse something I got to make if I hadn't pursued my rock dream.

Two dreams. One life. One purpose. Intertwined. One is the good you do for yourself, and one is the good you get to do for others. The desire to spend some of your valuable life for the benefit of others is already inside your soul. But only you can access it. This book is designed to help you find it and live it out. We—and again, I mean all 7.5 billion of us—desperately need your dreams. We need you to step outside of the planned path you've made for yourself into the uncharted path toward meaning. The chaos and cosmos, the agony and ecstasy, the rock dream and soul dream are the opposing forces that work together to form a meaningful life. So let's make sure your dreams don't become dreams.

Dr. Martin Luther King Jr. taught us that *I* am not who I am supposed to be until *you* are who you're supposed to be.[7] Our identity, our purpose, is realized when we help build a cosmos for others living in chaos. We find ourselves when we give ourselves away. When we willfully decide to step into the chaos of injustice—the brutality of hunger, the spiderweb of the foster care system, the terrorism of post-traumatic stress, the insidiousness of sexual violence—we are making an investment into our own personal hedge fund of meaning and purpose. Let's go find ourselves as we build a selfish plan to change the world.

CHAPTER 3

A POVERTY OF MEANS

December 14, 2012
Ghana
Lake Volta

"PULL, ISAIAH, PULL!"

His small, muscular hands reach into the cold gray water and grab two fistfuls of net. Isaiah digs his bare feet into the damp wood of the boat, stretches the whole of his four-foot frame, and pulls in another arm's length of net onto the boat's floor. His eyes scan the folds of net for silver flashes of Nile perch. "Pull, Isaiah," demands the tall man at the front of the boat. Isaiah catches a glimpse of the large vein bulging on the tall man's forehead in the moonlight. He never helps. Isaiah's heart rate increases when the net comes up again without any silver flashes. His little brother Joseph frantically flips the nets. Empty nets make angry masters. So he and Joseph pull faster, harder, when suddenly the net catches, causing Joseph to lose his balance. He nearly falls out of the boat. The net has caught on a tree submerged deep beneath the surface. As the tall man peers into the dark waters, Isaiah looks over to see the whites of his brother's eyes widening with fear. It's 4:00 a.m., when seven- and five-year-old boys are supposed to be asleep at home, near the safety of their mothers.

The night is eerily quiet, with only the achingly slow cadence of water lapping against the boat and the distant sound of other boys pulling other nets on other boats. In the daylight, these boats are deceptively resplendent, decorated with bright rainbow colors. Each boat has a name, such as *Trust in God, Jonah and the Whale, Woman at the Well*, with an accompanying painting of a biblical story on the side, such as the ascension of (a white) Christ. Isaiah's boat is called *God's Love*. A pink moon offers the last of its pale light hovering above the lake's horizon, with its sister moon slow dancing on the tips of gentle waves. The tall man turns on a tiny LED flashlight, affixed to his head with a sweatband, and scans the opaque gray water. He is like one of the crazy men from the market that Isaiah's father used to warn him about, wearing only a threadbare tank top and burgundy underwear. With the tall man's eyes still focused on the surface of the water, he waves his arms at Joseph, summoning him with his bony fingers. Joseph walks obediently to the side of the boat and carefully examines where the net emerges from the water. He turns to catch Isaiah's eyes, searching for someone to override his master's terrifying order, and then, without any more hesitation, leaps into the darkness of the lake.

The second that his brother disappears in the murky abyss, Isaiah's mind shifts into survival mode—a dream state where he imagines his life back home near Accra. He and Joseph shared a two-room shanty outside of the big city with their mother, two sisters, and three other brothers. Their father had left for work in Nigeria two years before and never returned. Isaiah would wake up with his family laid out like dominoes on the floor, nestled in closeness and safety. He used to play in the street with his best friend, Josiah, who lived a few shanty houses down from him. Josiah liked to pretend to be Asamoah Gyan, captain of Ghana's national football team, the Black Stars. They would pass the remnants of a football, held together with twine and wire, until dusk.

Isaiah came home one day to a tall man talking outside with his mother. She was wringing her hands as the tall man spoke. She only wrung her hands when she talked about his father. As Isaiah drew closer to the tall man, he could see Joseph listening from inside the shanty. The tall man's voice was high like a woman's and hurried like the men selling in the market. *Does this man know where my father is?* he thought. *Are we going to meet him in Nigeria?* He heard the tall man say that he had just come from Josiah's home and that Josiah was going with him. *Going where?* As Isaiah came to his mother's side, the tall man produced a soothsayer grin and got down on his knee, level with Isaiah's eyes, and said, "Do you want to go to school?" Isaiah nodded his head up and down without opening his mouth or looking directly at the man. "Good boy. I will collect you tomorrow morning." The tall man noticed Isaiah's brother peeking out from inside the shanty. "He can come as well," the tall man said. Isaiah looked up at his mother with the kind of excitement kids in America have when they get permission to sleep over at their best friend's house. But her eyes were sullen and glazed.

The next morning the two boys were the first to wake up. The tall man arrived early and stood outside with a wrinkled paper bag in his hand. He looked around nervously, as if not wanting to be seen. His mother handed the boys a blanket with its edges tied together. Inside were two shirts and two pairs of shorts. She softly put her hand on their heads as if touching statues, then gently pushed on their backs toward the tall man. Once outside, the tall man handed their mother the paper bag. "Come, boys," he said. Isaiah looked back at his mother one more time. She was wringing the paper bag with both hands, like when she cleaned his clothes. He was sad for her but knew he would see her soon during school break. Just before he turned out of their alley, she yelled, "Watch out for your little brother."

Isaiah looks now into the dark, dirty water as his tall master pulls left and right on the net. It has only been one minute, but it feels like a lifetime. The light of the flashlight scurries across the water, where the bubbles have started to slow. Isaiah thinks about his friend Josiah again. The tall master sold Josiah to another fisherman, who owned a boat called *Fiery Furnace*. Josiah's new master had his own children working on the boat, so it was always Josiah who jumped into the water to free the nets. One day walking along the shore, Isaiah stumbled upon

Josiah's swollen, lifeless body, wrapped haplessly in thin turquoise fish netting. The memory gives Isaiah's half-naked body a chill, and he quickly refocuses his search for more bubbles.

Lake Volta is the largest man-made lake in the world. Years ago the government built a dam filling massive valleys, but they neglected to clear the trees. Fishermen's nets are constantly getting stuck on the submerged trees, so they send down young boys to unhook the nets. The boys are sometimes beaten with an oar if they come up for air too quickly. Some of the fish the boys see below the surface are as big as the boys themselves. These huge fish, some larger than one meter long, will swim to the boys and try to bite them. Isaiah knows this all too well.

More than twenty thousand little boys, and some girls, are forced to work here on Lake Volta. Many are sexually violated. All are forced to work with only a subsistence diet to survive. The children's parents are often duped by men who promise they will enroll the children in school. Some of their traffickers even offer the parents money to take the children away. Isaiah's mother was paid twenty dollars for him and another twenty dollars for his brother, the money wrapped in a paper bag. She was told her boys were being taken to school, which meant two fewer mouths to feed and a chance at a better life for them.

This exploitation is nothing new for this region of the world. More than three hundred years ago, millions of human beings were collected here and shipped to North America and the Caribbean. Europeans ran a very lucrative triangle trade system, bringing guns from Europe to trade with the local tribal leaders. Those tribal leaders captured members of other tribes and traded them for the guns. Those captured souls were then held for months in the dungeons of Belgian forts along the Gold Coast, now Ghana, until the slave ships arrived. They were packed so tightly inside the dungeons that it was impossible to sit down. Sometimes the white slavers running these forts would send down guards to punish the slaves for moaning too loud because the noise was interrupting a worship service elsewhere in the fort. They were marched onto slave ships with names such as *Madre de Deus*

(Mother of God). Like many of the boys on Lake Volta, these Africans sailed on biblical-themed vessels and would never return home. They had to survive four months at sea chained together, with mere inches of room to breathe. Once the ships reached America or the Caribbean, they were traded for goods and commodities such as rum, which were shipped back to Europe. They were no longer Africans with a tribe and family; they were now property, valuable assets in the global economy. Slave labor was an expedient and profitable business, just as it is here on Lake Volta.

Google the words *fishing in Lake Volta*, and you are likely to find pictures of Westerners on fishing holidays, standing knee-deep in water, holding a gigantic tigerfish the size of a five-year-old boy. Isaiah has seen these fish several times when it was his turn to swim down and unhook the nets. His brother is smaller and could not possibly out-maneuver a fish that size. Plus, he can't see but five inches in front of his face because the water is so dark and murky. Isaiah's anxiety begins to fade into resignation that he'll never see his little brother again. His mother's last command echoes in his ear. He argues with himself that he should have jumped into the water first, but knows the master would have beaten them both for disobeying. He can't stand to see his little brother beaten. A few bubbles surface near the boat, then . . . nothing. Holding back tears, he slowly moves away from the side of the boat. He knows Joseph's dead body will be surfacing soon, and he can't bear to watch. Suddenly a small head and muscular shoulders spring from the water. Unable to speak and gasping for air, Joseph nods at the master to pull in the net. It's finally free.

Back on shore my film crew and I are getting ready for the day. We've come to the town of Yeji, on the west side of Lake Volta, to document incidents of child slavery and start developing a program to help. The Yeji shore is brimming with activity at 4:00 a.m. Calls to prayer blast from distorted speakers, stirring this little fishing town into action. Everyone is up for the morning haul. Silhouettes of wooden boats brimming with passengers move slowly against a backdrop of midnight blue.

The stony shore is dotted with the remains of fires where people slept. The dozens of boats parked along the shore look like an illustrated children's Bible. Jacob's ladder. Three crosses. Abraham and Isaac. Our local fixer is on his mobile phone, talking to our boat driver, who is driving toward our location on the shore. He tells us our boat will be arriving soon, so my team uses the time to film the scene around us.

Documentary work is not linear. You seldom have control of the places and people you seek to film. We have been bracing ourselves for a difficult day of searching a massive lake for child slaves. As I look around for a good shot, a young boy backs into me. He is slowly pulling in a net from the water, using all his sixty pounds as leverage. As I move out of the way, I realize there are children all around me, some as young as four, all pulling nets for their masters back at the fires. The children's arms and torsos are abnormally muscular, like little plastic action figures, sculpted by seventeen-hour days. Their man-bodies are incongruent with their soft young faces. It won't be difficult to find children in slavery today. They are everywhere.

Our wooden motorboat arrives just as the sun begins to break over the horizon. My team and I load our gear and pull away from the shore. Within minutes it begins to fill with water and our gear is floating around the basin of the boat. We methodically bail water as we push deeper into the lake's interior. We have no data with which to track boats with child slaves, so we rely on our fixer's hard-won knowledge. He works with our partner organization in Accra, led by a man who was a child slave on this lake not very long ago. After ten minutes on the water, we spot a small boat with a small boy off our starboard bow, so we change course to intercept. As we pull alongside, we notice the little boy is also bailing water over the side, while a tall man wearing a tank top and red underwear listens to a handheld transistor radio. The tall man monitors our approach with suspicion. The boy is wearing only underwear and a tattered sweatshirt with the words *Ship Ahoy* stitched across the front. His increasing curiosity about the white men approaching is at odds with the invisible control his master has over him, so he keeps bailing water while carefully stealing looks at us. His eyes tell us something his mouth is not allowed to—just like the eyes of the kids in my dream.

Once we come alongside their boat, our fixer begins to speak diplomatically in a local dialect with the tall master. The master speaks with jazz hands waving about, talking erratically about how the fishing here is difficult. While he elaborates on his fish tales, I kneel down to speak with the boy who still struggles to make eye contact and never stops bailing water. "What is your name?"

"Isaiah," he says without looking up.

I ask, "Is this your father? Are you going to school? When was the last time you ate? Where do you sleep? What do you want to be when you grow up?" As I ask him questions, I notice that his boat has another passenger, a younger boy lying motionless under the bow, his face buried in the folds of the net to protect against the sunlight.

"He's tired from working all night," Isaiah says without looking up.

I interrupt the tall man's Shakespearean lamentation about how hard his work is to ask him why the boys are not in school. He flails his arms in indignation, like a junior high student caught with marijuana, offering more excuses. I push a little harder, pointing out how small the boys are and that this kind of labor is not reasonable for them. He replies matter-of-factly, "If they do not work, I do not eat." At the sound of these words a crack breaks open from my brain and runs all the way through my heart. He enslaves because he is hungry. His poverty creates exploitation. While the tall man's reasoning is reprehensible, in his mind, he's justified. After all, he paid the mother forty dollars in a paper bag. These children are property, to use and discard, just as they would have been three hundred years before. On his boat, slavery is how you survive.

SYSTEMIC FAILURE

Isaiah's tragic plight is both common and hard to classify. It's slavery. It's poverty. It's lack of access to education. It's failed governance and lack of law enforcement. Perhaps above all, it's a level of injustice beyond our imagination. Righteous indignation and a sense of affronted morality rise up when we hear stories like this, but our morality has little power in Isaiah's world. This isn't just moral failure. It's systemic failure.

The system failed when Isaiah was unknowingly sold to work on a boat. The system failed when a tall fisherman was able to enslave two young boys in the open. The system failed when a young boy was essentially murdered, his body wrapped up in a tangled fishing net. These events are not merely unfortunate; they are failures. This is a whole-cloth breakdown of our capacity to be human to one another. The world failed them. That is not the world they were made for.

To understand what the world needs from you, and to know the true power of your soul dream, a new lens is required. This lens will help you view the world's challenges as problems you get to fix, rather than entrenched conditions that no one can affect. I don't look at some-one who is trapped inside of systemic failures such as extreme poverty, lack of education, lack of healthcare, or lack of justice as mere poverty. I see their challenges through a lens I call a *poverty of means*. This new lens is critical because it will help you focus in on your riot and build toward your life's purpose.

A POVERTY OF MEANS

Poverty is a loaded word. It conjures images of emaciated souls lined up along red dirt roads, waiting for USAID rations. For some, the word *poverty* can sound like a black hole that drains resources and goodwill. For others, it can sound like our brothers and sisters in broken zip codes of broken cities with broken systems proliferating broken racial lines. It can sound like rural communities in Peru where children carry dirty, infected water for three miles back to their village to drink and cook with. You probably have your own images of what poverty is. And while these images are unfortunate, they do not represent the full picture.

The definition of the word *poverty* is a great place to begin to understand poverty of means. *Poverty* is defined as scarcity. It is the fundamental nonexistence of something that's desperately needed. Someone is hungry because there is a scarcity of food. Someone is sick because there is a scarcity of medicine. Someone is in slavery because there is a scarcity of law enforcement. The word *scarcity* is important because it describes an absence where there should be presence, the missing puzzle pieces needed to create a complete and beautiful picture. Poverty simply means that something is missing.

Perhaps you grew up in or around poverty. My wife grew up in poverty near Oakland, California, which was famous at the time for consistently landing in the top ten poorest and top ten most violent cities in America.[1] Physical security and food security were always issues in my wife's home. There was a reason she grew up poor. (There is always a reason.) Her father's alcoholism was part of the reason. He ran off when she was three years old, leaving her young mother to raise four kids on her own. Her mother did everything she could to provide for her children. My wife remembers how her mom would often come home late at night from her job as a waitress with a doggy bag of food for her. They were not poor because some cosmic force in the universe decided that this little family should be poor and other families shouldn't. She grew up poor because she faced a scarcity of provision and safety. It's interesting that we as a society hyper-focus on all the reasons why people get rich but fail to understand that there are actual reasons why people face scarcity. From what I've seen, scarcity is never a twist of fate. It's simply something or someone failing to show up.

I like words, and one of my favorite words is *means*, as in "a means to an end." *Means* is a power word. Its definition is "an action or system by which a result is brought about."[2] When we want to achieve something very important, we often say we'll do it "by any means necessary"—in other words, we'll take whatever action is required to achieve the goal. Means is the action required to produce the desired result. So *poverty of means* is defined as the scarcity of an action or system required to change an undesirable situation.

Anyone whose daily routine revolves around obtaining basic health, justice, security, food, education, and shelter falls under a poverty of means. Children dying from a treatable disease such as cholera suffer from a poverty of means. Girls from rural Cambodia tricked into prostitution suffer from a poverty of means. Middle-class families who've fled genocide in Syria because of ISIS and now live in a refugee camp suffer from a poverty of means. Isaiah—who lacks affordable primary school, functioning law enforcement, and basic healthcare—and my wife as a child—suffer or suffered from a poverty of means.

People who suffer from a poverty of means are in need of an action or a system that will change their situation. Every day, eleven-year-old girls in Somalia wait for something to convince village elders to stop conducting ritualistic female genital mutilation, causing severe physical and social problems. Every day millions of people in Central Africa wait for their governments to clean up the corruption that prohibits them from access to basic food. Eleven children die every minute because they are waiting for systemic changes to curb their extreme poverty, which the World Bank defines as living on less than $1.90 a day.[3] More than 663 million people, twice the number of Americans, are waiting for access to basic clean water while facing preventable disease and death.[4] Every day, the planet waits for governments to actually reduce carbon emissions.

Hunger, injustice, disease, inadequate education, and planetary change are not the problem. The problem is we are using the wrong lens to understand these problems. We need to see them as a poverty of means, a scarcity of an action leading to a result. Poverty of means is our shiny new twenty-first-century lens that allows us to better understand the world's challenges. With this lens we cease to see these situations as misfortunes, causes, or issues to which our primary response is pity. We can now see these situations as challenges, where the most reasonable response is our participation.

Here is another reason why it's time to see these situations as challenges instead of misfortunes that require pity. Our most common and generous response to the misfortunes of others is a donation. Generosity is one of our world's everyday miracles, of which I have been a blessed participant and recipient. But charity alone can't get the job done. Amazing things have been accomplished with charity over the last fifty years, but we can't fix everything with charity. In fact, it's very difficult to create lasting change with charity alone. Rather, we need to find the *means*—an action or system by which a result is brought about—to remove these challenges. There is a means to establishing justice in places where the news cameras are not pointed. There is a means to convincing corrupt governments in East African nations to distribute wealth to its people. There is a means to creating systems of clean water for the world's thirsty.

When we see Isaiah through the lens of a poverty of means, we see the scarcity of justice around him. We see the scarcity of people in power enforcing the laws that should protect his life. We see the scarcity of a justice system set in place to protect him, the scarcity of economic opportunities that allow his mother to raise and provide for him, and the scarcity of an education so he can lift himself out of poverty. Each of these actions and systems would be a means to a better end for Isaiah.

When we think of poverty, we often think of desperation. Sometimes charity organizations use desperation to drive donations. Desperation can look like an emaciated child in rags, reaching out for something to eat. Of course I want to help that child, but desperation is not a strong motivator for sustainable change. When some charity organizations use desperation to convince us to give, they miss the full potential of who we are by focusing only on our potential donation. Participation becomes a transaction. I may give out of pity—I'm sure you would too—but I would only be reacting to difficult information. I don't think it's unreasonable to want to feel needed beyond my donation. In the charity desperation model, all I'm being given is information when what I really want is an invitation. I want to be invited to participate in stories that mean something. Many charity organizations understandably miss this. But we are entering a new era, where who we are matters as much as how much we can give.

Looking at the world's challenges through the poverty-of-means lens opens the door for ordinary people like me to participate. It creates an invitation for curious, passionate, and capable people who want to be a part of a bigger story. It means we can do more than donate. Challenges like Isaiah's are impossible to solve when viewed only as something that needs pity and donations. But when we see that there exists a *means* to a better end for Isaiah, we can build selfish plans to change his world.

I admit that I am bending the definition of *selfishness* here in order to break some taboos about do-gooding. Most examples of selfishness point to someone who is only concerned about himself or herself at the expense of others. Let's look at the first part of that definition of selfishness—the part about being concerned for oneself. I don't believe anyone can change the world without being self-centered. It's impossible. You are not a person without needs that must be met. Neither was Abraham Lincoln, Mother Teresa, or Bill Gates. We are needy all the way up until we breathe our last. We will always be motivated by what meets our needs, even if our need is for meaning and purpose. That's why we need plans that are "selfish," because if they don't somehow help *us*, they will never help the world. As performers, we used to say, "If I'm not rocking, the audience is not rocking." Same goes for changing the world.

Is it possible that we can feed the world and feed our souls? Is it possible that we can fight against someone's injustice as we also fight against the voices in our heads that tell us we've wasted our lives? Is it possible not only to give out of our charity, but also to give out of our talents and story? The answer is yes, and we are just getting started. We need solutions to change the world that simultaneously solve for a poverty of means and a poverty of meaning. This is the subject of our next chapter.

CHAPTER 4

DON'T TRY TO SAVE THE WORLD

October 11, 2011
Port-au-Prince, Haiti

THE SALT BREEZE GLIDES ACROSS THE SAPPHIRE WATERS OF THE CARIBBEAN, over the rusty corrugated roofs, white United Nations tents, open sewage, and pastel-colored shanty homes impossibly perched on the hill we are standing on. If you squint to look beyond the bruised city below us, you'd think you're standing on the top of Robert Louis Stevenson's Treasure Island. This tropical paradise could be a famous travel destination if it wasn't already famous for other reasons. We've just come from the ruins of the National Palace, which looks more like a folded accordion than a house of power. The park across from the palace, where the statue of Haiti's founding father and infamous slave revolt leader Toussaint Louverture stands, is now a tent city housing more than ten thousand Haitians. It's been eighteen months since the earthquake, registering 7.0 on the Richter scale, rocked Haiti and killed 160,000 people, displacing another 1.5 million. The poorest country in the Western Hemisphere became world-famous literally overnight. Round-the-clock CNN news coverage fed the world images of a people who before the earthquake were living on the brink of hell and had now fallen straight in. The world responded with more than $13 billion to help rebuild and restart Haiti, but from up here it's hard to see where the funds are going.

Haiti had it tough from the start, all the way back to the days when Christopher Columbus named the island Hispaniola—which today also includes the Dominican Republic. The French took control of the western region, now Haiti, and imported slaves from Africa to work on their sugarcane plantations. The slaves eventually revolted, and France was forced to abolish slavery. Napoleon lost a huge part of his fighting force trying to shut down the revolution. He needed to liquidate some assets, so he sold the Louisiana Territory, which comprised about a third of what is America today. If you live anywhere in Middle America, you have these Haitian slave revolutionaries to thank. People in Arkansas would be speaking French today if not for the Haitian slave revolt. The young and upwardly mobile United States of America purchased the territory for less than what Facebook pays for most of its acquisitions. In the years that followed, France found ways to financially punish the newly free Haitian colony through economic sanctions, keeping this new nation isolated from the ever-expanding global market. Systemic poverty forced families to make hard decisions in order to survive. A practice for helping poor children was developed during this time, which became an entrenched tradition in Haitian society. This tradition is why I'm here today.

Parents living in rural areas of Haiti during the colonial period did not have enough resources to feed, clothe, and educate all of their children. So they would send some of the children away to a city to live as domestic servants with a distant relative or a stranger. The child would do household chores in the host's home in exchange for food, shelter, and a chance at an education. This practice was called *restavek*, a term derived from the French words *rester avec*, which means "to stay with." This practice of sending your children away was woven into the fabric of Haitian society, and for a time it worked. Children with no opportunities were being given an education and hope. The restavek practice devolved over time, and by the twentieth century it turned into full-scale domestic servitude. Today young children are sent to strangers' homes to become common house slaves, with no identity and no chance for education. Slavery in Haiti is back.

Now, close to three hundred thousand children in Haiti are living as restavek slaves. Ranging from five to fifteen years old, they are the bottom of Haitian society, forced to perform labor-intensive chores like fetching water and cleaning latrines. Barefoot five-year-olds carry their body weight in water uphill for miles. Their host families are at best indifferent, but often cruel. These restavek children blend into the larger tattered fabric of Haiti's crushing poverty, making them virtually invisible. Fate in the form of an earthquake has given Haiti a chance to move forward, and the global community seems to want to participate in its new start. Haiti has a chance to rebuild its physical infrastructure, as well as its communities. We are here because we believe these three hundred thousand kids deserve to be part of Haiti's restart.

I'm filming a documentary for CNN on the plight of these children. CNN has already made a huge investment in this country by covering the earthquake. They humanized Haiti's challenges better than any other network. The camera operator for our documentary was the first to land after the earthquake. He recounts how the airport was completely abandoned when he landed at first light. Port-au-Prince looked like the set of a horror movie with broken and bloodied souls roaming the ramshackle streets. In addition to the CNN crew, I've brought along someone who can offer another lens through which we can view the challenged lives of these kids: Grammy and Academy Award–winning actor and musician Common.

A few weeks earlier I was in Calgary with another CNN camera crew to meet with Common on the set of his AMC television series *Hell on Wheels*. Common lives what he believes as well as anyone I know. He grew up on Chicago's South Side and experienced firsthand how broken systems can prevent children from reaching their potential. His mother, Dr. Mahalia Ann Hines, has been a leading voice for education, and she is a huge influence on his life and work. Common has a particular penchant and practice of helping young people overcome their challenges and reach their dreams. I asked Common on camera, on the set of *Hell on Wheels*, if he would come with me to Haiti to help these kids living in a broken system without access to an education. And so, here we are today, standing on top of a hill overlooking Port-au-Prince.

We are looking for restavek children whom we can help get into school. To achieve this, we'll have to convince their masters to let them go, which I know sounds backward and broken. It's actually illegal to physically remove children from their "caregiver" host families. A bunch of well-meaning and misguided missionaries tried to rescue kids right after the earthquake and wound up being accused of child abduction and held by Haitian authorities. Freedom is never a linear transaction. It's a series of small steps. So, getting restavek children into school is the first step toward ending the system of slavery in Haiti.

Despite our best efforts to be stealthy, we are rolling through Port-au-Prince with a big footprint consisting of a film crew, security, and social workers. This means we draw a crowd quickly wherever we go. The people of Haiti are fatigued due to eighteen months of visitors from rich nations, with their cameras documenting their suffering. We can seem like an intrusion, which means we can't stay in one location for very long. I believe that if you film exploitation without a plan to address it, you become an exploiter. If you aren't thoughtful, the filming of suffering can become a type of extractives industry, where the extractor (the filmmaker) wins, but the raw materials (the subjects of the film) do not. We are here to tell these children's story to the world and to raise the profile of the righteous local activists working tirelessly in the field. We have partnered with a dynamic local organization called Restavek Freedom Foundation, started by the indefatigable Joan Conn.

Joan and her husband, Ray, are from Cincinnati, where they raised a family and built a successful construction business. By all American-dream standards it's time for them to retire and hang out with the grandkids. A few years ago they were sailing around the Caribbean and decided to come ashore on Haiti. They were instantly overwhelmed with the level of poverty they witnessed. After learning about the restaveks, they decided to make a life pivot and apply themselves to building solutions. They have been here ever since.

Our guide into the slums is a local social worker with the organization and is walking Common and me through a maze of makeshift domiciles. Every home is made from found materials: sticks, food-aid bags, pieces of corrugated tin. We jump from side to side over rivulets of open sewage and trash. Our guide directs us into a home where a restavek child lives with a host family. For some reason the child is gone, but the mother of the house, or master, matter-of-factly shows us the table in the corner under which the child sleeps. She speaks without hesitation about how the child is not really part of her family and is treated as an outsider. It's hard to conceive of how a woman facing abject poverty can enslave a child. It's not something you want to believe is possible. Her poverty is overwhelming, making the distinction between slavery and poverty almost imperceptible. Injustice is a chameleon, masking itself to avoid detection.

Our guide's mobile phone rings. They found a restavek girl who is willing to talk with Common and me. Her master isn't at home right now, so this is our chance. We jump in our vans and drive to her location, where we set up our cameras behind some abandoned tents. Common sweetly asks the young girl questions while our guide interprets in Haitian Creole. "Where are her mom and dad?" he asks. She doesn't know who they are. She's been living with her master for four years. "How old are you?" he asks gently. She shakes her head at the interpreter. She doesn't know. "Do you dream of doing anything or being anything?" The young girl hesitates, then answers in a subdued and confused manner: "I don't have those kinds of dreams." Her poverty of means is so pervasive that she doesn't even possess the faculty to dream of a better life. It becomes clear that we will not be able to help this girl out of her circumstance by enrolling her in school. After our brief conversation, the young girl returns home to her host mother.

The hardest part of abolition work is walking away from children in slavery. I can remember the eyes of every child I had to walk away from. It's always the eyes. Despite the understandable desire to grab a child and run, you can't without permission from the police, who are sometimes complicit. As tragic as it may sound, we aren't here to be cowboys rescuing children. We are here to help expose the system of slavery. It's heartbreaking, but we aren't here filming just to break hearts. Heartbreak is a tool, not a destination. We are here to change something that's breaking kids.

We finally find a child working inside the city slum whom we may be able to help, but to get her to school, we'll have to get permission from the person who controls her. Common sits down with the girl's caretaker and asks if we can enroll her in school. After some deliberation the man agrees. We give the girl some items for school, including some pink barrettes for her hair. Her hand gently grazes the plastic barrettes as if they were precious stones. Seeing a child receive permission to hope for the first time is a dose of pure meaning. It is the payoff for helping create actual change in someone's life, and there is nothing else like it in the world. Tomorrow, instead of carrying water, she will be carrying books.

SAVING THE WORLD AND CHANGING THE WORLD

I am the world's worst fund-raiser, the Woody Allen of fund-raising. If I have to ask you for money, I will trip over my words, talk nervously with my hands, and offer to give you money instead. I have hosted fund-raisers for the organization I started, Made in a Free World, with billionaires in the room and barely raised enough money to cover the wine tab. I'm not shy and don't lack enthusiasm for our work, but I'm terrible at raising money for it. I can probably raise money for whatever you are doing better than I can for my own work. It turns out that fund-raising skills are good to have if you want to run a charitable organization.

It took a while for me to admit to myself, and to my board of directors, that I'm not interested in saving the world. I want to do something very different. I want to change the world. The projects, campaigns, films, and tools my organization built were designed to change the way the world works. They were designed to disrupt the system of slavery. Slavery exists due to the absence of a system, to protect economically vulnerable people, a poverty of means. The profits from slavery exceed $150 billion annually.[1] The amount of money raised to fight slavery is less than $200 million annually. It's not a fair fight. If we want to end slavery, we need to be faster and smarter than those who are enslaving others. I believe we need to challenge the systems of impunity, like the system of restavek in Haiti that allows slavers to thrive. If all we do is try to pull people out of those systems without changing them, more will just fall in. But if we can disrupt the system, we can change the world and save countless lives.

There's an easy way to understand the difference between saving the world and changing the world. To illustrate, let's say you are standing on the edge of a river and hear the voice of someone in trouble coming from the water. You see that a person is drowning, so you jump into the water to save them. Once you get that person safely to shore, you hear another voice coming from upriver. So you swim out to save that person, but before you can get back to shore, you see countless others coming down the river. What do you do? Do you keep jumping in to save them, one by one? That will eventually fail because at some point your energy will diminish and you won't reach them all.

There is another tactic. You can go upriver and find out why these people are falling into the river. You can focus your efforts on stopping what is pushing them in the river rather than pulling them out one by one. See the difference? Pulling people out of the river is saving the world. Running upriver to stop people from falling in is changing the world.

Some might think that changing the world and saving the world is a worthless distinction, but the difference is in the approach and the scale of the results. The end result—people not drowning—is the same in both approaches. Going upriver and preventing people from falling in results in more people staying alive. You can save people by pulling them out, or you can stop them from being pushed in. Two strategies, same goal. The important difference is in how many lives are saved. The challenge is that we are more comfortable with saving than we are with changing. Saving can be performed over and over, but changing a system requires risk and innovation.

Watching the little girl whom Common and I met attend school was incredibly powerful. No one can deny the merits of trying to save her and dozens more like her. After doing this kind of work for years, Restavek Freedom Foundation realized that it's impossible to go to hundreds of thousands of homes to get these kids into school and out of slavery. They also realized that once the kids were in school, Restavek Freedom Foundation would need to raise more money to support their ongoing education. They had to shift some of their over-all strategy by going upriver to change the restavek system. Shifting strategy is something Joan and her husband, Ray, understand well from building a successful business in America. To be successful in business, you need to think ahead of your competition. In the case of Haiti, the competition was the generational, deep cultural acceptance of the restavek system.

A few years after CNN aired our documentary, Joan gave me a call and asked if I would come back down to Haiti to judge a national singing competition. Joan and her team had created the equivalent of *American Idol* in Haiti, only these contestants wrote and performed songs about slavery and the restavek system. Haitians love music more than any country I've visited, and this national competition was a way to get the country singing about something that it rarely talked about. The idea was pure genius. Each of the ten districts in Haiti conducted their own regional singing competition. Attendance for each of these events averaged six thousand people. Radio is the primary source of media in Haiti, and it carried news about the regional competitions for weeks. This amount of free radio coverage about restaveks was unheard-of up to this point. The winners of the regional competitions went on to the national competition in Port-au-Prince at the national soccer stadium, where I was honored to serve as an international judge (that is, a white guy from America).

The singing contest lasted all day and was now being covered by international news outlets. The contestants looked fresh in their white suits and chiffon prom dresses, singing and dancing as if they were auditioning for *Hamilton* on Broadway. It was beautiful to see how the contestants took so much pride and ownership of their songs and, by proxy, ownership of the restavek issue. This was a game-changing strategy. What Joan did was give Haiti something fun to do while also achieving her larger goal of shifting societal norms around child slavery. Creating this contest was far from easy, but it accomplished much more than her team ever could have achieved going door-to-door.

Joan knew that saving kids one by one would never solve the problem, so she went upriver to where the problem originates. The system of restavek is woven into Haitian culture, so much so that one Haitian government official told me it's customary for a groom to give his new bride a refrigerator and a "little one"—that is, a child—as a wedding gift. Lest any American be tempted to feel superior, remember that fewer than one hundred years ago, America was sending its children into coal mines instead of schools. Exploitation of children is unequivocally wrong and must be ended, and our most effective change agents are people like Joan, who weave grace, innovation, and tenacity into action. By creating a participatory cultural event, she enlisted Haitians to speak out about restavek with their own voices.

We rarely change our behavior because we are told to do so. We change when someone who is trustworthy graciously shows us another way to live that works better. That's exactly what this singing contest did. It motivated individuals based on their own needs and desires—a cash grand prize and prestige among peers. Joan's approach is all too rare. Though we all like the grand pageantry of changing the world, we naturally default to trying to save it instead. Joan learned through experience that she would need to change the world to save the world. Her example is a gift to any of us who want to find our purpose. We may think our purpose is to save the world, but more than likely it's to help change it.

THE LIMITATIONS OF CHARITY

Charity is one of the great pillars of any society. According to the National Center for Charitable Statistics, American individuals gave $258.52 billion in 2015. This does not include corporate and foundation giving. In the last ten years, we have seen a renaissance in fund-raising strategies with new online tools and campaigns designed to encourage donations. You can donate your birthday. You can donate a bike ride. You can donate what you would have spent on lunch. You can donate instead of getting doused with ice water. A new generation of always-on and always-connected individuals has innovated philanthropy, making it easier and more exciting to donate to our favorite causes. These donations feed into organizations addressing a multitude of needs, from cancer research to bed nets in Central Africa. The transaction of giving and deploying funds has never been easier, and the world is truly better for it.

Charity has long been the device through which we save the world from its problems. This transaction is composed of a donor and a practitioner. The donor gives money and the practitioner does the work. To use our river metaphor, the donor gives the funds enabling the practitioner to wade into the river and save people. The donor receives a sense of satisfaction for helping save the world, and the practitioner gets the resources needed to do the difficult job. This charitable-transaction model has worked for generations, but we can do more. Much more.

As someone who has been a practitioner myself, I am well aware that our organization has counted on donors to fund our work. But as noted earlier, I have had a hard time raising money because our approach is more about change and less about saving. I've spoken at dozens of fund-raising events, sharing how we are "going upriver" to change the system and stop slavery from proliferating. The upriver approach we employ is utilizing the power of the world's supply chains to disrupt the business of slavery. While I consider myself a decent communicator, I have failed often at convincing potential donors about our theory of change. Sometimes after I've finished my heartfelt, pitch-perfect, Churchill-like speech about ending slavery, potential donors will come up to me and ask how I am going to help the kids. I think to myself, *I thought I just told everyone here how we are going to do it in my awesome, inspiring speech about going upriver.* I want to pull out my TED talk–esque presentation again and start over. It isn't the donor's fault. These are amazing people who genuinely want to do good things; otherwise they wouldn't have shown up at a fund-raiser. When a donor's heart is tuned to help save kids from slavery, someone prattling on about corporate supply chains is a distraction. They are simply following the time-tested protocol of all the other charity events that serve up dry chicken, white wine, and inspiring images. It wasn't that they didn't want to give. They came to give in order to save, and I wasn't offering opportunities for that.

Eventually, we found a way to serve the donors who wanted to save kids directly from slavery. We created projects with partner organizations working in the field and directed 100 percent of these funds to these projects. Each project we developed had a clear goal along with a transparent budget and timeline. People loved it, and we've been able to directly impact thousands of kids. This traditional charity model of saving the world works because it fits into our already very full lives. There are literally thousands of ways to give, which is a good thing; but it's not the only thing. The challenge is in understanding that changing the world is as important as saving it.

The change-makers who came before us believed that their humanity was wrapped up in the humanity of others. Dr. Martin Luther King Jr. said in his "Letter from a Birmingham Jail," "Injustice anywhere is a threat to justice everywhere." He went on to say, "We are caught in an inescapable network of mutuality, tied in a single garment of destiny. Whatever affects one directly, affects all indirectly."[2] By King's logic, the woman at work getting slighted in her compensation affects every woman. The young boy being shoved against a police cruiser for being born black affects every young black, white, brown, and yellow boy. The pimp who pretends to be a boyfriend to the fourteen-year-old girl who just ran away from home endangers every young girl. Those children are our children. Those boys are our brothers. The work of the change-makers noted previously was not built on merely feeling sorry for their brothers and sisters in need, but in walking upriver to create lasting change. Sometimes pity, or feeling sorry for someone, is what drives us to want to save others. Pity alone could not have created the civil rights movement. That historic movement, and others like it, was built on something far more powerful than pity. Change has always been built on something deep and powerful inside of every one of us. Change is built on parity.

PARITY AND PITY

Service is the rent we pay for being. It is the very purpose of life, and not something you do in your spare time.

—MARIAN WRIGHT EDELMAN, PRESIDENT AND
FOUNDER OF THE CHILDREN'S DEFENSE FUND

On September 2, 2015, before the sun climbed out of the Aegean Sea, Alan's father placed him and his brother, Galib, along with Alan's mother, Rehana, into an inflatable rubber raft with twelve strangers on a rocky shore a few miles south of Bodrum, Turkey. Reports are unclear if life vests were worn or who chose to drive the boat the 2.5 miles toward the Greek island of Kos. Alan's father, Abdullah Khurdi, paid the traffickers $5,860 for four of the sixteen spots on a boat designed to carry eight people. This was Abdullah Khurdi's fourth attempt to cross this small stretch of ancient sea, a leg of a journey that would hopefully end in Vancouver, Canada, where relatives were waiting. Abdullah chose this remote section of beach to avoid detection from the boat patrols off Bodrum. Getting caught would mean losing the fee that he paid to the traffickers and having to start over again. If the sea cooperated, they could reach Kos within thirty minutes. However, their voyage to freedom was over within five minutes.

According to Abdullah, the waves quickly became violent, making it impossible to steer with the small single engine. No one knew how to drive a boat, much less in rough open water. Few of the passengers had ever been in water deeper than their waists. The waves grew higher the farther they pushed into open water. In an instant, the boat flipped upside down, throwing mothers and children who couldn't swim into the Aegean Sea. Rehana had been warned by family members not to make the crossing, but her husband insisted. What options did they have? Crossing waters where thousands had drowned in the last few months in order to land in a foreign country with just the clothes on their backs, then enduring the purgatory of the refugee camps in Greece for years, was far better than staying in their hometown of Kobani in Syria.

Before the war, Abdullah was a successful barber providing a modest middle-class lifestyle for his young family. ISIS took control of the city almost overnight, forcing everyone to convert to their version of Islam. Abdullah was of Kurdish descent, making his family a prime target for ISIS. His option was either to face the imminent extermination of him and his sons, along with the likelihood of his wife being sold to ISIS combatants for sexual slavery, or to follow the path of hundreds of thousands of Syrian refugees into Turkey. He figured that once he walked his young family the 795 miles to Bodrum, he could pay human traffickers to get him to the Greek Isles. There, he could apply for asylum in Canada, where a family member was waiting. He knew he would have no bargaining power with the traffickers, who could force upon him their own price and terms, which included the barely operable overfilled boat.

Around 5:00 a.m., Turkish authorities near Bodrum began to receive calls that a boat had capsized. By 6:30 a.m. bodies were washing ashore. One investigator saw what looked like blue and red articles of clothing at the shoreline. As he drew near, he realized it was the drowned body of a three-year-old boy. Alan's little body lay facedown, his head turned slightly to the left, with his arms placidly tucked into his sides. The sweet and peaceful positioning of his small body there at the waterline expressed a false narrative. He looked as if he had fallen asleep in the car seat on the drive home and his parents had gently put him to bed with his clothes still on. He was lying in the same position that millions of other sleeping toddlers were sleeping in at that very moment all over Europe. A photographer on the scene took a picture of Alan and submitted it to the newswires. Within twelve hours more than fifteen million people viewed the photograph. Within twenty-four hours the still image of the baby asleep on the beach was international news. With this one image, the plight of Syrian refugees officially became a global crisis.

The migration caused by the war in Syria and Iraq was a crisis before Alan's dad put him in a raft. Most major news outlets were already covering the story, calling it the worst refugee crisis since World War II. There were stories of refugees drowning, images of infants with hypothermia being wrapped in blankets by Greek rescue workers, and aerial videos of Exodus-long caravans moving across Turkey. The refugee migration was news, but the world's attention was occupied elsewhere.

Overnight, the image of Alan on the beach slammed into the world's consciousness like a punch from a prizefighter's forgotten arm. For some reason, Alan's picture was different from all the other images of refugee children buzzing in the media every day for over a year. His timid frame captured something greater than our pity. He captured our sense of parity. The world was looking at their own child, their own nephew, their own grandson on that beach. I've watched my son sleep in that exact position countless times. I've stood over his crib, mesmerized with love and gratitude to the Almighty for trusting me with such a miraculous gift. Parents universally look at their children while they sleep. That common feeling of parental love is what the world felt when it looked at Alan's still body. Parents from all over felt that warm, deep love that we have for our own children, while also wrestling with the reality that this was someone else's child who had perished while fleeing from terrorists. Alan became our child.

Alan was the SOS message in a bottle that the world finally decided to read. The world reacted with donations. People began to work out their frustrations through generosity, activism, and creativity. They took the photograph of Alan and photoshopped it to look as though he were sleeping in the middle of the United Nations' General Assembly and on the president's desk. The famous Chinese activist and artist Ai Weiwei was photographed on a beach, lying in the same position as Alan. Other groups performed mass protests by lying on beaches, dressed in red and blue. The Syrian refugee crisis became a major campaign issue for Canada's 2015 national elections. No image has elicited such a response of parity since the 1972 image of a young naked Vietnamese girl running away from a napalm attack during the Vietnam War. There were plenty of images of children in the Aegean Sea that came before Alan's, but those only touched our pity. Alan touched our parity.

The natural reaction to the problems of people we don't know is pity. We feel sorry for them and their unfortunate circumstance. *Pity* is defined in the *Oxford English Dictionary* as "the feeling of sorrow and compassion caused by the suffering and misfortunes of others." Pity is merely a feeling. Somewhere along the way society has convinced itself that feelings are somehow an accomplishment. We believe that our pity, whether felt internally or posted to our social network, actually accomplishes something. When those we love are in trouble, do we just feel pity? Do we just feel sorry for them? No, we feel the need to help them because they are our people, and our equals. What happens to our people affects us. This feeling of mutuality we share is *parity*—the state or condition of being equal. When my son hurts his knee, I don't have pity on him, standing at a distance feeling sorry for him. I get involved with his pain and help him because we have parity. His pain is my pain. Pity is kind, and sometimes it's where we start, but pity alone is not very helpful. More important, we ourselves don't want people's pity; we want parity. Wouldn't you rather be understood than felt sorry for?

Parity is what happens when we believe that the problems of others are as important as our own. And this is where it gets personal. Does this mean our First World problems, such as an uncertain job market or facing the indifference of someone whom you want to love you, are equal to Third World problems, such as fleeing your home because of a terrorist group? Absolutely not, but neither does it mean that I should stop caring about my needs to care for the needs of others. It's virtually impossible not to take care of our own needs. I've yet to meet an entirely selfless person.

Even our legends of social justice had motivations for self-protection and self-betterment. Humanitarians worry about paying the rent, just like the rest of us. We'll discuss further how our motivations work in the coming chapters, but for now it's important to understand that we were built to see mutuality between ourselves and people we don't know. Why is this important? Because seeing others' challenges through the lens of pity is a double mistake. Pity lacks the power of truly helping others because it is only a feeling, and it lacks the power to produce any meaning in our lives because it requires zero vulnerability on our part. Looking at Alan through the eyes of a parent stirs up deep vulnerability and empathy. These are the deep waters of parity inside us that see the plight of his family as being as important as the plights we navigate for our own families.

You might think that though we can have a sense of parity with our families and friends, having parity with people halfway around the world—with different backgrounds, beliefs, and income brackets—is impossible. But the photograph of Alan Kurdi proves otherwise. That photo reveals that we can operate with a parity mindset for people we don't know, even if it's for a brief social media moment. We can feel a sense of mutuality for others by overcoming our emotional default setting of pity and pushing ourselves to venture upriver and find ways to create change for kids like Alan. This is what Dr. King meant by "an inescapable network of mutuality."

Here's a bonus tip: Parity comes standard on all makes and models of human beings. It's a feature we all possess, but it needs to be developed. On the day Alan's story traveled around the world, we all still went to work, went to school, paid our bills, and spent time doing things we like to do because life is always moving. What would happen, however, if we let stories like his stay with us a little longer than a brief social media moment? What if we did more than share Alan's image on social media by instead writing a longer post about how it affects us? What if his story became a topic at dinner that night? Though actions like this do not directly fix the refugee crisis, they do bring these struggles into our lives alongside our own victories and struggles. It positions Abdullah's hopes to make a better life for his family alongside our own hopes for our families. Small acts like these humanize our mutual struggles by focusing on our similarities. That's how our parity starts to come out of us. That's exactly how we begin to change the world, because we would do anything, or at least we would do something, for someone we feel mutuality with.

When Common asked the young girl in Haiti about her dreams, he asked from a position of parity. Parity says that her invisible life is as valuable as his highly visible life. Living for your dreams is what Common is all about. His life and actions demonstrate this. He gets up every day and continues to reach for his dreams, and he has the humility to know how blessed he is, giving glory to his Maker. He truly believes that if he can reach his dreams, then others can as well. This was evident when we went back to South Side Chicago and did a secret concert at a high school. We were able to sneak onto campus with a full concert production and surprise seven hundred students. His concert was a message of hope from an artist who sees his challenges and opportunities in parity with the challenges and opportunities these students face. This parity mindset helps us to see the world's problems as a poverty of means, a scarcity of solutions. Parity even reformulates how we view our lives with our own needs and motivations. Parity means we don't feel sorry for people. Instead, we feel connected to them. Think of parity as the human software we use to change the world and ourselves.

THE NEW ERA OF PARITY

We are living in the era of the everyday problem-solver. I work in San Francisco, where it seems as if we are finding new problems to fix every day. One morning I saw two guys standing on the street corner in front of our office, one wearing a pink blazer, holding a matching pink umbrella, and the other wearing a blue Windbreaker with a matching blue Razor scooter. They each worked for competing on-demand parking startups. If you want to park your car, you simply open the app from one of the companies and tell it where you want to drop off your car. A parking agent meets you there and drives away in your car to park it somewhere. Do I really want to give my car to a complete stranger in a blue Windbreaker and then recall my car on my phone hours later? Why, yes, I do! A few months before, it was unthinkable to hand my keys to a stranger on a blue scooter; now it makes perfect sense. Parking has always been a problem in San Francisco, yet now there is a solution (for a price). This is an amazing time to be alive because we believe we can solve almost any challenge. Previously intractable challenges, like ending malaria, colonizing Mars, and improving parking in San Francisco, now seem plausible. We are a generation that believes problems are meant to be fixed. In other words, we are a generation determined to reduce scarcities of solutions.

The Hebrew word for charity is *tzedakah*, but the actual definition of the word is "to do what is right and good, often through an act of goodwill." Further study of the definition of *tzedakah* reveals that the highest act of goodwill includes building a partnership with someone in need so that person will not remain in need. Somewhere along the way we started to define *benevolence* as donations, but it has always been about building partnerships through a lens of parity.

There has never been a better time in history to leverage our penchant for problem-solving for those struggling inside a poverty of means. I believe in a world where parking problems and child slavery can both be fixed with the same creativity and passion. By applying our problem-solving tenacity toward the problems of others, we fix our own struggles of purpose and meaning for our lives, a true win-win. Joan's singing contest proved that we can do more than just try and save the world; we can actually change it for good when we see others, like Alan, through the lens of parity.

Made in a Free World made a huge bet on parity when we doubled down on changing the world instead of trying to save it. We believed we could reduce slavery globally by influencing something that happens every nanosecond of every day. Consumers, businesses, governments, and organizations are purchasing goods and services constantly without knowing whether or not that purchase was produced with slavery. This question is just not something that people have thought about, until now. We determined that if we can influence those purchases with intelligence about the likelihood of slavery, we could eventually impact tens of millions of lives. Slavery and child labor are buried deep in supply chains, but previously no one had a way to look for it. So we built a software business intelligence tool called FRDM that companies use to identify risky purchases. When the company identifies a risk, they can then interrogate certain suppliers that might be benefiting from slave labor. This long-form upriver approach is designed to make it hard for bad guys hidden deep in supply chains to profit from slavery.

We wanted to change the world, so we had to harness the power of parity. This pivot in our approach to the problem of slavery might be why it was hard for me to fund-raise. (Or I'm just genuinely terrible at it.) We turned purchasers into practitioners because that's where the power is. Both individual consumers and large corporate buyers now have the power to influence the behavior of the companies they buy from. Who would have thought that business professionals doing the purchasing at companies had the power to impact kids' lives? If Made in a Free World was only focused on saving the world, then we would never have partnered with companies to make this kind of impact.

This is truly the age of the problem-solvers, the upriver change-makers. We see our stories wrapped in the stories of others. There are no rules to changing the world anymore. There are no schools from which you must get a degree. There are no mega-institutions where you need to intern. All that's required is a mindset of parity and a desire to be a part of a bigger story. That's it. If you believe that all 7.5 billion of us are part of a "network of mutuality, tied in a single garment of destiny," and if you want to find your spot in that tapestry, then you are ready to change the world. You just might have the ideas, skills, and the right amount of change in your pocket to genuinely improve the lives of others. To do this, we next need to learn how our own neediness can meet the needs of the world.

CHAPTER 5

A POVERTY OF MEANING

MARCH 12, 2008
AUSTIN, TEXAS
ALAMO DRAFTHOUSE CINEMA

I'VE SEEN THIS FILM A THOUSAND TIMES, AND I CAN TELL YOU THE EXACT second when Ashley Judd is going to cry. I know every frame, every note, and every word of the script. Tonight's viewing is a little different, though, because I finally get to watch it with an audience of strangers. This isn't a typical Hollywood screening audience used to test whether your romantic comedy will play well to Midwestern mothers ages twenty-five to forty. This audience has a very specific and refined palate. They've come from all over the world to attend the famous South by Southwest Festival (SXSW), one of the premier music and film festivals in the world. Musicians, film critics, visual artists, superfans, film executives, and music industry executives are here to view screenings of major and independent studio films, and watch bands such as Radiohead, the White Stripes, and the next Ed Sheeran perform. Their discriminating taste led them to this festival, and now they are filing into one of my favorite theaters in the world to watch the rockumentary I directed, *Call + Response*. My editing team and I have been stretching and tweaking this film inside a San Francisco editing suite for almost a year. This is the first time it has made it out of our editing suite and the bubble of our isolated scrutiny. This is a real audience in a real theater with real popcorn and very real opinions. You might say tonight is the film's theatrical bar mitzvah.

It was only nine months ago that I finished filming the last musical performance for the film right here in Austin. We had been shooting all day at a recording studio called Tequila Mockingbird with the brilliant performing artist Matisyahu. We had wrapped up our shoot and the vans had arrived to take Matisyahu and his band off to their show. The first van left with most of the band. Matisyahu and a few players were waiting for the second van when I got an idea. I asked him if he'd ever performed Bob Marley's "Redemption Song." He said he never had but was up for a try. So we raced back into the studio and stopped the crew from tearing down all the gear. Matisyahu, along with his guitar player and bass player, started into the song. I watched through the camera monitor as he gently fell into a trance singing Bob Marley's timeless question, "Won't you help to sing these songs of freedom?" Matisyahu was turning the lyrics into a prayer. It was immediately obvious that this artist was made to sing this song for this film about this cause at this moment. We were on sacred ground, capturing something transcendent to film. Tequila Mockingbird became a temple of remembrance for the transatlantic slaves, and for the millions we were now trying to help with this film.

Toward the end of the song, Matisyahu started beatboxing and freestyling. It felt as if the roof came off our recording temple, and a wave of collective effervescence flowed across the planet to people of all backgrounds and faiths. At that moment music was more than sound. It was a rallying cry for the cause of freedom. Once he finished beatboxing his last line, we all came back to earth and Matisyahu jumped into his van.

My producer drove me to the Austin airport, both of us still deeply moved by what we had just experienced. He said to me, "This footage looks good enough to be on the big screen." I knew the film was starting to become something meaningful, but documentaries, or even rockumentaries, are very difficult to get into theaters reserved for the latest superhero film. Now here we are, nine months later, just down the road from Tequila Mockingbird, with Matisyahu's rendition of "Redemption Song" as the film's closing performance.

Making a film is pretty hard to do, but getting a film into theaters is almost impossible, especially when you don't have any money. But we didn't make a normal film, where you come up with a script and then go out and ask someone to give you money or permission to make it. This film, just like Matisyahu's performance, wanted to be made. It only needed a few, or a few hundred, crazy individuals who had found their riot, listened to their soul dreams, and stepped into the chaos to create something that's never existed before.

Watching the film here in this theater is somewhat bittersweet for me. This wonderful experience is not my dream. I recognize that many people would love to make a film and have it screened here, but I never set out to be a film director. I had a rock dream, not a film dream. My entire life up to this point has been about making music. I would never have written this chapter into my story. And yet, I'm living inside this moment—with a musical doc-opera focused on a very difficult topic being distributed into theaters. What makes this chapter sweet in my life isn't the film itself, but the story of how it was made.

Creating this film has taught me a lot about the power of vulnerability, especially the vulnerability one faces when trying to change the world somehow. This type of vulnerability is raw and open because you can't do it alone. You need others. Here's how that worked for me. I didn't have the required money, power, expertise, or relationships that films typically require. I was still in my record contract when I got the vision for this film. What I didn't know was that this film was my riot coming out. I decided to take a break from recording and then called everyone I knew in the music industry to pitch my idea of filming live performances of music artists in order to bring awareness to modern slavery. Miraculously, my wonderful friends in the music industry started tapping their Rolodexes for me, reaching out to talent agents and production houses. This generosity from friends gave me the confidence to keep pushing further and risking more and more for the film. I think you can see where this was heading.

The more I worked on this film, the more time, money, and skills were needed. More and more artists wanted to perform. More experts wanted to lend their voices. There were film shoots in London with Natasha Bedingfield and Talib Kweli. There was an interview in New York with Nicholas Kristof from the *New York Times*. There was an interview with Secretary of State Madeleine Albright in Washington DC. The film project completely took over my life, and it was clear that this would not be a solo effort. I had walked out on a precipice with a reckless passion and an unformed riot. The film was taking off, and I was desperate.

Desperation creates vulnerability, and vulnerability creates opportunity for others to help. What started to happen around me was nothing short of a miracle. Camera operators who are used to receiving substantial sums of money showed up to the film set for free and then thanked me for the opportunity afterward. More Grammy Award–winning artists gave up an entire day to perform for free. Song rights holders, such as Radiohead and the Bob Marley family, gave me permission to use their songs for free. My cowriter, Shadd, gave up precious time that could have been used for other projects to work on the editing. When people learned about the story and vision of this film, they jumped in to help, sometimes for months on end. I've learned that when you step out into something bigger than yourself, people around you are attracted to not only your vision but also your vulnerability, which provides them a platform to participate with their own talents, financial resources, and networks. Your need becomes an opportunity for others.

Everything on the big Alamo Drafthouse screen in front of us is the product of a convergence of talent being leveraged to save people in slavery. No one was paid to make it. Not the crew, the talent, the performers, the camera operators, the film scorers, the editors, the colorists—no one. People found their riot and gave of their talents and networks to put a film about slavery into this theater. When I took the film to the MPAA to get its rating, I was certain they would rate it R for its content, but even they helped when they chose to give it a PG-13 rating because they *wanted more people to see it*. So, it's popcorn and Kleenex time for a few of us here tonight.

As the final credits roll, listing the hundreds of names of the people who helped make this film, I'm reminded that no matter who we are, where we are, or what we're good at, we all want to be a part of something bigger. We want to participate in something bigger than our best-laid plans (rock dream) and contribute to a timeless narrative (soul dream). As I look down the row from where I'm sitting in this theater, I can see tears in the eyes of the people who worked on this film. They are watching something they sacrificed for being screened during the world-famous SXSW Festival. As the houselights come up, so does the entire audience for a standing ovation. The film crew's investment will pay dividends for years to people the crew will never meet. This film will go on to travel the world, exposing the insidious crime of slavery. The lives of the crew have been enriched because they gave themselves away to something that will help others. I could never pay them what their talents are worth, but their response tonight tells me that they have been paid in something far better: they were paid in meaning.

THE POVERTY OF MEANING

Loneliness and the feeling of being unwanted is the most terrible poverty.

—MOTHER TERESA

I was once speaking in a Las Vegas hotel at a large conference of business executives hosted by the global software company SAP. My organization, Made in a Free World, had recently built a software platform to help businesses detect slavery deep in supply chains. I talked onstage to approximately four thousand business professionals about our mission to build tools that everyday consumers and business professionals can use to make the world better. I explained how our software platform called FRDM empowers business leaders to protect the lives of millions through their purchases. Keep in mind, these attendees are used to conference keynotes on topics like the latest cloud-based financial modeling tools, open APIs (application program interfaces) for mobile software engineering, or predictive algorithms. Instead of showing them bar graphs and *up and to the right* market projections, I talked about how millions of people trapped in slavery are connected to our daily lives through the products we purchase. I then petitioned the executives in the conference hall to join us by leveraging their companies' purchasing power to help kids live a life of freedom. My message seemed to be well received, and after shaking a few hands backstage, I headed out of the conference hall.

I'm really not a conference guy. I love speaking at them, but conferences are primarily designed for networking, which requires me to walk up to strangers and say hi. I'm terrible at this. So, as people began to pour out from the conference venue, I ran across the main hall of the casino to a coffee shop to grab a cup of my liquid social lubricant. I was standing at the condiments bar, mixing my milk-and-honey cocktail, when a woman who worked at the casino coffee shop came over. She got about three inches from my face and asked my name. It's hard to be an introvert when someone is three inches from your face, so I told her my name and asked how she was doing. Without altering her distance, she asked me what I do for a living, which is always a tough question. So I told her without any diplomacy that I work to protect kids from slavery. She stood back, her eyes as big as cherries on a slot machine, and said to me, "Oh Justin, God has plans for you. I'm going to pray for you." Then she put the sugar packs she was holding into their dispenser and walked back to the counter. I'm a big believer that we get direction for our lives from unexpected sources. Her unsolicited encouragement reminded me of why I was there, to employ others into the movement. In other words, "Justin, get over your introverted self."

The condiment lady gave me the courage to swim back into the river of business professionals flowing out of the conference venue. As soon as I did, a well-dressed man with pin-striped pants and a perfect polka-dotted necktie stopped me. This guy probably has almost everything that most people want in life. Good job. Good family. Good retirement plan. Success at work. Free trips to Vegas. Life is good. So I was surprised when I noticed he had tears in his eyes. After some small talk he asked me a question I hear so often: "What can I do to help?" He was using the same sales skills he deploys in his profession to sell himself to me saying, "I know I'm just a guy in a suit, but I really want to make a difference somehow." Here was someone who is slick, successful, and incredibly vulnerable. Here at a conference designed to inspire success, he shared his poverty with a total stranger—a poverty of meaning.

"What can I do?" is an ocean-deep, mountain-high kind of question. It belongs in the pantheon of life's biggest questions, alongside "Who am I?" "Do I matter?" and "Why am I here?" I feel a deep sense of responsibility to help people who go out of their way to ask me this question. Their eyes full of vulnerability. Their voices shaking. These are sacred moments. After listening to the businessman for a few minutes, I finally offered him my gilded answer, sent to me from on high on a marshmallow cloud of wisdom: "I don't know. Only you can answer that."

I hate this answer. Everyone who asks the question hates it too. If he had asked where he could donate, I would've had an answer—but he didn't ask that. He asked a much deeper and more vulnerable question. He wanted to know how he could participate in a bigger narrative, how his life could make a difference in the life of someone else. He wanted to know how to matter. He wanted to know what the world needed from him. That question reminds me of the famous Walt Whitman poem "O Me! O Life!":

> Of the empty and useless years of the rest,
> with the rest me intertwined,
> The question, O me! so sad, recurring—What
> good amid these, O me, O life?

Answer.

That you are here—that life exists and identity,

That the powerful play goes on, and you may contribute a verse.[1]

These kinds of identity questions aren't relegated to conferences, spiritual retreats, mindfulness seminars, or mountaintop experiences. We face these questions while looking at the magazine rack at the grocery store checkout line, watching reality television, sitting in a worship service, watching our children graduate from one grade to another, and about a million other unguarded moments. We want to know that we matter to the world we inhabit. We want to know that the world needs something from us. We want, in Whitman's words, to *contribute a verse*.

As noted earlier, I've come to identify this deep need to participate as a *poverty of meaning*. We have learned how the world's big challenges are best defined as a *poverty of means*, a scarcity of solutions. The needs of the businessman I met are also a form of poverty, or a scarcity. It's a scarcity of meaning. It's a conversation he is having with himself, during his unguarded moments. He is not alone. This poverty is faced by the hockey mom, the university student, the social worker, the retired veteran, the datable single, the social media celebrity, you, and me.

To understand what a poverty of meaning is, it might make sense to talk about what it is *not*. To begin, modern colloquialisms have hijacked the word *meaning*, defining it as something earnest and ancillary, like an emotional accessory we can wear when we want to feel deep-ish. "Oh, wasn't that religious service meaningful?" or "That exhibit in the museum was so meaningful, I cried my eyes out." These experiences and others like them are not meaning. They are feelings. Let me illustrate. I literally cannot move when I hear the Beatles song "A Day in the Life." If the song comes on, no matter what I am doing, I fall into a catatonic state, every synapse in my body paying obeisance to John and Sir Paul. I am Han Solo frozen in carbonite with my hands in the air. What I am experiencing in that moment is a feeling.

Here's another example. When I visit the Tate Modern in London, I walk out so inspired that I actually believe there is still time in my life to become the next Banksy. That's also a feeling (and a delusion). When I watch a movie like *Selma*, I become indignant, my fists clenched with rage. That too is a feeling. Just because I hear a song, visit a museum, or watch a film does not mean that I'm a Beatle, Banksy, or Dr. Martin Luther King Jr. Human beings are designed to be affected by the work of others, but being affected by something is a feeling—and feelings are not meaning. The primary reason for this is that we didn't pay anything for those feelings other than the price of admission. We didn't spend ten thousand hours playing dive bars in Hamburg. We didn't hone a craft worthy of the Tate. We didn't risk our lives marching for civil rights. Meaning comes from action, not from feelings. Meaning requires that we contribute something of value—or in Whitman's words, a verse.

When we become inspired by something, like a great story about someone overcoming odds, we feel a high—as if we too can overcome great odds. We are inspired. But inspiration is also not meaning. Inspiration is the soul's equivalent of cotton candy, having the appearance of food without anything to nourish the body. Calories laced with sugar. The problem is that we've been trained to move from one inspiration to the next, from one feeling to the next, and taught to believe that in doing so we are somehow contributing a verse to the world, when in reality we are just lip-syncing to someone else's risk and rewards. Inspiration can certainly be used to get us to act, but meaning is what we get when we act. Inspiration is not meaning.

Carl Jung, the founder of analytical psychology, wrote, "The least of things with a meaning is worth more in life than the greatest of things without it."[2] So why did the businessman come up to me with tears in his eyes? He, and many like him, have been relegated to a box. He has been financially successful, so society and many charity organizations have put him in the donor box. People like him are asked to give to charity all the time, but they are never asked to participate. No one considered a contribution of his skill sets, his business acumen, or his relational equity. So when he heard me talking at the business conference about how ending slavery requires business practitioners just like him, he saw a chance to build meaning into the story of his life. He thought that perhaps *who he is* and not just *how much he could give* would be helpful in protecting the children forced to work in supply chains. He, like many others, learned that meaning isn't hiding in a bird's nest at the top of a mountain of success and wealth. It's found when we act without reward for the benefit of others. This timeless wisdom has been tested in a place that looks much different from a supply chain conference at a Las Vegas casino.

THRIVING IN A DEATH CAMP

> Ever more people today have the means to live, but no meaning to live for.
>
> —Viktor Frankl

Viktor Frankl's massively influential book *Man's Search for Meaning*, formerly titled *From Death-Camp to Existentialism*, is a journey through the psychology of living inside Nazi concentration camps. Before the war, Viktor was a rising star within the psychotherapy circles of Europe. He published a paper on psychology in high school that gained the attention of psychotherapy's elite, including Sigmund Freud and Alfred Adler. Viktor's early work focused on meaning and values, which led him to organize several youth counseling centers in Vienna around 1930. Due to the success of these free counseling centers, student suicide rates dropped to zero that year for the first time.

In 1938 Nazis invaded Austria. Frankl was allowed to continue his work while his country was under Nazi control. Despite great risk to his own life, he often subverted strict Nazi requirements to euthanize mentally ill patients by declaring them healthy. In 1941 he met and married his wife, Tilly. They soon became pregnant but were ordered to abort by the Nazis. The next year Viktor, Tilly, and his parents were forced to move into the Theresienstadt ghetto, north of Prague. As a result of his incredible work and knowledge, in 1941 Viktor was offered a visa to immigrate to America. His parents did not have the same visa opportunities and would have to stay behind, so Viktor opted to stay, knowing that concentration camps were imminent. His father died in Theresienstadt in 1943.

In 1944 Viktor, Tilly, and his mother were sent to three different concentration camps. His mother was sent to Auschwitz, and his twenty-four-year-old wife was eventually sent to Bergen-Belsen. Viktor bounced around camps, eventually landing at a camp near Dachau, where he performed slave labor during the day and secretly worked on his thesis at night in the overpopulated barracks. The hope of reuniting with his wife and mother were his motivation to keep surviving.

Frankl made an extraordinary decision. He decided to turn his camp, designed to systematically destroy humanity, into a research laboratory to learn about humanity's need for meaning. In this "laboratory" he played two roles: curious researcher and tortured subject. The physical brutality Frankl's captors exercised on the prisoners was designed to obliterate the prisoner's sense of control. All external choices were taken away, such as what they wore, what they ate, when they slept, and how much they worked. Survival was predicated on mental health as much as physical health. But there was one choice his deranged captors could not control. Choosing how one viewed their circumstances was the only choice the prisoners could own for themselves. Their internal perspective on their external conditions was the place they could be free.

In his book, published after the war, Viktor explained the difficult mental shift one had to make: "What was really needed," he wrote, "was a fundamental change in our attitude toward life. We had to learn ourselves and, furthermore, we had to teach the despairing men, that *it did not really matter what we expected from life, but rather what life expected from us.*"[3] Frankl meant that the only way to survive was to believe that the world needed something from them. His mission in the death camp, as it was back in Austria before the war, was to save as many souls as possible.

Every prison has its own subeconomy, and Frankl's prison was no different. The prisoners were forced to do local construction jobs or build roads, train tracks, and ditches for municipal contractors. Their daily ration of food—a few ounces of bread and half a bowl of watered-down soup—didn't provide the calories and protein necessary to keep up with the strenuous forced-labor projects. To motivate productivity, the prison guards would reward prisoners with cigarettes if they willfully took on a difficult or dangerous task, such as digging a tunnel. These cigarettes were a form of currency in the camp that could be traded among the other prisoners for food and other resources needed to survive. If you worked particularly hard that day, you traded your cigarettes for another prisoner's food rations and lived to see another day. The tobacco trade was vital because if you were deemed too weak or sick to work, you were exterminated.

Suicide was common and even encouraged by the SS guards. If someone tried to commit suicide, the prisoners were not allowed to physically stop him. Viktor saw this as an opportunity to utilize his expertise in suicide prevention. He had to find a way to preemptively identify prisoners who were considering suicide. He discovered a startling pattern. The prisoners who opted to smoke their cigarettes were often the ones most likely to commit suicide. Instead of holding onto their tobacco currency to trade it for food, they would smoke the cigarettes and offer themselves one last illusion of control. Frankl identified these prisoners as high risk and worked to convince them of a higher purpose for their lives. He counseled them, saying that life still expected something from them, that they still had a verse to contribute. He told them that their suffering, as sadistic as it was, could one day serve some purpose if they chose to view it as such.

Frankl wasn't just encouraging his fellow prisoners to survive. He was teaching them to thrive, to live for something beyond their immediate challenges. Thriving in the midst of adversity requires a pursuit of something meaningful while in the throes of suffering. Thriving in adversity is about believing that your life's trajectory isn't solely based on existing data. It's the belief that no matter what the circumstances are, the world still requires something from you. Choosing to thrive in adversity means that your life matters. Adopting this perspective of thriving is the foundation of meaning.

Meaning isn't something we only need later in life. According to Frankl, meaning is what's required to survive at any age. While our lives look nothing like those of Frankl's fellow prisoners, we still face adversity and disappointment. Frankl's wisdom is a critical lesson if you want to change the world. One of the few things we have in common with those prisoners is that life doesn't turn out the way we planned. Frankl's findings about pursuing meaning in your life, regardless of the circumstances, are relevant to us. Knowing that the world needs something from us can give us purpose through the daily grind of our lives. The prisoners in Frankl's camp were always hustling for cigarettes to barter, but mere pursuit of survival was not enough to keep them alive. Likewise, the mere pursuit of living our rock dreams is not enough. Without meaning, many prisoners fell into a paralysis of despair, smoking their last cigarettes in a delusion of control. In a similar manner, many of us today are opting for a life of survival and control over a life of meaning.

Frankl followed his own wisdom. He himself thrived because he found purpose in working to save others in his camp, along with the hope of reuniting with his mother and wife. His own wretched daily existence in the camps was offset by his belief in his purpose on earth. It was his focal point for the three years he spent in the concentration camps, and it gave his shattered life meaning. His camp was finally liberated by Allied forces in 1945. Shortly thereafter he learned that both his mother and his wife had been killed one year earlier upon entering the concentration camps. Despite this tragic loss, Viktor Frankl went on to teach about meaning and purpose for the rest of his life until he passed away in 1997.

Frankl offers us a timeless truth: Meaning is required in order to thrive, no matter what life throws at us. Meaning isn't something we need when things are going well; it's exactly what we need when things are difficult. It gives us context in our difficulties, and balance in our successes. Understanding what the world needs from you (finding your riot) and working toward it (your soul dream) is how you thrive in every chapter of your life. Don't fall for the mistake of pursuing meaning once you have everything you want. It will be too late. Addressing your poverty of meaning is something you can begin now, no matter where you are. To understand our poverty of meaning, it might help to understand its distant cousin, happiness.

IF YOU'RE HAPPY AND YOU KNOW IT

If meaning is so important, then why are so many of us living below its poverty line? Before I answer that, let me say that I know what you're probably thinking: *Hey, look: I'm okay. I'm pretty happy. No, I'm very happy. Sure, some bad things have happened, and there are things I'd like to change about my life, but I'm happy and I know it, so back off.*

Happiness is great. I love being happy. We can't get enough, constantly chasing after our next fix of happy. But happiness comes in single servings. What made us happy yesterday may not make us happy today. Yesterday getting a puppy made me happy. Today the puppy used my pillow as a toilet. Yesterday eating pasta, ice cream, and three Slim Jims (a beef product rolled into the shape of a straw) made me happy. Today my stomach is boycotting my body, and I hate myself a little. Happiness, like sugar and campaign promises, doesn't stick around very long.

We've been sold the idea that drinking the elixir of happiness will bring fulfillment, but it fails the task miserably. A study originally published in 2012 in the *Journal of Positive Psychology* concluded that people who are focused solely on happiness "are takers rather than givers, and they devote little thought to past and future." The study further concluded that "happiness without meaning characterizes a relatively shallow, self-absorbed or even selfish life."[4] In short, the pursuit of happiness alone leads us toward narcissism and shallowness. Now remember, I'm not talking here about selfishness as we're defining it. That selfishness is all about tending to the needs of the self. The narcissism the study uncovered is created by an unbridled pursuit of happiness or tending *exclusively* to the needs of the self.

It's easy to make an unexpected left turn into the alley of narcissism. I've certainly spent some time there, but it's a terrible place to stay. If we aren't careful, we end up becoming the person people tolerate at parties because we can't stop talking about ourselves and all the things that make us happy. We can find ourselves prattling on, saying things like, "And when I was on my two-hundredth pull-up, this guy was totally noticing me, which reminded me that my followers were probably ready for another picture of my abs. . . . Then I was drinking a lemur-milk decaf latte at my favorite little spot with the yummiest avocado toast when my bestie called to tell me about a cute outfit with unicorns on it that she just bought for our Cabo trip. I guess the universe thinks I'm a unicorn, which is awesome because the unicorn is my spirit animal." Living in the moment and enjoying life is truly beautiful. But believing that we should get everything we "deserve" is a playbook for narcissism and extreme poverty of meaning. Frankly, that kind of thinking makes us a danger to society. The narcissism that prioritizes personal happiness over the well-being of others doesn't go away at a certain age or professional level. It just gets harder to deal with and much more sad.

The moments in between our digitally documented awesome happy times are what I call the *unguarded moments*: quiet moments when we ask ourselves questions about the true meaning and purpose of our lives. We lie down at night after running the same program we did the day before and ask what our days are adding up to. Happy moments work best when held together with something deeper. Meaning is the glue that holds our happy moments in perspective, that nothing is promised in life and everything good is a gift. Blindly pursuing happiness alone robs those we love, and the world, of our contribution to their lives. When we give our attention and energy to others, we see a world that's much bigger than our happiness could ever fill. A practical rule of engagement is this: happiness comes through attaining, but meaning comes through giving.

TWO POVERTIES

We were made for meaning, and if we don't find it, we are doomed. What's more, so is the world. Here is how it all works together: My vulnerability and inadequacy as an accidental filmmaker created opportunities for people in the film and music industry to perform their normal jobs to bring attention and help to free modern-day slaves. Looked at another way, the needs of the kids in slavery created an opportunity for the film and music industry to invest their talents, thereby creating meaning in their lives. A poverty of means provided an avenue for people to address their poverty of meaning, and vice versa. This is classic supply-and-demand economics. There is a means-and-meaning economy at play all around us. This economy has the power to simultaneously reduce the poverties of means and meaning.

Here's another example: A young boy in the Kibera slum has a need for an education, and a soccer mom with a teaching background and two discretionary hours a day has a need for purpose. The soccer mom spends her extra two hours a day tutoring the Kenyan boy via a remote educational program linked to a school wired with Google Fiber. The boy gets an education and the soccer mom gets a sense of meaning. Two needs are met. Reducing both poverties is the greatest win-win scenario in history.

We've been trying to save the world for decades with a mindset that goes something like this:

I am rich.
You are poor.
I give to you.
You are saved.
I remain rich.

Instead, our mentality needs to sound like this:

I am poor.
You are poor.
I have means.
You have scarcity of means.
I have scarcity of meaning.
I help reduce your scarcity of means.
I now have meaning.
You are not poor.
I am not poor.

The future of humanity is dependent on both poverties being alleviated with one transaction. This transaction is rooted inside of you. Acting on your riot becomes the transaction that reduces the poverty of means for others, while simultaneously increasing meaning in your life. We will never get away from our deep need for meaning, nor are we supposed to. Meaning is not a First World luxury; rather, it is life itself, as Viktor Frankl revealed. And if we seek meaning by giving ourselves to others, we get to change the world and ourselves. When a soccer mom spends her only open hours educating a boy in Kenya, both poverties are alleviated. When an advertising commercial editor whose day job is to sell condiments on television helps make a film that brings attention to the forty million slaves in the world, both poverties are alleviated.

As human beings, we are naturally motivated to help ourselves first. Doing so is not privileged or elite or "First World." It's human nature. And so is the desire to participate in the story of others. We are predisposed to both happiness and meaning. Biology and psychology all point to helping ourselves first, then others. Think of the air masks that drop when a plane loses altitude. You are told to put the mask first on yourself, then on your child. We need to change our perspective. We have placed such an impossible purity ring around "doing good" that most of us feel disenfranchised from participating because we aren't good enough. But our desire to help ourselves and our need to help others are two sides of the same coin—a coin with currency in the marketplace of meaning.

Friend, there is no quick path to meaning. It is like physical health, which needs to be built up through resistance and maintained. It's found when we participate in something bigger than our own advancement and temporal happiness. This is contrary to most of the popular messaging that bombards us hundreds of times a day to buy something new because it will make us someone else. When we participate in something other than our own happiness, we belong to others. When we belong to others, we are part of something bigger than ourselves. Happiness may promise you that you're part of something bigger than yourself, but when you wake up the next morning, you'll realize your heart is empty. Next, we will learn that we are naturally motivated to alleviate both poverties.

CHAPTER 6

YOUR NEEDS? WHAT ABOUT MY NEEDS?

August 2013
Goma, Democratic Republic of Congo
A Church

THE LAST MAN TO GET THIS CLOSE TO HER WAS HER RAPIST. NO, THE LAST men to get this close were her rapists. And now here I am, holding her face in close focus, looking into the pores of her skin. I'm sitting five feet away with my camera lens zoomed in, creating proximity to a story I can barely listen to. A story that nonetheless must be told. A story that would incite public outcries if it happened to a white girl in a white suburb, but in this place her story is no more tragic than bicycle theft. Her eyes are white marbles set into a stony gaze. They fall on me like fifty-pound bags of sand and carry an authority that's powerful and ancient. She is draped in electric green and turmeric yellow, colors you see on a horse jockey jersey. The patterns in the fabric are as packed with stories as an AIDS quilt, rich in color and backstory.

She sits like a queen on the dirty plastic chair in her bombed-out throne room, waiting patiently as the film crew sets up the lights. She looks out the second-story window to a point in the distance, past the bustling city of Goma, past the endless United Nations Displaced Persons camps, past the white peacekeeping tanks, and past the rebel militias hiding in hills surrounding us. She looks to a place called home, before all of this began. Green rolling hills. Deep, lush valleys. A farm producing avocados, mangos, and cassava. A village with children playing. A husband. A life. And friends who knew her by her first name, Blessing.

She waited four hours for us to arrive. This is Africa, where time is elastic. There are only a few stretches of paved road, and the rest are like driving on Mars, almost literally: much of the ground is covered in volcanic rock. In 2002 Mount Nyiragongo, an active volcano, erupted, sending six-foot-deep streams of lava into much of Goma, eventually ending its trail of destruction in nearby Lake Kivu. Roads, buildings, and even the international airport were damaged by the lava. Just walking up to this bombed-out church building was treacherous, as jagged shards of lava rock cover most surfaces. Children play outside of the church in their bare feet. It feels like a poor excuse, but this challenging landscape is why we were late.

The church we are in looks like a movie set from a World War II film. The rusted corrugated tin roof barely covers the two-story temple of dust, rebar, and concrete. The stairs to the second floor where we have set up our cameras are half-finished, with fingers of rebar protruding. In fact, rebar is protruding everywhere in Goma. Buildings get started but never get finished. You never know who will be in power from one day to the next here, the government or one of the militias. So many projects are left unfinished. It's a place operating without a concept of tomorrow. There is no glass on the windows of the church, just more strands of rebar. If you look south from here, you can see where Goma ends and the white tent camps begin. That's where Blessing came from on a motorcycle taxi. She's traveled far and waited long to tell me her story. She wants the world to know what is happening here. It's not safe for Blessing to travel after dark, and the sun will be setting soon. This section of the globe was ranked as the most dangerous place in the world to be a woman.[1] We need to get started.

My interpreter is a local Congolese social worker doing peacebuilding in town. He has been helping to rehabilitate victims of violence for years and makes every effort to project meekness and love. He gently pulls me aside before we start the interview and offers me a tip: "Justin, when you speak to her, make sure that you lower the level of your eyes. Look up at her, not down." A few other women draped in color are waiting to be interviewed after Blessing. They've brought along some of their children who are too young to be left back at the camp. There's a lot of distraction, but right now I have to give Blessing my full attention. I check the camera monitor and adjust my posture, sitting a little lower in my chair in front of Blessing. After expressing my gratitude for her bravery in coming here, we roll cameras.

A few years ago Blessing lived in a rural village about a hundred miles from here. She had a small family who all helped with the subsistence farming. They grew enough food to sell in the local market, which provided them a small and coveted income. Civil war had been raging in the Democratic Republic of Congo (DRC) for years. From time to time fights between rebel groups and the government would break out near their village. When this happened, they would either stay with relatives in another village or try to find somewhere to hide until the rebels left. Still active today, these rebel groups are not just bloodthirsty mercenaries; their campaign of terror is pragmatic, with a laser focus on money and power. They are fighting for control of the DRC's mineral-rich land, where open-pit mines dot the landscape. Children and forced laborers work in these mines to extract minerals such as coltan, gold, tin, and tantalum. These minerals get bagged and smuggled into the black market, and finally into open markets. The raw materials end up in just about all electronics products from mobile phones to football stadium Jumbotrons. The money obtained from selling these minerals funds the militia's operations.

One night Blessing and her family woke to the sound of semi-automatic rounds being fired. They ran out of their house, but it was too late. A militia from a group called M23 was already ravaging their village. Somehow Blessing and her husband got separated in the chaos. She was able to run up the hill with her three children and hide in a ravine. She held her hand over the younger children's mouths all night until the sun came up. When she felt it was safe to return, she headed back to the ash heap of her village, where women and children paced between burned buildings and the ashes of loved ones. That's when she learned that her husband never made it out.

Without the safety of a husband and village, Blessing decided to join a caravan of other women and children heading north to Goma. They heard of a United Nations Displaced Persons camp there where they would be safe until the fighting subsided. She's remained there ever since. The camp looks as if the United Nations is colonizing Mars. Endless white tents dot the lava rock surface in every direction, like a sea of surrender flags. Blessing's new home for herself and three children is a ten-by-ten-foot section of lava rock with five pieces of plastic that serve as walls and ceiling. Her neighbors are only a few feet away in every direction, mostly women with stories similar to hers. Their husbands were all exterminated, and many of their sons were conscripted as child soldiers by the rebel militias.

Blessing isn't just a survivor. Like Viktor Frankl, she's a thriver. Despite having little control over her circumstances, she committed herself to providing for her family. Everything she had, including her husband, was gone. She had to start over. Despite the abject depravity of her new situation, she committed herself to improving the conditions for her family. She heard how some of the women were going into the hills just outside of the camp to collect sticks. They would bring the sticks back to the camp to sell as firewood. So she went along on these expeditions, hoping that the money she earned could provide some extra food or another plastic sheet for the tent roof. The rainy season was coming.

As she speaks, I can see that Blessing is becoming distracted, looking away from me and wringing her hands in her lap. Her attention is drawn to one of the toddlers playing between the broken pews. The other women see that she has paused, and they look over as if to offer some unspoken form of support. Daunted, she draws a breath and begins to tell me the next part of her story.

Blessing's camp was flanked on one side with hills. That's where the M23 militia preferred to set up their camp, which made it easy to descend into Goma on raiding parties. That's also where the sticks were. All the sticks close to her camp had been pilfered, so Blessing and the other women pushed farther into the hills away from their camp. It was there that militiamen came out of the forest, surrounded the women, and methodically gang-raped Blessing and the other women.

Rape in this region is not just violence against women. It is a weapon of war. The militias use rape to break down families, spread disease, and tear apart communities. By killing the men and raping the women and girls, they build an effective brand of terror, allowing them to gain more territory with less loss of their own militia. Fear of these militias has spread throughout the region, causing the villagers to give up without a fight when they see them coming.

In addition to the sexual violence Blessing suffered, and the crushing poverty she endured in her new home, she now had to face life as a social pariah, a victim of rape. Word spreads quickly in a camp with a million people and nothing to do. Blessing was beside herself and began losing any reason to go on.

Soon women in the camp began to visit her tent to share their own stories of sexual violence. Story after story made its way to Blessing's tent. Many had been raped before they reached the camp. What these women could not know was that their neighborhood had become the rape capital of the world. More than 40 percent of women have experienced sexual violence in eastern Congo, affecting 1,152 women and girls every day. These women were living in the worst place on earth to be a woman. The camp they were living in offered little solace. They were surrounded by fear. Outside the camp were rapists, and inside was the stigma from being raped. There was only one thing that could possibly make matters worse for Blessing.

A month after the rape, Blessing noticed that she was getting sick every time she ate her cassava rations. This mother of three knew it could mean only one thing. She was carrying the child of one of her rapists. The challenge of another mouth to feed was overshadowed by the fact that children of rape carry a stigma as well. They are ostracized by their community and face tremendous social barriers.

The camera crew and I are interrupted by some noise coming from the young toddler playing between the dirty pews and rebar. His mother tries to quiet him down. We find out later that this boy is a child of rape too. His name is Israel, which in Hebrew means "struggle with God." Blessing begins to talk about how her faith in God has led her through the valley of the shadow of death. She is not dead, but she knows the cold, dark shadow that death throws. I hear what sounds like weeping behind me and turn around to see that my producer has vanished. I walk over to find him curled up in a ball behind one of the pews. All he can say is, "I don't believe in God in America, but I believe in God here." Faith is easier to find in temples of rebar and dirt.

Once he recovers, I return to my interview with Blessing and look once again into her eyes, which have been communicating a deep truth this entire time. It's always the eyes. I finally recognize what I see in them, something rare and powerful: I am interviewing a woman of immense authority. This woman, who possesses little control over her life, has more authority in her eyes than anyone I've ever met. It's a power that says, "I've seen more pain in one day than you will see in a lifetime, and it hasn't killed me." What she has done with her power is even more amazing.

She invites us to visit her camp the next day. When we arrive, she is waiting like the proud mayor of her camp, an island of misplaced souls. She is flanked by an adoring entourage of electric-colored ladies. As we walk through the endless alleyways of tents, she shares the third act of her tragic story. Despite her challenges, Blessing did not give up on finding ways to provide for her family. Gathering sticks for income was and is too dangerous. She needed a new strategy. She needed a new entrepreneurial model that not only would help her, but also benefit her newfound community of ostracized women.

She walks us into a small, dilapidated room on the edge of camp, near the base of the militia-infested hills. Inside are fifty or so women wearing expectant looks and horse-jockey colors. The women are giddy and joyful. It feels as though we just walked into a birthday party on Mars. All have similar stories to Blessing's and want the same opportunities for their struggling families. As soon as Blessing walks in, they break into their fight songs of worship and hope. Blessing joins in, throwing her arms heavenward in reckless abandon. I notice small strips of plastic—strands of pink, blue, and yellow scattered around the room—like the material used to make Easter baskets and plastic beach bags. Blessing motions to the room to quiet down the way a president calms down a cheering audience. She wants to show me the startup business that she and her band of beautiful thrivers have created.

Blessing saw a market opportunity inside her camp of displaced people. She noticed that everyone was carrying something. Food. Rocks. Small sticks. Children. Everyone literally had their hands full. If she could make carrying these items easier, she could make money, or at least barter for items she and her band of thrivers desperately needed. So Blessing decided they would make multi-use carrying bags. Most bags were made from the plastic woven sheeting used for tents, which tears easily. Her bags would be different, improving the lives of both the owners and the makers.

Blessing found an outside source for the bright-colored plastic strips. She then created a collective of ostracized women—her thrivers—to hand-weave these bags. She proudly hands one of the bags to me with the enthusiasm of an inventor showing you her latest invention or a songwriter playing you his latest song. Everyone in this displaced persons camp carries the weight of their poverty of means. Blessing and her band of thrivers just made that weight a little lighter.

HIERARCHY OF NEEDS

There is a motive behind everything we do. These motivations determine our behavior. When we sign up for a spin class, for instance, signing up is the behavior, and the desire to feel healthy and maybe look good is the motivation. Determining the motivations behind our behaviors is a major focus for many industries. Marketers want to know our motivations so they can influence our purchasing habits. Politicians want to know what motivates us in order to influence our vote. Charity organizations want to know what motivates us to encourage a donation. Put plainly, knowledge of people's motivations is a gold mine. There are a million tools, books, conferences, and websites designed to help us understand why we do, or don't do, certain things. When I searched for "motivational books" on one book retailer's website, I received 197,851 results. There are books to test your personality type, yoga retreats to help you find mindfulness, and apps reminding you to reset your brain.

Understanding one's own motives, and piecing together the data around someone else's motives, is an essential step toward discovering meaning and changing the world. I see this every day. My number-one job is to motivate people to end slavery. Everyone I talk to, other than the slavers, agrees with this goal. I've learned that each individual's motivations to accomplish this goal are different, because each individual's motive to end slavery is mixed with their other motives. For instance, the supply chain executive's motive to end slavery could be a mix of her motivation to perform well at work and bring shareholder value to the company. The university student's motivation to end slavery may be mixed with his motivation to also be recognized as a global citizen. The billionaire's motivation to end slavery may be mixed with the desire to leave a meaningful legacy for possible grandchildren. Before you jump to the opinion that the motivation to end slavery is more important than the other motivations mentioned here, it may be helpful to first learn how our motivations work.

Motivation has been a primary focus of modern psychology. Sigmund Freud connected our motivations to sexual energy. Ivan Pavlov's research revealed the nature of conditioned responses, when we do certain things because of triggers in our minds (think Pavlov's dog salivating at the sound of a bell). B. F. Skinner gave us the concept of radical behaviorism, which suggests that human actions are reactions to previous external stimuli. ("Ice cream tasted good yesterday . . . so I want ice cream now.") For all their contributions to psychology, these early psychologists focused on the human being as a robotic bag of problems. They focused on what was wrong with human beings rather than looking for what was right.

We are self-centered creatures. Almost everything we do is designed to benefit ourselves, from eating and sleeping to working and raising a family. There is practically nothing we do that doesn't somehow bring some benefit back to us. Even meditation and worship return benefits. But somehow we've adopted the idea that doing something for the benefit of others is a selfless act. We describe acts of benevolence and charity as sacrifice and selflessness. I don't believe that. I believe that participating in the benefit of others is a *selfish* act because it inherently makes our lives better too. In fact, finding one's riot and stepping into the chaos of others is a need we all possess, much like our needs for affection and esteem. As stated, the return we get for helping others is meaning, which Viktor Frankl proved is essential for survival and thriving at any stage in life. I'm not the only one who believes this.

In the middle of the twentieth century, a psychologist named Abraham Maslow came along who was interested in learning what makes human beings great, as opposed to a robotic bag of problems. He believed that we are driven by motivations beyond immediate rewards or unconscious desires. He wanted to understand how individuals who contributed much to society—such as Teddy Roosevelt or Harriet Tubman—operated. So he created a chart to measure motivations, called the hierarchy of needs, which has become a highly regarded measurement for understanding human motivation.

He assembled a human's needs into five ascending hierarchical levels, like a pyramid.[2] Any deficiency at one level of needs prevents movement to the next level of needs. This hierarchy has come to be known as Maslow's hierarchy of needs. Our first basic level of human need is *physiological needs*. These needs include what we need to stay alive: food, shelter, warmth, sleep, and air. Charities and incorrupt governments are designed to assist with these base-level needs. If anyone is missing any of these physiological needs, then that individual's sole motivation will be to acquire them. People in Blessing's displaced persons camp were primarily motivated to address these basic physiological needs.

Once we have met the basic physiological needs, we can move on to the need for *safety*. This includes our need for law, order, protection from physical harm, and freedom from fear. This is the kind of need that a functioning justice system is designed to fix. But for people like Blessing, who live within a poverty of means, fear of violence and injustice is rampant. People in the developed world can get stuck at this level in the hierarchy too. Fear is a liar masked as a motivation, and without safety you can't move to the next level in the hierarchy.

The next level of needs is *social*, which includes our need for love and belonging. These are the needs that certain Barry White songs try to fix. Social needs can be addressed through friends, families, relationship partners, or children. They can also be met through spiritual communities, religious gatherings, and support groups. When this need is not adequately met for a prolonged period, a dangerous "warm body" syndrome can arise to meet it. Any warm body can serve as a substitute for love and belonging, such as when Aunt Winnie gets divorced after thirty years and starts to date her twenty-two-year-old trainer at the gym. A basic level of affection, love, and support is required to move on to Maslow's next level of needs.

The need for *esteem* is the next level in Maslow's hierarchy. This level is all about our need to be respected—to which Aretha Franklin can attest. At the root, this need relates to how we see ourselves and how we imagine others view us. Countless souls are stuck here in a feedback loop of approval seeking, be it through endless reaching for fame, recognition, social media affirmation, or some kind of prestige.

Unmet needs for respect create fertile ground for depression and narcissism, and keep us from progressing to the final (highest) level in the hierarchy.

The uppermost level in the hierarchy is *self-actualization*. Those who are motivated to address this need are trying to determine their physical, intellectual, spiritual, and professional limits. People who are motivated at this level tend to have a strong sense of self and knowledge of who they are. This is about finding the ideal version of yourself. I want to make an important distinction here: The highest level on Maslow's hierarchy is *self*-actualization, not *someone else*–actualization. It is about finding your own potential, not trying to reach someone else's. And our potential is essentially a mystery to us and others.

Maslow's hierarchy of needs isn't perfect, but it's the best model I've found for explaining how addressing our poverty of meaning can address others' poverty of means. Maslow has made this easy for us to understand by putting all of humanity's needs in order, first with what he called "survival" needs (physiological, safety, social) and then ending with the "being" needs (esteem and self-actualization). The survival needs are where the poverty of means operates, and the being needs are where our poverty of meaning operates.

We can survive physically without respect, but we can't survive without food and safety. In the same way, the man enslaving Isaiah in Ghana isn't likely to be preoccupied with needs for self-esteem. The women picking up sticks outside the displaced persons camp in Goma are not likely to be thinking about whether or not they are hitting their peak physical potential or career goals. Likewise, the retired insurance broker living in Florida probably isn't worried about how to access clean water or avoid contracting Ebola. The point is this: We live in a world full of immense needs. Even those blessed not to live in a poverty of means still have a deep need for Maslow's higher motivations, a scarcity for meaning that needs to be met. I believe these higher needs are our motivations for meaning. It's impossible to find meaning without a bigger vision for our lives, beyond our rock dreams.

SHOW ME A SIGN

He who has a Why to live for can bear almost any How.

—FRIEDRICH NIETZSCHE

If you are reading this book, then I can reasonably assume you didn't wake up thinking about whether or not you will eat today or wondering if the police will break into your home and drag you to jail for no reason. Your physiological and safety needs are likely met; therefore, you are not living within a poverty of means. According to Maslow, as we move up the hierarchy of needs into the esteem and self-actualization levels, we focus less on survival and instead begin to examine how we fit into the world. You may quibble with the accuracy of Maslow's specifics, but the trajectory he observed is undeniable. Even if you aren't looking for food and shelter from month to month, you are likely still motivated to fulfill your very critical need for meaning.

We may not be living on dirt floors, but we still feel the need to hustle. We tend to believe that acquiring more food, more safety, more affection, more approval, and more affirmation will somehow provide us with meaning: more stuff equals more meaning. I call this the *meaning placebo*. It's the never-ending pursuit of more. Many of us get locked in a feedback loop of *survival needs* and never step out into a bigger narrative, our soul dreams. Instead we try to draw meaning from things like comfort food, entertainment, or the endorphin surge we feel when a post receives a thousand likes. It's a dangerous trap for a life to fall into.

Those of us living within a poverty of meaning do not struggle day to day to survive, but our hearts struggle day to day to locate something bigger. The transition point on the wealth spectrum between those living within a poverty of means and a poverty of meaning is hard to pin down. It's impossible to determine how much is enough, but a Princeton University study in 2011 determined that $75,000 is the amount of money an average American needs to earn a year to be happy.[3] Earning more than that amount did not result in greater contentment. Constantly focusing on the survival needs leaves us unfulfilled, and in some cases, according to Maslow, it can even create mild to severe neurosis.

Giving to charity can seem like a reasonable response to our need for meaning. Donate to a particular cause, and you will feel good. As expressed earlier in this book, charity is incredibly important, but it doesn't always satisfy our *being needs* for esteem and self-actualization. These being needs are about who we are as people—not how much we can give. Allow me to illustrate. My wife's friend Shannon is an amazing artist and muralist. She lost her husband when she was in her midforties. Her kids have since started families, and she now faces being a grandparent as a young widow. Like Blessing, she is a *thriver*. She knows pain intimately and keeps on living and giving life. About once a month she volunteers her talent and skills to paint the bedrooms of children who are terminally ill. These kids often have only months to live, but Shannon will transport the room in which they will spend their final days into a princess castle, a Warriors basketball court, a scene from Star Wars, or anything else the child loves.

Shannon's husband died slowly from amyotrophic lateral sclerosis (ALS), sometimes called Lou Gehrig's disease, over the course of three years. She knows what it's like to be stuck in a room with death looming, but she found a way to transpose her painful backstory with her artistic talents and create something beautiful to be briefly enjoyed. Shannon could donate money, but she donates herself instead, and in doing so reaches her potential as an actualized human being. She's not independently wealthy and could be using that time to provide for herself, but she chooses to invest in someone else. In doing so, her being needs are met. She finds meaning. We will never find our human potential, or meaning in our lives, if our motivations are constantly focused on our own lower survival needs.

I want to return to our dear sister Blessing. Anyone who understands the difference between a poverty of means and a poverty of meaning would rightfully place her in the former category. But if we look at her story against Maslow's hierarchy, we see a very different trajectory. Blessing was clearly motivated to address her basic physiological needs. After the militia destroyed her village, she knew that she needed to find food and shelter (Maslow's physiological and safety needs) for herself and her family. So she headed toward the United Nations Displaced Persons camp. Her economic and physical safety inside the camp was insecure, so she was motivated to search for wood to sell, resulting in sexual violence against her and a negative stigma within the camp. Her social need for belonging was addressed when she built a community with the other women who faced the same violence (Maslow's social need). By creating the carrying bag co-op with the other survivors, she addressed her need for esteem and betterment by self-manufacturing an opportunity for herself (Maslow's esteem need). This co-op improved the lives of other survivors of sexual violence, which helped Blessing find her potential by helping others (Maslow's self-actualization need). Blessing lived up to her name, and without knowing it, she climbed Maslow's hierarchy of needs.

One of our greatest needs in life is to be needed. Viktor Frankl was convinced that if we live as if we were meant for some greater good, then we will thrive regardless of our circumstances. He understood the symbiotic relationship between those living in a poverty of means and those living in a poverty of meaning. Investing ourselves in others isn't some selfless, earnest act we do once we get all we want in life; investing ourselves in others is, in fact, investing in ourselves. This is good news. This means your life has a much greater meaning, a greater purpose, than you could ever have imagined. You may not have found your riot yet or discovered your soul dream, but both are within you, and pursuing both is actually something you need to do.

If a woman living in the most dangerous place on earth inside a hundred-square-foot plastic tent with a lava rock floor and four children can be motivated to address all her needs, including the being needs, then certainly we can as well. The greatest, most efficient method for addressing our needs for purpose and meaning is to invest who we are into the lives of others—be they survivors of sexual violence in Goma or a child dying of cancer in the suburbs. When we invest ourselves in the lives of those living in a poverty of means, two poverties are alleviated.

Pursuing meaning for your life by finding your riot and listening to your soul dream is how we will change the world in the twenty-first century. Your selfish plan to change the world is the most economical and innovative approach to dealing with seemingly disparate challenges at the same time. With this new approach, we can address poverty-of-meaning challenges while also dealing with poverty-of-means challenges such as global illiteracy—which costs the world over $1.2 trillion a year.[4]

We need a movement of people with selfish plans if we want to survive and thrive in the twenty-first century. But the world isn't currently receptive to this new approach. It's still operating under an antiquated zero-sum-game approach, where doing good for others is a cost to you and not a benefit. In the next section we will learn how to work around the old operating system that is prohibiting us from making our selfish plans to change the world.

PART 2

WHAT KEEPS THE WORLD FROM CHANGING

CHAPTER 7

BREAD AND CIRCUSES

AD 106
Rome
The Forum

IT'S A BEAUTIFUL SUNNY DAY ON THE BUSIEST AVENUE IN THE MOST POW-
erful city of the Roman Empire. Everyone who is anyone is out.
Patriotism blows like the summer wind through the eight-hundred-
year-old Forum. Mythology says the city's founders, Romulus and
Remus, were babies when they were thrown into the Tiber River and
washed ashore near here, but the story gets weirder from there. (Think
drinking milk from a she-wolf and being fed by a woodpecker.) The
Etruscan pioneers thought this little plot of land next to the Tiber would
be a good place to put down roots and maybe build a city that would
become the center of the world. Now those roots stretch throughout
most of the known world.

Rent is high here in the center of town, so the commoners have traveled in from surrounding villages to shop, sunbathe, play, and marvel at
their self-congratulatory statues and monuments. The seemingly endless
columns, arches, buildings, and sculptures in the Forum remind citizens
of the glory and power of the empire. Buildings housing government,
commerce, and religious activities flank the perimeter of the Forum.
We're standing in the heartbeat of the most powerful empire in history,
though many have simply come here today for the entertainment.

The one-percenters have come down from their palaces on Palatine Hill, looking fabulous in the latest designer purple sashes. Tyrian purple, as the upper crust call it, is reserved for the rich alone, due to the laborious dying process required to produce the deep saturated color. Dyers take the secretions of rare sea snails and mix it with human urine to produce the regal hue. The smell lasts about as long as the color, which elicits nose-plugging from commoners—a covert gesture of solidarity among the ninety-nine-percenters. But today everyone is an august Roman, walking through the city center as if it were Mount Olympus itself, beaming with pride over their republic and all its glorious fringe benefits.

Juvenal, Rome's Jay Z, is standing in the shadow of the columns supporting Basilica Aemilia, the Whole Foods of Rome. He is finding it hard to concentrate with commoners passing by discussing their favorite gladiator and eating eel on a stick. He is looking over small scrolls of text, studying the words, then reciting them under his breath as he looks out at the growing crowd in the Forum. Juvenal is known for dropping wisdom in dactylic hexameter about lower-class life in the Roman Empire, and he has generated quite a body of work. He looks across from the basilica at the House of Vestal Virgins and grins, a favorite subject matter for Rome's poet laureate. Who could resist material about virgins hanging out in a temple, keeping an eternal flame going? Juvenal has recently released an autobiographical satire about his upbringing and run-ins with the law that's become a modern hit.

> Dropped to earth on a Tuesday, not a big news day
> Born to take the stage from a fiddler who plays with fire.
> Mama told me of my he-man, said he was a freed-man
> Sowed his seed and left our field, had somewhere else to be, man
> Now he lookin' at me, man
> Hail, hail Master Quintilian, taught me how to make my millions
> Horace and DJ Persius wrote the verse for the rest of us

Speaking truth to the sycophants, the yes
    men who forgot their pants
Bowing to the purple demigods high upon the hill
Sending down purple rain to break plebeian will
Now my words are flaming arrows, bringing
    light into the narrows
Emperor Trajan preferred shadows, sent
    me to the land of pharaohs
Exiled on Egyptian main streets, but no
    Roman here can blame me
Are we Brutus or Mark Antony? Slaves pretending we are free?
A thousand vestal virgins couldn't wake me
    from this Roman holiday daydream

Word has spread that Juvenal was going to give a rare free performance today in the Forum. He's decided to debut his latest, "Satire X," on the growing crowd. He takes one more glance at his scroll and steps out of the shadows and onto the steps of the basilica. His eyes drink in the sea of commoners who are still unsure of who he is. Mothers, merchants, stonemasons, fishermen, carpenters, soldiers, prostitutes, administrators, lawyers, and farmers are all eager to hear the latest from the Roman Empire's Young Hov. Across the Forum he watches smoke rise from the eternal fires inside the Temple of Vesta. He smirks as the smoke glides gently upward against Palatine Hill, covering the palaces of the purple people. Juvenal steps out farther onto a granite podium and levels his gaze at his audience. A slow hush wafts across the crowd and he begins to speak.

They shed their sense of responsibility
Long ago, when they lost their votes, and the bribes; the mob
That used to grant power, high office, the legions, everything,
Curtails its desires, and reveals its anxiety for two things only,
Bread and circuses.[1]

They listen intently as Juvenal throws out double-barbed hooks of verse, telling his audience that they have given up their power for something unimportant. He calls them out for their lack of civil engagement and willful dismissiveness about the affairs of the Roman leaders. Instead of raising their voices for change, they've raised them at sporting events while filling their stomachs with free food. The poet entreats them to look up from their bread and amusement to see that they are being played by their leaders. Bread and circuses were cheap devices designed by the Roman leaders to control a growing populace.

Running the Roman Empire is not easy. There are foreign civilizations to subjugate, aqueducts to build, roads to pave, and temples that need worship. The list goes on and on. Life isn't like it once was for Rome's founders, who merely had to fill marshes, fight natives, and farm the land. Now Rome is everywhere, and controlling the empire requires new strategies. Roman territories spread from what will one day be northern Africa, Iraq, and an island called the United Kingdom. There is also a massive populace to keep in line, all of whom have opinions and muscles. The last thing you want as an emperor is for the commoners to start noticing the economic injustices, the military-industrial complex, and the salacious excesses of the powerful that would make the raunchiest reality-TV star look like a saint. The Roman emperors have figured out that by providing entertainment and free food, they can pull the people's focus away from their political maneuvers. By keeping the ordinary folk, the plebeians, distracted with activities ranging from crucifying insurgents to massive *cirque-de-so-slave* performances, the government can carry out its business unencumbered, expanding the empire any way it pleased.

So the emperors got into showbiz and built the Flavian Amphitheater, more commonly known by its nickname, the Colosseum. Construction of the Colosseum was conveniently funded with spoils acquired from sacking the Jewish temple in Jerusalem. The Colosseum, just to the left of where Juvenal is standing, has a seating capacity of close to eighty thousand, nearly twice the size of another coliseum that would one day be built in the great city of Oakland. Anyone can walk down on a weekend with the kids and get in for free. You can grab some fried boar sticks and watch spectacular gladiators from all over the world battle each other to the death. The irony that's not lost on Juvenal is that commoners are being entertained, and feeling empowered, by watching the death and dismemberment of other commoners. The people running for their lives on the Colosseum floor are foreign commoners, conquered warriors, slaves, and the poorest of the poor.

As if the Colosseum weren't enough, another pleasure dome was recently constructed not too far from here, called the Circus Maximus. The circus has a capacity of 150,000 people and is part shopping mall and part *Mad Max* pleasure dome, with businesses and stores located inside its massive structure. Violence and spectacle are the draw, and the public just can't get enough. The show designers have to outdo their spectacles week after week. When they want to reenact a ship battle, they simply fill the circus with water and ships to sail around and fight one another. How about a full-scale reenactment of the Battle of Placentia or a massive hunting expedition of wild animals? No problem. No expense is spared if it will amuse the Romans.

Another perk of being a Roman is free bread. Roman leaders are not just trying to be nice. When people don't have enough to eat, they get hangry.[2] When people get hangry, they start looking for someone to blame. If the people look for someone to blame, it's going to be the government and the purple people. Free bread stops the hangry.

Something very powerful and insidious is machinating behind this distribution of free bread and the productions in the circus. A culture is being meticulously orchestrated behind the curtains of power— one bred to depend on delight and desire. Those in power don't want the plebeians to look around at what is actually happening within the Roman Empire. These seemingly innocuous public offerings of amusement and food are carefully designed to keep the populace satiated, happy, and distracted.

In "Satire X," Juvenal is dropping wisdom on his brothers and sisters, warning them about the dulling of their senses through their addiction to bread and circuses, also known as comfort and amusement. He goes on to say, "Who'd embrace virtue simply for itself, if you took away all the reward? Yet nations have been destroyed by the ambition of a few, by their desire for fame and a title." Juvenal is throwing verbal rocks at glass towers, declaring that the leaders are running their beloved republic into the ground because of their vanity. They are getting away with it because everyone is too intoxicated with bread and circuses to notice what their leaders are doing. The Roman Empire has amassed control over most of the Mediterranean world and is showing no signs of stopping. Their tactics are swift, pragmatic, and cruel. Their leaders are divas who view themselves as deities, and parade their power like inebriated trust-fund kids at a rave on Ibiza. Roman society is being carefully engineered to tune out questions about injustice or equality, and it is losing its ability to see itself clearly because of free food and spectacles of violence. Juvenal is asking his people, "Where is our leaders' virtue? Where is our moral excellence?"

Juvenal lifts his head up to the statues, arches, and citadels of wealth, government, and religion that tower above the crowd. He finishes with these last few lines from "Satire X": "Fortune: it's we who make you a goddess, and grant you a place in the sky."[3] He drops the proverbial mic and walks off the podium. At first a few confused hands clap, followed by a slow crescendo of applause and affirmation. He walks away from the crowd dejected and slowly descends the ancient Via Sacre that leads toward the monstrous Colosseum. It's obvious to him that his audience has no idea that these words were written about them. He stops to look up at the five-story Colosseum and mutters under his breath, "Where are the heroes?"

COMFORT AND AMUSEMENT

Today comfort and amusement are the modern equivalents of Rome's bread and circuses. They are so woven into our lives that we can barely recognize them. While seemingly innocuous, they can become destinations rather than rest stops, and they can divert us from our purpose—our soul dream. We need to heed the two-thousand-year-old wisdom of Juvenal and not become distracted from seeing the world as it truly is.

Comfort is a hard word to define because it can mean different things to different people. The best working definition I have for comfort is "any consumption above our basic needs." Comfort is someone keeping your cocktail glass full while you lazily look at the Caribbean Sea. Comfort is a new-car smell. Comfort is a volcano of nachos. Comfort is the room you come home to in order to connect with family or friends. Comfort is a certain number in our bank accounts. Comfort is living within the protection of a functioning rule of law. Comfort is elusive and never satisfied.

Amusement is anything that entertains us. We have a device in our possession at all times that constantly beckons us to consume amusement—not only video games, but also media and communication activities as well. We've become so amused that it's becoming harder and harder for anything to hold our attention. In one study by Microsoft, researchers interested in attention spans surveyed two thousand participants to determine that the average human attention span has fallen from twelve seconds in 2000, or around the time the mobile revolution began, to eight seconds in 2015. Goldfish now officially have a longer attention span than humans.[4]

To be clear, there's nothing inherently wrong with comfort and amusement. Our bodies and minds were designed to pursue and enjoy them both. The challenge here is that if we are not careful, these delights can become ends unto themselves. We get distracted from our lives' larger narrative when comfort and amusement are the destination, rather than rest stops on a life filled with meaning. When comfort and amusement are the goal of our lives, our dreams and ideas get replaced by the dreams and ideas of others. To find our soul dreams, we need to know and respect how powerfully entrenched comfort and amusement are in nearly every moment of our lives.

In the twentieth century, comfort and amusement were the rewards American society received for graduating out of its agrarian age or industrial age and into its information age. America moved into the information age around the middle of the twentieth century, when much of the workforce was moving out of the family farming business and into service and manufacturing jobs. Before this period, most of people's time was spent doing whatever job was in front of them to provide for their families' survival (survival needs). That started to change around the 1940s, when the majority of families were no longer all working on the family farm.

My grandmother Genevieve came of age during this transition. She was born in 1917 and grew up on a farm in northern New Mexico. Her parents acquired several acres of land from the United States government as part of a land rush, when the government gave land away to people brave enough to farm it. Her house was a 336-square-foot, two-room dugout with a dirt floor, which she shared with seven other family members until she left for university. She didn't want to be a rancher's wife on the family farm, so as a teenager she worked several jobs to pay for her high school fees. She rode a horse to school every day, sometimes in the snow. She worked her way through college and served as a schoolteacher until retirement.

My grandmother lived at the apex of America's conversion from an agrarian/industrial age to an information age. Once her brothers and friends came home from the war, they went to college and found jobs in the service sector. She was part of the first generation in America to benefit from a legal five-day workweek and a nine-to-five workday, which gave her generation more discretionary time and resources than previous generations had enjoyed. These discretionary resources created a new age demographic between childhood and adulthood called *the teenager*. The term *teenager* had never existed before the 1940s,[5] and it quickly became an important sales target for advertisers. For the first time ever, teenagers like my mom had discretionary time and resources to spend in the marketplace, and consumer brands have been lining up to win their loyalty ever since. There has also been an increasing supply of comfort and amusement.

The blessings of comfort and amusement are not just an American or Roman phenomenon. I grew up with parents who tried to guilt me into finishing my dinner because little kids in China were starving. They were correct. Children were starving in China, but China was also emerging from its agrarian age with more families finding work in the cities. China's economy grew at an exponential rate and began its own relationship with comfort and amusement. In 2015 China represented 20 percent of the luxury goods purchased globally.[6] It's expected that China will soon exceed the United States to become the world's largest movie market. China is building twenty new movie screens a day.[7] The desire to turn our bodies and imaginations over to visual storytellers is universal. The human spirit's longing for comfort and amusement is global.

EYES ON THE PRIZE

How much comfort and amusement is enough? This is a tough question to answer. Every society has its own *haves* and *have-nots*. The commoners who came to hear Juvenal had gathered under the shadow of Palatine Hill, which could just as well have been Beverly Hills, Pacific Heights, or the Upper East Side. Much like today, Rome wrestled with socioeconomic tensions between the purple people on the hill and the plebeians in the streets. Roman people were fixated on upward social mobility, though there was a sizable gap between the classes. Lower-class Romans were fed the idea that if you worked hard enough, you too could wear purple, smell like snails and urine, and live on Palatine Hill. This same upward-mobility dogma is propagated today when people argue that acquiring more comfort is akin to moving up socially. If you buy more, you may not be climbing the class ladder, but you will feel as though you are. *If I can just get that new pair of shoes, I'll feel richer. If I can just get that vacation I've dreamed of, I'll feel richer. If I can just get that promotion at work, I'll feel richer. If I can just get that bigger house with a home theater, underground grotto, and helipad on the roof, I'll feel richer . . .* This comfort-climbing can feel endless because there is always someone with more comfort.

Our twenty-first-century Circus Maximus is video games, content, and social media—especially the sharing of our images. The perils of narcissism derived from constant campaigns for affirmation via social media are well documented. More recently, narcissism has been considered an epidemic on par with obesity.[8]

Video games can offer us false views of ourselves, which allow us to experience the *feeling* of creating justice without paying the cost. When playing video games, one experiences an endorphin rush that triggers the pleasure centers of the brain, which also offers a sense of accomplishment. According to a report that came out in 2015, 155 million Americans regularly play video games. That's nearly half of the entire population. Forty-two percent of Americans play for at least three hours per week. When our natural desire to pursue justice is satiated through role-playing games, we feel no need to find our own riot for justice. A great example of this is a friend of mine who teaches skiing in Aspen, Colorado. He's told me stories about how frequently he encounters first-time skiers who think they can do X Games–style backflips because they've played the video game at home. This confusion of real-life bravery with the virtual bravery on the circus floor was precisely what Juvenal was warning his fellow Romans about. Why risk participating in real battles for justice when you can watch your favorite gladiator rip his opponent to shreds or role-play a brave character in a video game?

In addition to games, content can obstruct our soul dreams. Access to fantastic content from around the world allows me to feel risky and brave without the cost. I can be in San Francisco, open an app on my phone, and watch live streaming video of someone dressed in white with a red sachet belt running down a cobblestone street chased by bulls in Pamplona, Spain. I can even watch firsthand footage of towns in Iraq being liberated by Kurdish female fighters. I'm served up live events as they happen from wherever they happen. When there is a riot in Cairo, I'm there. When there is a migrant crisis in Greece, I'm there. When there is a tsunami in the Philippines, I'm there. Except, I'm not *really* there. I'm only a spectator. I may feel as though I'm part of something dangerous and crazy, but I'm actually just standing in line to order my Kenyan dark-roast single-origin pour-over made by a guy with a bachelor's degree in applied philosophy from Rutgers. The gladiator battles of social media and the twenty-four-hour news circus allow us the feeling of engagement without the cost of actually being there. I can be aware of everything but engaged in nothing.

ONE MORE CIRCUS: APPROVAL

Approval is social dopamine. It is the elation we feel from the endorphin rush that occurs when we post a picture that gets multiple hearts, likes, shares, and fist bumps. As the counter of our digital affirmations rises, so do the tiny rainbow-colored geysers of love in our souls. Alas, our elation disappears as fast as it arrived when we notice a post from a friend whose approval stats are reaching Justin Bieber levels. We obstruct our soul dreams when we rate our love-worthiness against the comforts and amusements of others. The fact that our lives are on display is not the problem. The problem is that a constant digital campaign for approval is another form of bread and circuses.

Comparing our lives with the lives of others goes back to the Roman Empire and beyond. When our focus is on others' lives, we neglect our own stories. Know this: The blessings of comfort, amusement, and approval masquerade themselves as *meaning*. While each are part of what makes life enjoyable, they are poor substitutes for finding your own story, your own riot, your own soul dream, and your own contribution to a bigger narrative. I love movies and forwarded videos. I love hearts, thumbs-ups, likes, fist bumps, and flowers, but they are not my story. They are not yours either. If we want to live a full life, we have to risk a little comfort, amusement, and approval. When we do, those enjoyments come back in a form that's far more satisfying. They come back to us as meaning.

Comfort and amusement are just a few of the obstacles that can keep us from changing the world and finding meaning for our lives. You might be surprised to learn that altruism and the idea of *do-gooders* are obstacles as well.

CHAPTER 8

ALTRUISM (AND OTHER LIES WE TELL OURSELVES)

February 15, 2009
Monrovia, Liberia

WAVES OF HANDS SWAY LIKE FIELDS OF DRY WHEAT UNDER A CORRU-
gated tin roof reflecting raised voices and offering shelter from the
blistering West African sun. Hands punch in the air in sync with every
vocal cue being amplified from the wood stage supported on cinder-
blocks. A voice cracks through the overpowered speakers hanging
from wire coat hangers: "And you shall know the truth, and the truth
shall make you free." A mixed chorus of moans, cries, screams, howls,
and cheers emanates from the congregation, some eyes closed in con-
templation, others fixed in suspicion of the man in white pants holding
the microphone. "If I can change, anyone can," he says. Islands of sweat
on each of his shoulder blades move in a continental drift toward each
other as he stalks up and down the aisles of plastic chairs. The congregants keep looking upward, some in worship and some in fear of
making eye contact with the messianic preacher. The man preaching in
this dirt-floor temple located in the capital of one of the world's poorest
countries is professing, and testing, the power of redemption.

Pastor Joshua Milton Blahyi grabs a towel from the podium and
mops his shaven head, which along with his rugby-player body could
knock down any wall or person in his way. The congregants have all
come today to hear and vet the apostle Paul of Liberia. Outside this

open-air church, the city of Monrovia is frenetic with hustlers, bustlers, and survivors. He preaches with the intensity of someone with one foot in heaven and the other foot in hell, both of which feel fantastically proximate. The euphoria inside the church is palpable, with worshippers lost in abandon to a God who forgives all sin—while outside is a scene that could only be described as a living hell.

Monrovia is an exercise in extremes. For every church like this one, you will find a brothel within a stone's throw. Christianity is the primary religion, yet most believe that without United Nations peacekeeping forces, this nation of 4.5 million people would fall back into bloody civil war. Liberia was founded by freed slaves from America as a sort of freedom colony and a new start. Even its capital city, Monrovia, is named after a US president, James Monroe. These American "free blacks" brought not only the American South's Christianity but also its business practices, which included plantation slavery. In the 1980s the country underwent the toppling of several leaders, until in 1989 rebel leader Charles Taylor took control. Taylor is famous for using blood diamonds and child soldiers to fund his hold on power in Liberia and neighboring Sierra Leone throughout the 1990s. Eventually he was elected president in 1995 under the campaign slogan "He killed my ma, he killed my pa, but I will vote for him." In 1999 several different rebel groups mounted an assault on Taylor, breaking the country into full-scale civil war, each group being led by its own theatrical and barbaric warlord.

Everyone in church today was touched by these conflicts. Fatherless children. Single mothers. Grown men raised on steady diets of violence and gang rape. Pastor Joshua appears to be an antibiotic in the open wounds of war, not for his infectious enthusiasm but for the three words he seems to work into every sermon: "Please, forgive me." He knows that the survivors in this congregation are more than just his audience; many are very likely some of his victims. Pastor Joshua's designation as the Liberian apostle Paul was earned in part by his time as the Liberian Saul of Tarsus, better known as the warlord General Butt Naked.

General Butt Naked was one of Liberia's most feared and maniacal warlords. His bloodlust for power was literal, convincing his child soldiers that no bullets would hit them if they ran into battle naked. After the war, when Joshua was brought before the Truth and Reconciliation Committee to account for his crimes, he admitted to killing at least twenty thousand people. Much of his story is difficult to verify, but his very public effort of contrition is obvious. His fellow Liberians, and nearly anyone else who hears his story, don't know what to make of him: heretic or hero, Christian or charlatan.

General Butt Naked's Liberia was very likely the worst place in the world to live during their fourteen years of civil war. More than a quarter-million people were murdered, and General Butt Naked was driving much of the chaos with sinister inventions of terror. Before every battle Joshua would find an innocent child, cut their heart out, and feed it to his brood of child soldiers, also known as the Butt Naked Brigade. Mayhem was the rule. These child soldiers were often high on opiates, wearing costumes and cartoon masks, and brandishing semiautomatic rifles as tall as they were. General Butt Naked was not the only warlord to take on colorful and fictitious titles. There was General Rambo and General Bin Laden. General Mosquito was a particularly terrifying nom de guerre here since mosquitos spread the deadly scourge of malaria. General Mosquito's nemesis was named, predictably, General Mosquito Spray. All were on a rampage of death, cannibalism, and rape. More than 70 percent of females in the country were raped during this time—a literal hell on earth.[1]

Joshua's alleged Damascus Road experience occurred during the early moments of one of his barbaric battles. Before the battle he sneaked into a river where young children were playing. Swimming underwater, he surprised and abducted a young girl to use for his pre-battle ritual. Once his boys had consumed her heart, Butt Naked led them screaming and shooting into battle. He was screaming and running toward his enemy, but when he tried to fire his pistol, it malfunctioned. As he examined his gun, he heard a voice behind him calling his name in his native tribal tongue. He turned to face the voice and saw a man with a burning light coming out of him who asked, "Why are you a slave?" Butt Naked responded to the man, saying that he was not a slave but a king who commanded an army and took what he wanted. The man responded, saying, "It's true you are meant to be a king, but you are living as a slave. Stop what you are doing." At once the man disappeared, and Butt Naked felt something he had never felt before: fear. According to Joshua, at that moment he was a changed man.

Much as the apostle Paul had done when he fled to Arabia after his conversion, Joshua put down his soldiering and fled to a neighboring country for a time, away from the people he had terrorized. He returned years later as a born-again believer. He started a family and committed his life to Christ's work, preaching and running a mission for former child soldiers. His detractors believe his conversion was pure theater, a dramatic act playing on Liberia's predilection to Christianity, in order to avoid punishment.

Pastor Joshua's tent-revival-preacher theatrics and passion draw worshippers and skeptics alike, some of whom would like to see him dead. He has reinvented himself by transposing his former warlord skills of inspiration, conviction, and leadership into fire-and-brimstone preaching. His detractors claim that all warlords must reinvent themselves after war, and this charismatic preacher is a mere invention of convenience. Many believe this lamb is still a wolf, this messiah still a maniac.

The very existence of redemption and forgiveness is being tested in the hearts of these congregants and victims. "I believe the Bible strongly, and it says God has forgiven me," he proclaims from the stage, and the congregants cheer in response, perhaps in the belief that if God can redeem someone like Joshua, then maybe they can be redeemed too. Drugs, violence, and prostitution are waves upon the sea of everyday life, with each worshipper navigating his or her own course. In order to survive, you must believe. To believe, you must suspend doubt. If God can truly redeem anyone in any state of depravity, then Joshua is a deep-sea diving bell testing the depths of forgiveness. Everyone here is desperate for a God that big. In this dirt-floor temple amid the chaos, they are making fundamental commitments to changing their lives for the better based on the words of a former rapist, cannibal, and genocidal maniac.

DETERMINING A MOTIVE

Would you take spiritual guidance from an admitted cannibal who had killed more than twenty thousand people? Joshua's story is deeply disturbing not only because of his heinous crimes, but also because of his apparent apostle Paul–esque redemption. It's almost impossible to accept his claim of atonement because doing so requires us to know his motivation—which is difficult to truly know. Is Joshua a true evangelist giving his life for others, or is he just playing a role to avoid international criminal court? Is it possible that, despite all the good work Pastor Joshua is doing to rehabilitate child soldiers, he might have mixed motives?

Much of the Bible Joshua preaches from was written by someone with a story similar to his. As we've already learned, the General Butt Naked of the Bible was Saul of Tarsus. Saul would be considered a terrorist by today's standards, walking around Israel with the power and authority to maim and kill at his discretion. In Acts 22:4–5 he says, "I persecuted the followers of this Way to their death, arresting both men and women and throwing them into prison, as the high priest and all the Council can themselves testify. I even obtained letters from them to their associates in Damascus, and went there to bring these people as prisoners to Jerusalem to be punished." I remember learning this story in third-grade Sunday school with sanitized cartoon characters in bathrobes lobbing smooth pebbles at a guy named Stephen until he was dead. I'm grateful today for the soft focus of these children's illustrations, but what I was really learning about was an incident of state-sponsored terrorism. Saul eventually had his bright-light conversion, and just like Joshua, he returned to the people he had been persecuting. This resulted in Saul receiving some death threats as well, so he skipped town for a few years. He returned with a message of redemption, but people still didn't trust him. He changed his name to Paul and became one of the most influential people to ever draw breath. We have two thousand years of hindsight on the apostle Paul to determine if his motives were authentic. We don't know how Pastor Joshua's story will end, though he's shown signs of commitment to his cause.

The point is, we want heroes with pure, distilled motives, but they just don't exist. I'll offer an example. I was once in a creative meeting with an advertising agency, explaining my organization's work, and told the stories of some of the kids we've been able to help. When we wrapped up the meeting and were heading out of the conference room, one of the creative directors said to me, "Boy, you really can't screw up. If you do, it's all over." I was confused and asked for clarification. He explained that since I've committed my life to doing so much "good" for others, I therefore can't ever screw up in my personal life because the whole world would fall apart. When I asked what "screwed up" meant, he said, "You know, like hookers and hard drugs." By his logic, if I ever did anything morally bankrupt, the very notion of a "good person" would cease to exist for him. I assured him that he had nothing to worry about regarding his specific examples, but that he had a lot to worry about if he thought I was *more good* and that somehow he was *less than good*.

The saintliness that my creative director friend mistakenly believed he saw in me is something called *altruism*, the unselfish concern for others. Altruism is the idea that a human being can somehow get outside of his or her own self-centered motives by genuinely caring and acting on behalf of others. We use the term *altruism* to describe people such as charity workers, philanthropists, and religious workers, including pastors, priests, and nuns. The perception is that they are forgoing anything that might benefit them so that they may benefit others instead. The problem is that altruism is a fantasy, a bad fantasy we use to make-believe our way through a very challenged world. Altruism is social idolatry. The reason is because motives are invisible, and many seemingly altruistic actions are sometimes based on reciprocity rather than selflessness. It's important to understand why society believes in altruism, and why it's better to view do-gooders with eyes wide open. The fairy tale that people who work for charities, nonprofits, and spiritual institutions operate from completely selfless motivations is patently untrue and very dangerous.

Our desire for our heroes—or at least our do-gooders—to be pure and selfless is understandable. We want examples of authentic people living for others to inspire us to become better people ourselves. I certainly want that. But the reality is that pure altruism simply doesn't exist because it's impossible for anyone to be truly selfless. As Maslow made clear, we are needy, and our needs drive our motivations. That's why the lines between selfless and self-interested are blurry. They are so blurry that we ourselves may not fully know our own motivations. Doing good for others is a selfish act, and that's okay. It's okay to benefit from doing good. In fact, it's better than okay; it's exactly what the world needs to improve.

FINDING THE SELF IN SELFLESSNESS

I'm an extroverted introvert, which means I'm comfortable onstage but terrible if I have to network in a room full of people I don't know, as mentioned earlier. I become like one of those kids at summer camp who can't assimilate into the larger group and ends up playing with matches by himself. One of the tasks of running a human rights organization is that I need to travel to events, which are full of really smart people with considerable influence on culture, government, and business. Trying to enter a conversation in a room like that is like trying to jump onto a fast-moving merry-go-round. I keep looking for a good spot to jump in, but the speed of thought in the conversation means I'm likelier to land on my butt than on a salient point. This is more a reflection of my own insecurity than what anyone else thinks of me. I often just talk myself out of talking at all.

I came out of the music industry, where my job was rhyming and counting to four. (Okay, it was a little more than that.) The world I later found myself in was much different, filled with wonderfully intelligent people who want the world to work better. But I spoke a different language. I'm a quick learner, but I didn't always learn quickly enough. For example, I once sent a birthday card to a high-ranking official in the State Department telling her that she was an "insufferable advocate for justice." I meant to write that she was *indefatigable.* The vocabulary police should have handcuffed my mouth for that; I clearly have no business driving words that big. The official said it made her day—which says more about her than me—and she showed it to everyone in her office, without revealing who sent it, of course. Another time, a gracious friend invited me out to dinner with some influential individuals after an event at the United Nations. Someone across the table who works with George Soros was talking about some of their philanthropic work. I quietly leaned in to my friend and whispered, "Who's George Soros?" Without looking at me or breaking eye contact with the person who works with George Soros, she whispered, "Google him."

At another high-profile networking event, I was introduced to someone for whom I have great respect. A mutual friend introduced us, and while we were shaking hands, I blurted out that I had read half of his book. To be honest, I don't finish most books, so my getting halfway is a compliment. He didn't see it as such and balked, making it clear to the others around us that I had offended him. I felt terrible. It wasn't until later that night when I was replaying the scene in my mind that I realized I'd had two glasses of red wine and hadn't eaten that day, which might have affected my judgment. I'd actually read several of his books; it's just that his last book I couldn't finish . . . but I probably shouldn't have led with that.

It wasn't his books that impress me, clearly. I'm most impressed with what he's done with his life and how he uses it to help others. I had tried to convey this to him, but it was clear the damage was done. It was strange, though, how easily I offended someone I have so much respect for by simply not finishing his book.[2] That awkward experience taught me that heroes, and everybody else, possess self-interest just like the rest of us. I've learned that we are all operating somewhere between selfless and self-interested. I also learned that I should try to eat something before drinking red wine and then trying to compliment someone I admire.

I used to believe that people whose jobs are to help others are special, until I became one of those people. I wanted to believe in heroes with selfless motives out there doing the right things for the right reasons. I wanted to believe in altruism. In 2016 researchers from the University of Zurich ran an experiment to try and test for altruism in humans by tracking subjects' brain activity.[3] They hypothesized that there are different motivations for altruistic behavior, which can be tracked. The lead researcher, Ernst Fehr, said, "Motives have a neurophysiological fingerprint. The whole notion of a motive is that it's a mental concept you cannot observe directly. And we were able to show that we could make this visible." Through a series of experiments they found that altruistic behavior is driven by at least two types of motivations: empathy and reciprocity. They watched brain activity on test subjects who had to choose whether or not to help someone in need. The researchers found that some of the test subjects acted altruistically because they saw someone in need and empathized. No surprise there; empathy is often associated with altruistic behavior. Other test subjects, however, acted altruistically because of reciprocity: they saw that they could expect to get something out of helping someone in need. Same results, different motivations. Basically, not all behavior that looks altruistic has pure empathic motives. Sometimes we help others because doing so helps us.

THE SOUL'S ENDORPHINS

Every week there seems to be another book or article about empathy, and I try to read most of them. I even finish some of them. Most define *empathy* as one's ability to share another's experiences and emotions, and most argue that we are facing a global empathy deficit. American psychologist Carl Rogers describes the effects of empathy this way: "When a person realizes he has been deeply heard, his eyes moisten. I think in some real sense, he is weeping for joy. It is as though he were saying, 'Thank God, somebody heard me. Someone knows what it's like to be me.'"[4]

The adversary of our empathy is fear—usually fear of what we might lose if we give something away. This fear creates a world of extremes: extremist terrorists, extremist politics, extreme workloads, even extreme workouts. It seems as though we are a people of extremes, and when you are so far off in one direction, it can be hard to look at someone else and say, "Me too." Empathy isn't really something we can switch on. Empathy is a state of being, woven deep into our motivations. This is significant, for it means that we don't have to be perfect to be helpful. Changing the world has nothing to do with how good of a person we each think we are.

What if our motives for doing good also included reciprocity? What if we actually get something of value for ourselves out of acting on behalf of others? What if we were honest about it? Sure, we've all heard the cliché that you get what you give, and we've listened to the Beatles' assertion that the love you take is equal to the love you make, but I don't think people really believe that. We tend to think that doing good for others means that you are somehow losing something and not getting anything you need from the effort. This is a broken thought. Allow me to explain.

If ever there was an icon of altruism, it was Mother Teresa. She's been the byword for selflessness for generations. We admire her not only for her accomplishments, but also because she seemed to know more about the depths of humanity than we do. She dug deep into the mud and discovered buried veins of irrefutable truth. One of those truths is that you cannot give what you don't have. In other words, her tireless work was impossible to accomplish without reciprocity. Even she received a return on her investment of service to the poorest of the poor. She had been known to say, "I have found the perfect paradox, that if you love until it hurts, there can be no more hurt, only more love." Mother Teresa received something back from her experience of cleaning crap from between the toes of the world's untouchables. She experienced a form of reciprocity. She found the soul's endorphin rush.

Reciprocity doesn't mean one necessarily receives back something tangible, like money. Mother Teresa said she received the greatest of all returns: love. And isn't the desire for love the reason we do most things? While spiritual fervor is what drove her into service, it wasn't what sustained her.

When she died, Pope John Paul II immediately began the process of making her a saint. The church pored over her letters in search of evidence of recorded miracles—a requirement for sainthood. Instead they found something even more remarkable. In her letters she claimed that at a young age she heard God's voice telling her to serve the poorest of the poor, but soon that voice fell silent—leaving her to feel distant from God throughout the rest of her life. What I find *miraculous* is that she served the poor in Calcutta her entire life without the spiritual encouragement she had received early on. Given that, it's possible to conclude that it was reciprocity, at least in part, that kept her going all those years. Based on her own words, she received love and found purpose in her service.

By the same token, we might conclude that a young preacher from Atlanta, Georgia, in the 1960s, influenced by this woman who worked in India, must have personally benefited from all the community organizing and speaking he did while becoming the leader of the civil rights movement. Despite Dr. Martin Luther King Jr.'s substantial burdens, he found great joy in preaching the gospel of equal rights around the country. His sacrifice of activism and the joy of using his talents were two sides of the same coin used to help purchase the rights of others. Our motives need not be selfless to be effective. Waiting to be perfect is waiting for the impossible.

We see reciprocity even in the realm of business. Clear, bold lines exist between the purpose of a business and the purpose of a charity. The purpose of a business is to increase profits and drive returns to its owners. The purpose of a charity is to generate impact for the common good. You can determine a company's worth by looking at its bottom line. The *bottom line* refers to a business's net earnings, net income, or earnings per share. The bottom line for charities is harder to measure, but it usually includes some measurement of improvement against a baseline—such as the number of malaria nets distributed in an area that previously had zero. A new model has recently emerged, where entrepreneurs are working to blend the motivations of doing well financially and doing good socially. This new model is called the *double bottom line*.

Investors and entrepreneurs involved with double-bottom-line companies are looking to produce both financial and social returns. The Rockefeller Foundation was an early investor in double-bottom-line companies. Judith Rodin, the president of the foundation, said, "We recognized, if you put a price tag on all the social and environmental needs around the world, it is in the trillions. All of the philanthropy in the world is only $590 billion. So, the needs far exceed the resources."[5] These investors and entrepreneurs have started companies you might have heard of. Companies like Warby Parker, Patagonia, and Ben & Jerry's all have double bottom lines and are the envy of their competitors. There is reason to believe that these companies are performing better because of their social mission.

JIUJITSU AND THE BUYCOTT

When my organization decided it wanted to make a scalable impact on slavery, we knew it had to be in the marketplace. We estimate that the annual global profits reaped by slaveholders exceeds $150 billion.[6] Compare that number with the estimated $200 million a year in charitable donations, and you have an unfair fight. We knew we had to leverage a much larger amount of money to fight slavery, and those kinds of numbers only exist in the marketplace. On average, global commerce from consumers to businesses (C to B) and business to business (B to B) is more than $80 trillion a year. Now, that's a number to work with! So we focused our efforts on leveraging that number to end slavery.

Activists are accustomed to using tactics of shaming and boycotting to get a company's attention. This simply doesn't work in our case because the bad guys in this story aren't the highly visible companies. The bad guys are operating deep inside supply chains, where they benefit from the labor of kids like Isaiah in Ghana or the kids living in DRC. These bad guys hide their exploitative behavior from the companies they sell to. Sometimes governments are complicit in the practice of slavery and child labor, making it even harder to find and address these challenges. We had to find another method to engage and enlist companies into building a free world together.

Our opponents are skimming more than $150 billion off the global marketplace every year through the use of slave and child labor. We needed to use our opponents' purchasing power against itself. Our field of battle would be the global marketplace. The only way to achieve this was to empower companies to leverage their own purchasing power. We needed the power of an $80 trillion marketplace to place a choke hold on traffickers. You can't do that with a boycott.

Boycotts are sometimes polarizing because they assume a pure motive on one side (activists) and a sinister motive on the other side (company or government). Now, I'm not against boycotts. They can be powerful tools, such as when they were used to help end apartheid in South Africa. But boycotts are difficult to pull off today mainly because it's very hard to sustain anyone's attention for long enough. Boycotts are like karate, which involves direct attack. We needed a new tactic based on Brazilian jiujitsu moves, where you use the power of your opponent (the bad guy deep in supply chains) against himself. We needed to work *with* the power of the marketplace, not against it. What we needed was a "buycott." What if, we wondered, consumers and companies made their purchases with companies focused on protecting freedom in supply chains? Doing so would make good businesses the heroes in our story. What if the answer was for everyone to just *buy better*? Easy, right?

Steve Jobs used to say that storytellers are the most powerful people in the world. They shape culture, politics, and values. The story of freedom is a narrative that's woven into every human being. It's natural for this story to appeal to us as humans, but we needed to construct a story that appealed to companies—which technically are not human. So we started building tools to help them. I've already mentioned in earlier chapters about the FRDM software we built. Since most companies have no idea where slavery might be entering their supply chains, we built FRDM to help companies detect risks of slavery based on what they are buying. We built the world's largest database on the subject, which analyzed everything a company could purchase, from industrial refrigerators to wool scarves, copy machines to diapers.

We also created a brand that inspires. Our strategy was to create value around our brand, such that any company or organization publicly associated with us would be identified with the value of freedom. We knew that if we could create a positive and hopeful story around us, then companies would want to be associated with us. We were right. Fortune 500 companies began to come to us for help with their supply chains, which ended up impacting the marketplace and making it harder for bad guys to make money. Within a short time we were helping companies buy better by leveraging hundreds of billions of dollars in the marketplace.

Social and environmental progress today is about building a coalition of the willing. This happens when enough power becomes consolidated to do something good. To build coalitions of the willing, you need to build something called *moral suasion*. I love this idea. Moral suasion is an appeal to morality to influence or change the behavior of governments, institutions, and businesses. It is essentially an appeal to a preferred behavior. Moral suasion has been used to change environmental laws, establish women's rights, and scale abolition in the 1800s.

It manifests when a society says to itself, "Hey, we can do better here. We aren't living up to our ideals." Moral suasion is the process of appealing to motivations. Changing large systems doesn't happen overnight. You have to take the long walk upriver and learn how the system is broken. To change those broken systems, you have to understand, and in some cases empathize with, the motivations of the people working within those systems.

We didn't need altruism to make a difference. We didn't need perfect people. We just needed to find the correct kind of reciprocity. The story of Made in a Free World is a story where everyone wins. Consumers win because they know their slavery footprint and now have companies to buy from. Companies focused on their supply chain win because they get tools to protect their values and validation for their efforts in the marketplace. Victims of slavery win because the power of the marketplace is enlisted to put their captors out of business. So that makes it a win-win-win. Upgrade!

WE ARE GOOD ENOUGH FOR DOING ENOUGH GOOD

In Aristotle's writings on ethics, he said, "We ought to have been brought up in a particular way from our very youth . . . so as both to delight in and to be pained by the things that we ought."[7] He is saying a life well lived delights in participating in the things that matter in this world. It matters when people are facing a poverty of means, and our participation in fixing it will bring us delight and meaning. I'm not talking about the good feeling we have when donating to a cause here or there. I'm talking about a delight that comes from a fire in our bones. Aristotle says that if we allow the pains of others to affect our daily lives, our lives can become more delightful, more meaningful.

Altruism is an idealist fairy tale that disenfranchises us from participating in the delight of helping others. We don't have to wait for our motives to be selfless to participate in changing the world. Let's

131

face it: We think about ourselves often, and so does everyone else mentioned in this chapter. Pastor Joshua's motivations are mixed, as are mine. I don't go to work every day thinking only about others. As an artist, I know that my greatest joy is to make things that don't exist and then give them to others to use and enjoy. I used to make things as a songwriter and performer, then as a filmmaker, and now with business intelligence software; but the delight has always remained the same. The thread running through all of these efforts is my delight in making something for others. I'm getting something out of helping them, while good things are happening. The idea that we have to be second-century martyrs to help others is pure fallacy.

Life is about how you leverage your assets, which includes everything that's happened to you up to this moment. Pastor Joshua's motivation may be to truly live out forgiveness in Liberia with the ones he hurt. He may also be trying to reinvent himself in order to survive. Our motivations to help others don't have to be pure; they just have to be present.

Everyone is looking for a win-win, double-bottom-line result for their lives, and there is absolutely nothing wrong with that. The brilliant billionaire philanthropist, the bleeding-heart activist, the warlord preacher, the supply chain executive, and the accidental abolitionist all have something to gain by helping others. Financier Michael Milken famously served time for securities fraud and was dubbed the "junk bond king" of the 1980s. When he got out of prison, he committed his life to philanthropy, specifically medical research. *Fortune* magazine called him "The Man Who Changed Medicine." He says, "Giving yourself to others is the most important thing. When you give, you get something in return."[8]

A tweet from the famously mysterious street artist Banksy, who is never quiet when it comes to speaking truth to power, said, "Be good, do good, look good."[9] The lines between our motivations to do good for others and do good for ourselves have always been blurred. Society will always see the moral polarity between Mother Teresa and human traffickers, but the majority of us operate with some invisible mixture of motives. When we act on our desire to improve others' lives, we are acting in alignment with our primary desire—which is acting for ourselves. The key is to be okay with knowing you can do good, feel good, and look good at the same time.

CHAPTER 9

A SPOONFUL OF FICTION

DECEMBER 6, 2013
JHARKHAND, INDIA
MICA MINING REGION

MY BUNK JOLTS ME FROM AN AMBIEN-INDUCED SLUMBER. NOTHING around me looks familiar, making me wonder if I'm still asleep. The bunk rattles again like a car wheel missing half its lug nuts. My cognitive engine is slow to warm up as I reconstruct the events leading up to going to bed in a room with a stranger—or strangers, to be more accurate. The haze of sleep slowly dissipates as I use the light from my phone to survey the room. I'm either on a flying zeppelin or a train. (Please let it be a zeppelin.) Nope, it's a train. A woman sleeps in the top bunk across from me, wrapped in a burnt-orange sari and curled in the fetal position around what looks like a large woven satchel. Beneath me are two kids, maybe three and five years old, also sleeping. Next to them is a man on his back, dead to the world. They are clearly better at sleeping on trains than I am. Dark silhouettes of power lines and the occasional tree against a moonlit sky roll past the small window. I check my iPhone, but it's not picking up a signal, so I have no idea what time it is. My brain's hard drive is starting to come online, and I now remember this family was asleep when I boarded the train at midnight, so despite the fact that we all slept together, it looks as if we won't ever get to meet. Using my iPhone screen for light, I gingerly

135

cascade off my bunk, grab my gear, and tiptoe out of the cabin like a cartoon robber.

The train's hallway is a sea of humanity in every direction, huddled masses sleeping on top of overstuffed bags in positions that would impress the most enlightened of yogis. I move past men, women, and children of every age wrapped in yellows, reds, and blues, unfazed by the constant shimmy and shake of the train. I open the doors to the compartment between train cars to find my film crewmates who never went to sleep, opting instead to smoke and tell stories all night. We watch the dark midnight blues and blacks of eastern India's landscape race by and laugh at one another's stupid jokes for hours.

Our train pulls into the deserted station around 5:00 a.m., where our fixers are waiting for us. A fixer is like a local guide who speaks the language, knows the customs, and keeps you out of trouble. We quickly move our gear off the train and into the awaiting vehicles. Our fixers respectfully demand that we quickly get inside the van with the tinted windows. Even though it's only a few blocks to the hostel and it's still predawn outside, we need to stay out of sight. If we are spotted, our cover will be blown, along with our much-needed element of surprise. They load us into the hostel, being sure to put our room at the end of the hall behind their rooms, a blockade of sorts. They are taking every precaution. Once settled, we climb to the roof to get our first sense of where we are. The sun begins to emerge from behind the maze of power lines as the slow crescendo of constant car horns heralding the day's first light. This is our first glimpse of Jharkhand, India.

Jharkhand came on the scene in 2000, making it the youngest state in India. It's India's version of Alaska, in that everyone in India knows about its beauty but hardly anyone goes there. It was carved out of the state of Bihar, the poorest state in India. The Bihar region was once a center of power and culture. It was the India from our children's books, full of ancient temples, tigers, waterfalls, elephants, and Indiana Joneses. During the time of the British colonization, the region devolved into a feudal state due to deindustrialization. Artisan jobs such as spinning and weaving were essentially exterminated, leading to the loss of Bihar's valuable exports. Anyone involved in agriculture was also screwed over by the establishment of a new class of landlords only interested in collecting rent on land, not exporting goods. Due to bad trade policies, the mineral-rich land did not receive the financial benefits provided by the industrial age that other Indian states enjoyed, kicking Bihar farther back into the backwaters of progress. The British eventually left, but the landowner mentality remained, meaning that most people in the region worked for a few landowners who got rich off their labor. Most of the people here have remained in extreme poverty for generations.

Another challenge to the region, resulting from the power vacuum left by the British departure, is the rise of violent terrorism by Communist Maoist rebels who seek to overthrow the government of India. *Maoist rebels* sounds like something from an early James Bond film, but they are very serious business. The Communist Party of India formed in 1967 with a focus on redistributing land to landless farmers and miners, and rallied support from poor farmers to violently attack their landlords. The Maoists' political platform today remains essentially the same, declaring that imperialism is still the cause of the massive disparity between the wealthy and the poor. The Maoists claim that this disparity proliferates an ancient caste system, which perpetuates social and financial discrimination against lower castes, such as the Dalits. The Maoist rebels that operate here purport to be fighting for the people of Bihar and Jharkhand.

It's these rebels our fixer is trying to hide us from. Several months ago Maoist rebels blew up the same train we just arrived on, killing several people. Recently they blocked off a small bridge in the forest, kidnapping and killing more than a dozen people. Kidnapping to collect a ransom is one of the Maoists' go-to income generators, and our fixers are not being subtle about the potential price on our heads. We are grateful for the caution but remain focused on our task. The world doesn't need more white cowboys with cameras, but it does need the truth told with authenticity and empathy. This is the job we've come to do, and due to safety concerns, we have a very narrow window of time to do it.

Made in a Free World has been hearing about children forced to mine minerals in this region. The Indian government assures us that the mines that used children have been shut down for two decades, but our intelligence says otherwise. I've brought my film crew with me to capture the stories of these children and to find a solution that people back in the West can participate in. Americans and Europeans have no idea how much they participate in the tragedy of the story we are here to tell. The mineral the children are mining is called mica, and it is used in many of the different products you enjoy every day. You see mica every day because mica *is* sparkles. Those glittery sparkles you see in nail polish and cosmetics? That's mica. About 40 to 60 percent of the world's sparkles comes from this region. So basically, children are mining sparkles to make us look pretty. That's unacceptable.

Once the sun is fully up, we jump back into the vans and drive for two hours into the rural mining communities. As we drive through forests and small villages, I can't help but think about the movie *Indiana Jones and the Temple of Doom*. Indiana Jones is asked by a remote village in India to retrieve a sacred Shiva Lingam stone recently stolen from the shrine in their impoverished village. In addition to the missing stone, the community's children have been kidnapped and now labor in a Dante's *Inferno*–like mine, filled with rivers of lava and human skulls. Indy agrees to retrieve both the children and the stone, and nonstop adventure ensues. The film's director, Steven Spielberg, tried to film the movie in North India not far from Jharkhand, but the Indian government kept demanding script changes, so he filmed in Sri Lanka instead. We don't expect to go on any wild rides in mining carts here in Jharkhand, and we hope to avoid any fights involving bullwhips. But we do expect to find precious stones, evil masters, impoverished villages, and child laborers.

As we drive closer to our destination, we begin to notice that the dirt on the side of the road is sparkling like tips of waves reflecting the sun. Mica looks like stacked sheets of transparent plastic glued together, and it is acquired by digging holes deep in the ground until a vein is struck. The International Labor Organization has two definitions for *child labor*. The first definition is for situations where children are working with their parents to help provide for the family. This is the reality for many kids whose families cannot generate enough income to provide basic food and shelter for the entire family, so the children work to fill in the income gaps. The second form of child labor is defined by the ILO as the *worst forms of child labor*, which include "work underground, under water, at dangerous heights or in confined spaces; work . . . which involves the manual handling or transport of heavy loads; work in an unhealthy environment which may, for example, expose children to hazardous substances, agents or processes or to temperatures, noise levels, or vibrations damaging to their health."[1] In order to mine mica, children dig narrow "rat-hole" mines with prehistoric axes and spikes. They then must climb down into these dark, narrow tunnels. Deep inside the darkness of these confined, dusty spaces, the kids pickax the surface in search of mica veins. These rat-holes have no ventilation, are unsupported, and sometimes collapse.

One of our fixers is in another vehicle serving as a scout about five minutes ahead of us. He's just spotted children working in a mine. He tells us to park about a hundred meters away and come on foot to avoid detection. We grab our film gear and head down the glistening trail as quickly and quietly as we can. By the time we reach the mine, it's as empty as a ghost town. We see tires spinning on bikes thrown down in haste. Tools dropped where they were being used. Large piles of mica in the process of being bundled lay bare. Whoever is running the mine was tipped off about us coming and sent the children into the forest to hide just minutes before we arrived. We accept defeat and quickly make our way to the next location, only to find it also emptied out minutes before our arrival. This goes on for hours.

Now it's a few hours before dusk, and we are driving along back roads in an attempt to disguise our approach to the next mine. Out of nowhere several men on motorbikes block our way and demand that we all get out of the vehicles. These men say they work for the contractors who run the mines. The mines where these children and adults are working are not owned by families or tribes. They are owned and controlled by "contractors" who either manage or own the land, and they will use any labor necessary to get mica out of the ground. These contractors typically stand atop the mines under the shade of their umbrellas, watching children work, while thugs like these guys on the motorbikes protect their interests. These thug messengers tell us that all the contractors in the region know that we are here, and they are calling one another to warn of our arrival. They also inform us that they've told all the children that the white men are coming with candy loaded with explosives that we will detonate with our mobile phones. If I were eight years old and someone told me that, I'd run for the forest too. The thugs try to intimidate us a little more, then ride off.

A few minutes later we get a call from our scout that he's found a mine with children and no contractor. We race over to the mine, carry our gear down a steep hill for about a half mile, and find what we've been looking for. About a dozen children are climbing in and out of holes, dragging huge pickaxes and hammers. As I get closer to the children, a half-naked man wearing only a loincloth, wielding a pickax and a mobile phone, emerges from what looks to be a fifty-foot-deep rat-hole mine. He looks directly at me, dials his mobile phone without taking his eyes off me, and starts talking in Hindi. My team and I push past him to meet the kids and film their stories.

Kids are the same everywhere I go in the world. They are genuinely sweet, shy, and giddy around us, showing me all the mica they've mined in hopes of impressing me, which they do. All of the girls are dressed in beautiful beaded saris more appropriate for a prom or a Bollywood film. I notice one girl dressed in deep blues and reds coming out of a mine. Her eyes are fierce and she never breaks a smile. It's obvious that she's tired from swinging an ax all day. I can't help but notice that her face is glimmering. The mica dust has glued to her sweaty face, causing her cheeks and eyelids to sparkle. I'm struck with the irony that the mica she's unearthed will soon be painted on the face of another girl about her same age halfway around the world. That Western girl from London or Chicago, whose life consists of school, makeup, pop stars, and boys, will likely never know that another girl with similar hopes and dreams swung an ax in a mine so she can sparkle.

Our fixer tells us it's time to go, and we climb back up the hill, where we encounter the half-naked guy with the ax and mobile phone again. This time he is standing next to a well-dressed and very angry contractor. This is the half-naked guy's boss, whom he's been calling. It's clear that the contractor rushed over to stop us from going into his mines but was too late. We move past them and quickly get into the vans. As we drive away, our fixer tells me what the half-naked man was saying into his phone earlier on the way down into the mines: "The white devils are here. Should I chop them up?"

PEOPLE OF THE SECOND ACT

There is something in us, as storytellers and as listeners to stories, that demands the redemptive act, that demands that what falls at least be offered the chance to be restored. The reader of today looks for this motion, and rightly so, but what he has forgotten is the cost of it. His sense of evil is diluted or lacking altogether, and so he has forgotten the price of restoration. When he reads a novel, he wants either his sense tormented or his spirits raised. He wants to be transported, instantly, either to mock damnation or a mock innocence.

—FLANNERY O'CONNOR

We are hardwired for stories. Stories are how we do everything from learning to believing. We want to be transported when we engage with a story. Just like comfort and amusement, stories—in particular, fictional ones—have the power to inspire or distract us from finding our riot and soul dream. Separating truth from fiction has become more difficult with the proliferation of media. Sensationalism is used by nearly every format of media to attract viewers, blurring the lines between fiction and reality. We've had to create terms such as *fake news* to describe this phenomenon, an oxymoron if there ever was one. This blurring of lines has dulled our sense of tragedy, which, in turn, dulls our sense of purpose. It's hard to know what the world needs from you when you can't understand what's really happening. Despite this misuse of fiction in our society, we cannot afford to lose our sense of true story. Stories drive us to change ourselves and the world. So it's important to understand how stories can either inspire us to change the world or amuse us into apathy.

Famed founder of the Story Seminar and go-to expert for screenwriters, Robert McKee says, "A culture cannot evolve without honest, powerful storytelling."[2] In his courses students learn how to put together good stories in three acts. Act 1 sets up the characters and defines the protagonist and antagonist. In act 2, the protagonist finds himself or herself inside of a problem that he or she cannot solve, which is also called the "character arc" or the development of the character. In act 3, the protagonist overcomes these challenges in what's called the climax, and the story ends in resolve. In act 1 of *Indiana Jones and the Temple of Doom* we meet Indy; the co-protagonists, sidekick Short Round and romantic interest Willie Scott; and the antagonists, who have been enslaving children in mines. In act 2 we see our protagonists getting captured and Indy getting brainwashed into performing the antagonists' bidding. Act 3 has an awesome mine car chase, fight scenes, and a climax in which the antagonist is defeated.

Have you ever tried to read a novel by reading just the first and final chapters? Of course not. It's the tension we experience in the second act, when the protagonist is facing an impossible problem, that makes the third act so enjoyable. The tension of the second act is where we find out what kind of person the protagonist really is. They have to struggle without certainty of success. If it's a good story, we will experience tension on behalf of the protagonist, our hopes and imagination following along until a resolution is reached. We humans are hardwired to rally alongside protagonists in three-act stories, and we have been doing so since the beginning of time.

As we've learned, people suffering within a poverty of means—like the young girl in the mica mine, Blessing in a displaced persons camp, or Isaiah on a boat—are trapped in life-threatening situations, otherwise known as second acts. They can't get out of their situations alone. What will happen to the little girl in the mine or the little boy in the boat? It's important to remember that these kids are the protagonists of their own stories. They are the lead characters, and they are waiting for an outside character to come help them get to their third act—just like in the movies. In *Temple of Doom*, Short Round helps Indy awaken from an evil spell to save the children. In *The Empire Strikes Back*, Yoda offers vital guidance to Luke Skywalker in the form of the Force so that he can defeat the Dark Side. We are not the protagonists, like Indiana Jones or Luke Skywalker, in our selfish plans to change the world. We are the helpers, like Yoda and Short Round.

We will never find our purpose and meaning if we believe that we have to be the hero to change the world. It's impossible to change the world and find meaning if heroism is your motive, or if *saving* the world is your goal. We can only participate if we enter the second act of others' stories as helpers. But here's the problem: while we love watching second acts, we hate having to operate inside them. Changing the world means getting used to being inside of second acts, where the ending, or third act, is uncertain. To help us overcome our aversion to the second act, I've identified two specific challenges we can work on.

The first challenge is that we've been trained to avoid second acts unless there is a guarantee of resolution (i.e., a third act). Second acts feel desperate because, well, they are. The hero is stuck and doesn't know how to go on. We don't naturally gravitate toward desperation unless we know it will somehow work out in the end. That's why the charity model works so well, because we are offered certainty that our donations will move the recipient to their third act. We need to become acquainted with ambiguity if we want to find meaning and change the world.

When we read a book or watch a film, we enter into a silent agreement with the writer that the story is going to resolve somehow. We willingly offer our emotions and time to the story because we know it will be okay in the end. One of the reasons we are willing to follow the protagonist of the story into the tension of the second act is because we know something the protagonist doesn't know. We can see the book has several more pages or the film has several more minutes left for a third act. We basically take the god-position in these stories, seeing the length of the story as a whole. Our predisposition to the god-position in stories is challenged when we meet real people stuck in their second act. For instance, when I introduce the stories of kids in Jharkhand to someone new, the first question that persons asks is, "How do you save the kids?" People don't like seeing the kids stuck in their second act. As with any great story, helping someone from the second act to the third act isn't only about saving; it's about taking down the system that hurt them in the first place. (Spoiler alert: Indiana Jones not only frees the kids but also destroys the mine along with its slavers.)

The reason I went to Jharkhand was to help create a third act for these children. To do that I needed to introduce these children to people back home, just as characters get introduced in the first act of any story. It's hard to invest in someone's second act if you can't relate in some way. I needed to connect our world in the United States with the world of these children mining the sparkles that bedazzle our lives. Most people have never thought about where their sparkles come from. So we produced a short film and a campaign to help consumers connect the dots. This wasn't meant to enrage; it was meant to engage. The stories of consumers in the United States and those of the children in Jharkhand became connected and, as a result, we were able to make an impact on the lives of thousands of children. Little girls in America started their own fund-raisers for the little girls in Jharkhand. Hair salons started telling their clients where sparkles came from and raised money for bikes so the kids could get to school. Not only did we build schools, but we also met with the cosmetics and electronics industries who source mica from this region. Because of this, a new third act was written for many of these kids where they now go to school instead of working in mines. I was able to attend a school ceremony where we gave bikes to the kids in Jharkhand. Spielberg himself couldn't have written a better third act than the one I saw that day.

The second challenge we face with real-life stories stuck in a second act is our tendency to process the stories as fiction. When a person's story is so tragically different from our own and we cannot find a resolution for it, our brains can put the person's story onto the *fiction shelf* of our minds as a means of self-protection. If a situation feels too desperate, and there is no easy way to help, what else are we supposed to do? The migrant crisis in Europe is a story stuck in a second act. Fiction shelf. People suffering from poor sanitation in the Kibera slum is a story stuck in a second act. Fiction shelf. The girl sold into a brothel in Calcutta is stuck in a second act. Fiction shelf. It's not our fault that we fictionalize difficult information about distant people with distant problems. We've been conditioned to fictionalize difficult stories from some of the earliest stories we were told. It might help to learn a little more about how we've been conditioned.

CHIM CHIM CHER-EE-DICULOUS

Mary Poppins might have ruined an entire generation of babysitters and teachers. Children who watched Disney's *Mary Poppins* in 1964 were later disappointed to discover that their actual teacher or babysitter couldn't sing or fly or lead penguins wearing bow ties in a big dance number. Who could possibly live up to that? My babysitter Leah Mello was fun, but she wasn't packing a magic umbrella. Arguably one of the best scenes in the film is the resplendent chimney sweep dance number performed by Bert, played by the incomparable Dick Van Dyke, who danced like a praying mantis on Red Bull. In another scene Bert, covered in soot, walks the idyllic streets of London with two polished upper-crust children, singing the undeniably catchy song "Chim Chim Cher-ee." You probably just hummed it in your head. The song was a smash hit that won an Oscar, but dancing Bert wasn't telling us the whole story about his sooty trade.

Chimney sweeps were far from lucky, and the lives of their apprentices were a living hell. The magic of Disney, which I love and pay fealty to, turned a dirty, dangerous job into a snappy, happy dance number. The film wasn't written as a documentary, so it's unfair to be too hard on *Mary Poppins*, but it's a great example of the power of fiction to serve, in the words of Ms. Poppins herself, "a *spoonful of sugar* to help the medicine go down." To understand the true story of Bert's trade, we need to reach back to another, less-popular storyteller from an earlier time.

One hundred seventy-five years before *Mary Poppins* flew into theaters, a poet and painter named William Blake released an important series of poems about life in London. Blake belongs today in what one might call the Dead Artists Guild—a group of artists, like Vincent van Gogh, whose work became widely appreciated only posthumously. Blake was what we would call a struggling artist: a contrarian of his day who took aim at uncomfortable topics such as gender bias, racism, and religiosity with his words and art. Sadly, his peers held little regard for his work with its overt focus on activism—which was not even a word then. Popular artists of his day were more focused on painting with realism, like a painting of a bulbous white guy wearing a bonnet, sitting next to a plate of finely cut meat while a sullen Saint Bernard dog sleeps under the table. Blake, however, went to great lengths to express his point of view in his work, regardless of how it was accepted. He was committed to introducing his audiences to the second acts of real life.

Blake published a series of illustrated poems entitled *Songs of Innocence* focused on the fragile conditions of the impoverished youth of his day. The poems portray intimate stories of children's vulnerabilities while also telling larger lessons about cultural indifference and abuses of power. Poems such as "The Little Black Boy" and "The Little Lost Boy" paint pictures of vulnerability and innocence in both flesh and spirit. One poem in particular, "The Chimney Sweeper," describes how the poor children of his era were considered discretionary commodities. The poem highlights the innocence of these vulnerable children.

> When my mother died I was very young,
> And my father sold me while yet my tongue
> Could scarcely cry "weep! weep! weep! weep!"
> So your chimneys I sweep & in soot I sleep.
> There's little Tom Dacre, who cried when his head
> That curled like a lamb's back, was shaved, so I said,
> "Hush, Tom! never mind it, for when your head's bare,
> You know that the soot cannot spoil your white hair."
> And so he was quiet, & that very night,
> As Tom was a-sleeping, he had such a sight!
> That thousands of sweepers, Dick, Joe, Ned, & Jack,
> Were all of them locked up in coffins of black.[3]

Five years later Blake published another set of illustrated poems entitled *Songs of Experience*, which centered on the condition of children who'd lost their innocence and now faced a world of sin, depravity, and struggle. Once again, he wrote about child laborers in another poem entitled "The Chimney Sweeper."

> A little black thing among the snow,
> Crying "weep! weep!" in notes of woe!
> "Where are thy father and mother? say?"
> "They are both gone up to the church to pray.
> Because I was happy upon the heath,
> And smil'd among the winter's snow,
> They clothed me in the clothes of death,
> And taught me to sing the notes of woe.

And because I am happy and dance and sing,
They think they have done me no injury,
And are gone to praise God and his Priest and King,
Who make up a heaven of our misery."[4]

Here again Blake takes the voice of a young chimney sweep, sold in his youth by his parents, who now worship in a church. The family, benefiting from the forced labor of this child, a child who climbs and cleans three-story-tall, twelve-inch-wide chimneys, is praising the God who delivers his people from bondage. The boy is invisible in plain sight. His parents and the people who benefit from his labor have created a convenient fiction for themselves by believing all is well. Blake, an artist of fervent faith, was driven to write about the hypocrisy and injustice of parents who sell their children to work in frightening and dangerous circumstances and yet somehow manage to worship God as a loving Father. Blake wanted to reveal society's tendency to write a false narrative of their world in order to protect a convenient fiction. All around were children suffering a poverty of means, stuck in a second act; Blake used his voice to hold up a mirror to society. It's no wonder his career didn't take off.

Menial and dangerous jobs in nineteenth-century urban centers were considered appropriate for children. In rural agrarian economies, children working on the family farm was normal and paramount to the family's survival. When agrarian families moved to the cities during the Industrial Revolution, they still required their children's labor to contribute to the families' basic needs. So children were put to work in coal mines, in factories, as domestic servants, as rat catchers, as living scarecrows scaring birds from fields, in laundry services, as pickpockets at rail stations, in textile mills, and in prostitution. This was the era of Charles Dickens, whose famous characters included Oliver Twist, a cute little orphan pickpocket who ran with thieves in London and was controlled by child traffickers and pimps.

If Blake and Dickens were alive today and writing about our age, would they write about the girls from the mica mines? Would they admire our technological advancements and connectivity but question us about the millions of invisible slaves working openly in our global village, providing for our comfort while millions hasten off to church to worship a God renowned as a rescuer? The reality of a poverty of means is nothing new to us. We have been watching and reading about it our entire lives. The problem is that we've learned to skip over the second act of the tensions in our world, distracted by glossy dance numbers and viral videos. I'm not saying *Mary Poppins* should have included a subplot involving child slavery. I am saying that we are conditioned to prefer stories that always land on the resolution of the third act, even if the resolution is make-believe. We prefer a spoonful of fiction over a teaspoon of tension.

The greatest stories of our time, like those of the girls in Jharkhand, are stuck in the second act, waiting for the arrival of the third act. William Blake and Charles Dickens gave us stories of the second act, and who knows? Maybe Dick Van Dyke with his bow-tied penguins and Indiana Jones with his sidekick Short Round do something similar, exposing the world to child labor in some way. But Blake and Dickens would ask us directly to pay attention, because the real kids who are in trouble aren't dancing on rooftops or escaping slavery on a roller-coaster mining cart. They are living inside of real second acts, in need of a helper with a riot. So the next time you watch something like a whip-happy archaeologist or a chimney-sweep dancer, remember that real life is being served up there with a spoonful of fiction. We operate in a very nonfiction world.

ONE LAST THOUGHT

One of the reasons we feel a barrier between our lives and the lives of those stuck in second acts is that we don't know what a third act looks like. Not all problems come with solutions. If someone is hungry, they need food. If someone is sick, they need medical care. But what if someone is stuck in slavery because they belong to a lower caste in a system that justifies their exploitation? What if orphaned children in Haiti are expected by Haitian society to work as house slaves, to the point where children can't even dream of a better life? These are hard questions and complicated issues. Their third acts are not written yet. But you may be the person who helps write a third act for someone facing a punishing second act. It will require you to find your riot and believe in your soul dream. If you do, the narrative of your life will change forever, as will theirs. In the next section we will begin to build a plan out of your riot that can create third acts and change the world.

ONE MORE LAST THOUGHT

Hundreds of years after William Blake penned his two sets of poems, *Songs of Innocence* and *Songs of Experience*, U2 would plan two records with exactly the same titles and themes. In 2014 they released an album called *Songs of Innocence*, which focused on their early lives growing up in Ireland. This album was famously given away to everyone who had an Apple iTunes account in 2014, which some would say backfired. It turned out that not everyone wants something for free. The band immediately began putting together a second album, called *Songs of Experience*, exploring the process by which the once-vulnerable boys became men in a strange land. It's interesting that this eighteenth-century poet, relatively unknown during his life, would have an homage to his work given away to almost five hundred million people from artists with a track record of making the invisible visible.

PART 3

HOW TO CHANGE
THE WORLD

CHAPTER 10

YOU WERE BORN FOR THIS

AUGUST 7, 1939
NEW YORK CITY
CAFÉ SOCIETY CLUB, GREENWICH VILLAGE

SOMEWHERE IN THE DARK, A PIANO EXHALES WEARILY THROUGH WAVES
of cigarette smoke drifting above the stage like fog over the Golden Gate
Bridge. Minor chords stolen from a Dixieland funeral dirge rise and
fall in steady procession. It's 1:00 a.m., and for the first time tonight,
the nightclub has fallen eerily quiet. Waiters have stopped serving.
Houselights have been dimmed. The standard riotous exchange of banter and libations is being pulled into the vacuum of the dissonant piano
chords. The only visible image onstage is the head of a small-framed
ingénue draped in a solitary light. Her eyes are closed, but the eyes of
every black, Jewish, Irish, and Italian patron rest on her silken skin,
the fresh gardenia in her hair, and the ruby lips turned ever so slightly
south. But this young singer is far away from here—150 blocks north
and six years back, to be exact—running down an alley off of 204th
Street in Harlem.

She remembers how she was trying to catch up with her young
mother, who was running ahead. Her emaciated preteen legs eventually gave out. Within seconds the police were upon them both. Just
moments before the cops arrived, she had been putting on her ruby
lipstick in a small room on the fourth floor, getting ready to service her

sixth john of the day—another five dollars for the brothel she and her mother lived and worked in . . . or *used to* work in.

As the music slowly swells inside the nightclub, she is taken back to the feeling of those viselike white hands grabbing her malnourished arms and throwing her into the paddy wagon. The piano plays a gentle crescendo, A minor to E major[7], telling her it's time to come back to the present and pour everything she has into a song that carries a backstory as dissonant as its chords.

A few years ago, a Jewish schoolteacher from the Bronx came across a photograph of the lynching of two African American men in Indiana. The image portrayed the bodies of Thomas Shipp and Abram Smith hanging from a tree. Both had been accused of murdering a white man and raping his girlfriend. The men had been placed in a jail cell along with a sixteen-year-old alleged accomplice named James Cameron. That night an angry mob came with sledgehammers, broke into the jail cell, and took the three men. Thomas and Abram were strung up and hanged in a field, but the sixteen-year-old escaped. A photographer was in the crowd, which included women and children, and took the iconic photo that Abel Meeropol held in his trembling hands. Abel, an amateur poet, had always been disturbed with racism in America. The image "haunted me," said Meeropol. He knew then and there that he had to do something.

Meeropol had written poems before, but never one like this. Racism in 1937 didn't register as a problem to be dealt with by the general public. It was just a condition that most white Americans accepted as normal. Besides, the world had bigger problems to deal with in 1937, such as the ongoing economic depression, the struggle to find work, and a megalomaniac in Germany who was garnering increasing attention and concern. But Abel felt compelled to wrestle with the riot raging inside of him and shape it into something beautiful and good. He wrote a poem inspired by that haunting photograph and published it in a teachers' union publication. He then decided he'd take it a little further and put some music behind it, transforming his words into melody. White people just didn't write songs like this in the 1930s. It was dangerous. People could get dragged before government officials when they questioned the status quo. Abel published the song under his pen name, Lewis Allan—the names of his two children who died at birth. He then played the song for the influential talent scout and record producer John Hammond. John was so impressed with the song that he decided to have a young girl he'd just discovered in Harlem include it in her set. That young girl is onstage right now with her eyes closed.

John stands in the back of his nightclub, next to the bar. Café Society is an integrated nightclub, one of the few of its kind. John, a consummate musicologist, opened this club because he believes music can find new frontiers when you bring different races together on and off the stage. He will go on one day to play a role in the discovery of other artists, such as Dylan, Franklin, and Springsteen. For several weeks he's had his young rising star close her shows with Meeropol's song. John makes all the servers and bartenders stop serving during the song. He dims all the lights in the club except for a single stage light that illuminates the teenager's face. Her eyes have now opened and have leveled onto the crowd, revealing a wisdom far beyond her nineteen years of life. The red gate of her mouth opens to release Meeropol's song into the misty fog, which begins with the line, "Southern trees bear a strange fruit."[1]

The cadence of her phrases, the push and pull of each word, hypnotizes her listeners. Her voice sounds as if it were formed inside a bottle of jazz-infused gin. She is led by a spirit, a specter of chaos and loss, that turned an innocent young girl into a Harlem hustler. Survivors' voices often carry an authority untethered to class convention and social norms. They have touched the murky river bottom of disappointment, where the bones of dreams lie buried in the mud, and have pushed themselves up toward the surface of a new life. Survivors know depth and disappointment. This young woman will go on to say, "I've been told that no one sings the word *hunger* like I do." There is not a soul on the planet more qualified to sing Abel's lyrics tonight. All of who she is, her talent and her story, qualifies her as the messenger. She was born for this.

The crowd is leaning into every line, slowly decoding Abel's cryptic lyrics. They nervously look at one another as they decipher the meaning. People aren't supposed to sing about such things. This topic isn't supposed to get brought up in public, not onstage, and certainly not by a girl of her color. People today want to hear the hits, like Benny Goodman's "Sing, Sing, Sing" or Count Basie's "One O'Clock Jump." It's one o'clock all right, but ain't no one jumping in this here joint. The ice slowly melts in the audience's Manhattans as they try to reconcile how this teenage singer, nicknamed Lady Day, could get away with singing a song about lynchings. This young woman, with the authority of her backstory, is giving the audience no choice but to look directly at this strange fruit, *a strange and bitter crop.*

The single light above her head turns off on cue with the last word of the song. The entire club is in total darkness for a few pregnant moments, silent, before the houselights come on. The drink service and banter slowly come back. The singer's name is Billie Holiday, and the song is "Strange Fruit."

Though she didn't write it, she owns it. Her life up to this point has embodied the meaning and message of this song. She will go on from this performance to face discrimination in the face of her determination to make this song heard. "Strange Fruit" will become one of the most important songs of the century. It will take another eighteen years for the civil rights movement to start in earnest, but the power of these lyrics and her performances will lay a foundation for the movement. We have witnessed a social alchemy tonight, where the raw and difficult elements of both the writer's and the performer's lives have been formed into a song that will pave a way for the rights of others yet to be born.

BACKSTORY TO A BIGGER STORY

Building a plan to change the world involves multiple steps. Once you have found your riot, as Abel did, the next step is to understand and believe that *you were born for this*. I'll get to the other steps in the next chapters, but we are going to first learn how you were born to live out the story of your life. Despite our best scripting and chasing of our rock dreams, we are not fully in control of our stories. There are chapters in each of our stories we'd prefer were never written, but these chapters create the tension that can produce incredible third acts—both for ourselves and for others. Nobody sang the word *hunger* like Billie because she knew hunger intimately. There is something you can *sing* like no one else too, because all of your circumstances, good and bad, can lead to something much bigger.

I did a very aggressive press tour in 2008 before the release of my film *Call + Response*. We had zero money for advertising, so I basically had to take every interview request we were offered to get the word out. Sometimes I had to do radio interviews on my mobile phone in strange places: an airport bathroom, a friend's closet, sitting in traffic on the 405 in Los Angeles, the lobby of a hotel. Once I was in Nashville for a screening of *Call + Response* at the Country Music Hall of Fame. The only quiet place I could find to do my scheduled NPR phone interview was in the parking lot in the back. The interviewer asked me why I used musical performances in a documentary about modern slavery. I talked about how the hammer and nail of a songwriter are verse and chorus. That's what we use to make songs. Verse and chorus are direct descendants of call and response, the musical form used by slaves in America. So, by my estimation, verse and chorus are, essentially, products of American slavery. As a songwriter, I had made a living using these products, so it seemed right to use them as a tool to end slavery. I talked about how my background as a songwriter was now being used to support the freedom of people I would never meet. I said all this in the back parking lot of a building built with verse and chorus. The radio interview wrapped up a few minutes later, and a friend in California who was listening sent me a text with the words, *You Were Born for This.*

I never felt like I was born to make a film, or to help end slavery. To my recollection, no one wrote in my yearbook, *Have a great summer, Justin! Can't wait to see your next film, and good luck fighting those sex traffickers!* Sometimes aspiring filmmakers would come up to me after a screening and ask me how I did it. How did I get to direct a film that went into theaters? I'm pretty sure they expected me to offer some trick to fast-track a career or maybe an introduction to someone in the film industry. They seldom liked the answer I gave. "This isn't my dream," I'd tell them. I had a different plan for my life, and the plans changed.

I was living out my dream writing and performing songs, but those chapters of my life got hijacked by the crime of slavery. What started as me trying to help out a fledgling movement for a few months turned into several years. The more I helped, the more my career in music faded in my rearview mirror. The truth is, I never reached the goals I had set for my music career. As I mentioned earlier, I had put all my teenage and adult years into a career that was no more. I don't get those years and sacrifices back. My soul dream, however, was always guiding my life, and my story pivoted into amazing new chapters that I would have never imagined. That said, the exit from a career in music was a disappointment that will never go away. I imagine that you have disappointments that won't go away too. I've yet to meet someone older than ten whose life has gone as they planned. I have, however, learned that there is good news for all the bad news we've dealt with. The good news is that the backstory of our disappointments can build a much bigger story than we could have ever imagined for ourselves and others.

Despite what we're told via some of the snake-oil-self-help content, we weren't born just for the good times of our lives. It's impossible to live out a bigger story without the deep authority that comes from disappointment. Billie Holiday was an impoverished child prostitute, but she is known today as one of the greatest singers of all time. The misfortunes and disappointments of her life were a travesty, to be sure. But her story didn't stop there, and ours doesn't have to either. The sum of our stories isn't the good parts minus the bad parts. It's the good parts plus the bad parts. Disappointment has a purpose when it informs our purpose. It can shape us and give us authority.

We are living in a multidisciplinary age. The days of having only one career or one ambition for your life are over. We've learned to operate in fields that used to be open only to professionals. Today everybody is a photographer. A writer. A cinematographer. An Op-Ed contributor. A content curator. A critic. A hotel owner. A chef. A taxi driver. Most of the people I know have jobs they do during the day, and some kind of income-earning activity they do in off-hours. A software salesman is learning to become a master chef at night. A stay-at-home mom creates a revenue-generating blog. A tax accountant teaches a sweaty cirque-du-so-cycling class on the weekends. This multidiscipline ordering of life is a relatively new phenomenon. We are no longer single-story individuals. According to the Bureau of Labor Statistics, the average worker changes jobs every four years.[2] That's like repeating high school your entire life! Elon Musk, our modern-day Thomas Edison, cofounded PayPal, then got into space exploration (SpaceX), electric vehicles (Tesla), and high-speed travel (Hyperloop). In the middle of all that awesome, he had some miserable public failures and disappointments (like rockets blowing up), and he's certain to have more in the future. The plans we have for our lives are just that—plans. Plans change.

You really don't know what you are capable of until you kick off the murky river bottom of your disappointments. Disappointments lead to new chapters. The problem is when we believe that our backstories, with their painful personal and professional disappointments, are our only stories. I started as a musician, then became a filmmaker, activist, television producer, supply-chain transparency leader, and digital platform creator. Every title after *musician* was never planned for. Titles are just references to things we do. It's the output of titles that matter. And it's the disappointments of my backstory that best inform my actions today. My background of performing live helped me to direct and edit my film in a way that kept people's attention. My understanding of how to harness the energy from live audiences has been a huge help in promoting our organization's efforts. My background in song craft informs how I develop digital content and communication tools. My backstory was training for what I do today.

So when I hear someone say I was *born for this*, I take it to mean that I was born for a story that's bigger than my own plans. I was born for a story that includes disappointments and other unexpected chapters that lead to a bigger story. To change the world and develop meaning in your life, your story will require chapters that go off the script of your original plans. I'm not talking about being generous here or there, as important as that is. I'm talking about putting your own plans on the line for the benefit of someone else. Living out chapters where you risk and sacrifice for others is where you will find that your disappointments might actually serve some purpose. They can actually make a difference in someone else's story. Every day I get to reach back into gains and losses from the past and use them to help change the way the world works. Anyone can do this, but first we have to decide if we are going to stay in our backstories or move into our bigger stories.

SHOULD I STAY OR SHOULD I GO?

Life will give you a few unguarded moments when you get to choose between focusing solely on the plan you made for yourself (rock dream), or an adjusted plan that leads to the benefit of others (soul dream). Everyone has these moments, from university students in Idaho getting ready to graduate to Mother Teresa hearing the voice of the divine at a young age. Life hands you a choice when you have to ask yourself: *Should I stay or should I go?*

That moment came for me shortly after I learned what human trafficking was. I knew a bit about human trafficking, but I didn't see how it intersected with my life. I had placed the issue of slavery on the fiction shelf in my heart, where I put other disturbing tragedies that didn't affect my everyday life. Events like the genocide in Darfur seemed impossible to me. It also seemed impossible that labor brokers could go to impoverished regions of the world promising work to desperate people, only to trick them into slavery. And then I saw it for myself.

Shortly after the recording studio revelation, I went to Russia to perform a set of shows. Each night after the band performed, we would hang out in the town square with some of the new local fans. They were fascinated with America and desperate to find a way there, ready to do anything to get out of their impoverished backwater towns. Most of our fans were university age. When I asked them about their job prospects, a few of the girls began to tell me about the men who came to their town offering them jobs in America. These girls were so desperate for a better life that their families were willing to put up thousands of dollars, a fortune for them, to pay these brokers for the opportunity for their daughters to get one of these jobs. This caught my attention. What the girls described sounded very similar to stories I had read and placed on my fiction shelf. These girls had no idea what these men would likely do to them. It was as if I had information that could save these girls from a living hell that they were completely unaware of. It was terrifying. This was my unguarded moment.

The stories that I had shelved as fiction were now presenting themselves to me in real time. Should I stay or should I go? Should I intervene, or just believe that it's a coincidence that I had recently read about labor brokers going to impoverished towns to lure girls into forced prostitution? I decided I would intervene. I decided I would warn these girls of what likely awaited them if they went. I sat the girls down in a circle in the town square. I gently informed them that they were likely heading into a bad situation. I could see their eyes welling up with fear and embarrassment. That look of vulnerability quickly turned into a look of indignation. I expected them to say thank you for the warning, but instead they responded with, "Look around us. There is nothing here. Thanks for the warning, but we'll take our chances." When I got home from Russia, I got busy trying to figure out how to solve this.

I'm not the only one who has had an unguarded moment. Abel Meeropol, the writer of "Strange Fruit," had an unguarded should-I-stay-or-should-I-go moment in his life as well. It was 1951, and the Red Scare in America was at a fever pitch. Since the end of World War II, Americans had become obsessed with fighting the scourge of Communism, domestic and abroad. Senator McCarthy led the charge in Washington with his infamous list of people suspected of being Communists. A married couple named Julius and Ethel Rosenberg were indicted for passing secrets about America's atomic bomb program to the Russians. The trial made international news, and the couple was convicted and sentenced to death in the electric chair. It was the first time a married couple had been given the death penalty for spying. They left behind two young boys, Robert and Michael, six and ten years old. These young boys now had few places to go in a country that wanted no association with anyone or anything remotely related to Communism.

A few years later, Abel and his wife were attending a Christmas party at the house of W. E. B. Du Bois, the famous civil rights activist, who happened to be on Senator McCarthy's blacklist. The Rosenberg children were at the party and met the Meeropols. After hearing about their plight, the Meeropols knew this was their unguarded moment. Their backstory included the disappointment of having lost two children of their own. Now they had an opportunity to start a new story with two children America didn't want. They knew that adopting these children would put anti-Communist crosshairs on their backs. Their decision was a diversion from their current story, an unexpected and unplanned chapter, leading to the redemption of two boys and the creation of a beautiful family. They had lost two children at birth and had now gained two children who themselves had been lost. You don't get stories or third acts like this without backstories of disappointment. And you can't live a bigger story without being willing to stand inside the unguarded moments—like the one I had in Russia, or the one the Meeropols had in W. E. B. Du Bois's house—and say, "I will go."

YOU WERE BORN FOR THIS

Part of building a selfish plan to change the world is recognizing that you were born to live your life—not someone else's life or even someone else's opinion of your life. You were born for your life, with all its valleys and peaks. You were born to live inside your song, with its dissonant chords of disappointment building to an anthemic chorus of sweet release. Great songs are the perfect blend of tension and release, verse and chorus. A full life is the same. We were made for tension and release, verse and chorus, and the call and response. Our lives are not full unless we experience and use both. A bigger story is not about the filtered highlights on social media; it is the hidden backstories mixed into paths we take into our future. If leveraged correctly, your backstory can help build a better story for someone else and yourself.

We aren't promised certainty in this life, yet we tend to chase it like junkies. We can't be certain that we'll be healthy, find love, or gain the possessions we want. No matter how much advertisers, politicians, and greasy prosperity preachers try to convince us, certainty is uncertain. Try as we might, we simply cannot mitigate the risk in our lives down to zero. So let's not waste our lives trying to avoid disappointment. Let's use it instead. Don't let yourself or anyone else tell you that the pain in your life is meaningless. It might be the raw element in your life that will change you and the world. Billie sang about hunger better than anyone else because she knew the pain of it; likewise, some of your pain can be used to create something beautiful and powerful for someone else. Friend, you were born for this.

CODA

You never know what will happen when you step out of your disappointments and step up for others. Remember James Cameron, that sixteen-year-old boy who got away from the lynch mob? He and the other boys were severely beaten and dragged to the town square. The mob put a noose around James's neck and was ready to hang him when a woman in the crowd yelled out that James was innocent. Miraculously, that shout-out was enough for the lynch mob to let him go. He would later go on to say that it must have been the voice of an angel. One voice speaking out against the injustice was enough to save this boy. That voice was a voice of dissent in a crowd bent on violence. James went on to work in the civil rights movement and establish the American Black Holocaust Museum.

Robert Meeropol, the adopted son of Abel Meeropol, went on to fight for social causes and established the Rosenberg Fund for Children, which has protected hundreds of children who have been unfairly attacked for their parents' activism. We never know the effects our backstories can have on the stories of others. We never know the impact our lives will have until we begin to step out of our histories and invest ourselves in the stories of others.

I've seen people find their riot and begin to leverage their backstories only to get stuck at the next step. Sometimes we get stuck looking for someone to give us permission to change the world. We'll next learn that we don't need someone's permission to change the world.

CHAPTER 11

DON'T WAIT FOR PERMISSION

ALICE IS WALKING BACK HOME AT A SURPRISINGLY QUICK PACE GIVEN THE long walking suit she's wearing. Her white outfit and bonnet cast a vivid contrast against the red earth and dark green jungle around her. One of the boys from the mission station has just given her news that a visitor from one of the local tribes is waiting for her on the veranda. She is used to meeting the concerned fathers of her students, who have reluctantly allowed their children to be educated. But this would be no such meeting. And with her husband away on business, she would have to meet this man on her own. Alice is not scared in the least. She's traveled alone in this jungle many times without incident. Besides, the man isn't asking for her husband. He has asked to meet her, and only her.

Nsala is waiting at the bottom of her veranda steps. He is clothed in a single loincloth, covering his groin and nothing else. His hair is wild, full of the twigs and dirt acquired from the jungle. He is incapable of making eye contact with Alice, instead keeping his focus on a large plantain leaf, wrapped several times around something she can't identify. Alice motions with her hands for Nsala and his other tribesman to come up the steps to the veranda. His eyes never leave the leaf. Once he reaches the top of the steps, he sits down and begins to methodically unfold his precious package. With plaintive motions, as if he is submitting evidence to a court of law, he reluctantly lays open the plantain leaf on the veranda floor. At first Alice is unsure of what she is looking at. She takes one step closer and quickly takes two steps back, covering her mouth in shock. She knows what she is looking at but has no language to explain it. Lying inside the leaf is a severed hand and foot. They belonged to Nsala's young daughter. His eyes never leave the foot and hand as Alice collects herself and slowly moves closer again. She doesn't need an explanation from Nsala. She knows what's been happening. She has heard the stories. She has been asking the locals about it for some time. That's why Nsala came to her. He heard that she's the one, the only one, who cares.

The Free State of Congo is a lush and verdant land full of natural resources the rapidly expanding modern world desperately needs. Most of this huge territory is landlocked, except for a small stretch of land that touches the Atlantic Ocean. A massive river runs for 2,290 miles throughout this territory and terminates at the Atlantic, allowing for easy transport of the valuable commodities procured from deep within the interior. Steamboats are a common sight, moving up and down the mighty Congo River, full of missionaries, sportsmen, and curious Europeans. Steamboats in the late nineteenth century are a symbol of progress and adventure. Joseph Conrad's recent novel, *Heart of Darkness*, is about one such steamboat that travels up the Congo River, deep into the abyss of the mysterious Congo.

By the late 1800s, Congo was one of the only African territories not yet colonized by a European country. King Leopold II of Belgium saw that all his neighbors had colonies in Africa, which made him feel left out—like a child who didn't get picked to play on a baseball team. The problem was that colonizing was becoming an increasingly less acceptable practice, so Leopold came up with an idea. He found a way to trick the world into believing he was being a humanitarian, while secretly executing his imperialistic schemes. He created a shell company called the International African Association, claiming to bring scientific and philanthropic benefits to the region. He purported to bring Western civilization and religion to the Congo, while, in truth, he was setting up one of the biggest land grabs in history.

Leopold needed someone to help him scope the region first, so he hired famed explorer Henry Stanley, best known for saying, "Dr. Livingstone, I presume," when he found missionary Dr. David Livingstone in the middle of Africa. After surveying what would become the Free State of Congo, Stanley came back to Leopold with his version of great news: not only was the land rich with natural resources, such as rubber and ivory, but there were also millions of people that King Leopold could enslave to do the labor-intensive work of extraction. This pleased Leopold, but since all the other Western nations were slowly winding down their slave trade, he would need to keep his activities hidden. So Stanley spent years upriver getting local tribal chiefs to sign treaties that turned over their land to Leopold. If you have enough guns, you can claim just about any land for yourself, which is precisely what Leopold did. He named this new territory the Free State of Congo, but this part of the world was far from free.

Elsewhere in the world, bicycles were becoming the rage due to the invention of the rubber tire. Automobiles were just starting to hit their stride as well, creating a new age of mobility for Europeans and Americans. The demand for tires and tubes was spiking, which was great news for *exploit-trepreneur* Leopold. His new Congo fiefdom was rich in rubber trees. Extracting the sap from the rubber trees was an arduous process requiring a huge local labor force. Within a few years' time, Leopold established a thriving rubber exportation business by enslaving millions of men, women, and children through brutal armed force. King Leopold was making a fortune.

Alice and her husband, John, came here as British missionaries. Both felt a divine calling to this place. Their mission has been to bring the love of Christ and, if necessary, use words. The last thing Leopold needs is the Walkers and other missionaries exposing his massive slavery system. He has set up a local police of sorts, called the Force Publique, whose job is to protect Leopold's charade of bringing "scientific and philanthropic benefits" to Congo. They accomplish this by keeping a tight hand on the missionaries to prevent any word from getting out about the genocidal tactics being employed. The Force Publique also makes sure that the natives are hitting their rubber quotas. Failure to do so is punishable by death. The Force Publique is allowed to use any means necessary to reach the monthly quotas. Alice and John have been aware of the abuses to the locals, but are unsure of the severity and unable to prevent it. John initially tried to intervene by writing a rather diplomatic letter directly to King Leopold, saying, "I have just returned from a journey inland to the village of Insongo Mboyo. The abject misery and utter abandon is positively indescribable. I was so moved, Your Excellency, by the people's stories that I took the liberty of promising them that in future you will only kill them for crimes they commit."[1]

The pressure to fulfill the impossible rubber quotas now falls on the Force Publique, who use rape, torture, mutilation, and murder to force the natives to work harder. Once, a Force Publique soldier was overheard speaking to a man he was about to kill, saying, "Don't take this to heart so much. They kill us if we don't bring the rubber." Leopold holds the Force Publique to strict accounting standards. Everything has to be accounted for, including bullets. The sole purpose of the bullets is to murder lazy workers. Leopold doesn't want his Force Publique using bullets for any other purpose, such as hunting game. To prove the bullets are being used for this purpose, Leopold requires a severed hand or foot for every victim murdered. So, to save time, the soldiers stockpile baskets of hands and feet that can later be used to account for the bullets. This accounting atrocity has created an insidious economy in severed hands and feet.

Alice feels something rise inside her as she looks at the small hand and foot of Nsala's daughter. A power. A riot. A churning of molten lava at the base of her soul is about to emit from this demure British missionary. Nsala is sitting on the veranda steps, beset with grief, full of the shame a man feels when unable to protect his family. In addition to killing his daughter, the Force Publique has murdered his wife. Nsala is ensnared inside a system of supply and demand that he cannot possibly understand. How could he possibly reconcile that the rubber trees he grew up playing on are now the reason for the death of his daughter? How could he know that people halfway around the world would take the sticky substance from these trees and vines and build tires for riding around their beautiful cities? Nsala is trapped inside a ruthless poverty of means. Alice knows an expression of grief from her would be so inadequate that it borders on disrespect. There are dozens of questions to be asked, but only one question is apropos. So Alice asks herself the most human question possible: *How can I help?*

Without saying a word, Alice runs inside the station and returns with a small, leather-clad square box with a circle cut out of the front. The Kodak Brownie camera she is carrying is the first mass-produced camera of its kind. It costs a dollar, which means that any amateur photographer can get their hands on one. Alice asks Nsala to sit down on the steps again next to his daughter's hand and foot. She carefully adjusts the shot inside her two-square-inch focus frame and captures perhaps the most important picture taken on a Brownie camera to date: a bereft Nsala sitting on the steps of a veranda, looking helplessly at his daughter's hand and foot.

Alice doesn't stop there. She goes into the jungle to document more of Leopold's terror that is being visited upon other tribes. She captures images of children whose right hands have been cut off by Force Publique sentries. She documents mass graves. She films tribesmen shackled together. Much like the photographers who will walk into Nazi concentration camps forty years from now, Alice is capturing incriminating evidence of full-scale genocide.

This young woman with no background in human rights, no class status, no professional photography skills, the wife of a missionary reverend, and a stranger in a strange land is collecting images in order to topple an evil king she has never met. There is no plan, strategy, certainty, or guarantee of success. In fact, her actions do much to increase her chances of dying in the Congo. News about the atrocities is starting to reach Europe, which keeps King Leopold busy. He is doing all he can to suppress the European newspaper accounts of his exploits. He uses intimidation, power, and money to quell the media and keep his lucrative fiefdom a secret. Alice and her husband realize that the only way to ensure that the word gets out to the world is to take these photos directly to the public. It's time for a road show.

Churches. Town halls. University lecture halls. Parlors. Halls of government. There isn't a room that Alice isn't willing to bring her magic lantern show to.[2] Alice is building a grassroots movement one blade of grass at a time. The people who come out to witness her images and stories experience a sense of power just by being in the same room as this fearless woman whom no one has ever heard of before. Her story spreads quickly, making its way to the most famous person in America, Mr. Mark Twain. He contributes his own verse to the cause by publishing a pamphlet called *King Leopold's Soliloquy*, which credits the Kodak Brownie with exposing a genocidal maniac. Newspapers begin to feature Alice's pictures. Human rights organizations are formed. Political and social pressure builds against the mad king's maniacal exploits. King Leopold II will ultimately be responsible for the deaths of close to ten million people, but his stranglehold on the people of Congo will come to an end because one woman with a cheap camera refused to wait for permission to help others.

THE VELVET ROPE

Once you have found your riot and moved toward the chaos, you need to act on it. It's a vulnerable position to be in. When you begin to change the world, you are putting more than just your time and talent on the line; you are putting your purpose, your soul dream, on the line. You have decided that something is broken in the world and that you are the person to act on it. Behind you is your life up to this point, with its victories and disappointments. In front of you is an unknown second act, waiting for you to play your part. This is when the temptation to wait for someone or something to give you permission to act begins to rise. You will want someone with authority to tell you it's okay to act. In the changing-the-world space, a person in charge might look like a United Nations official, a government agency leader, a religious leader, someone who works at a charity organization, a donor, an expert on the topic of your riot, or someone who just seems to have it together. We think of these changing-the-world people as professionals, and it's logical to want some form of approval before you start acting on your riot. This is understandable, but a big mistake.

I like to think of this apprehension to step out as a velvet rope. We've all seen velvet ropes lining the sidewalks of a Hollywood film premiere or a VIP event. These ropes serve one function: to let everyone who is *on the list* get in and keep everyone else out. Velvet ropes tell anyone outside that they don't fit the criterion required for entry. I used to reasonably assume that if one doesn't possess a degree from Harvard's Kennedy School of Government or some title at the United Nations, then one simply isn't qualified to change the world. It's true that higher learning and career experience are useful, but they are not the rule. Here is a little secret: No one is an expert at changing the world. No one! Anyone who says otherwise is territorial and should probably be avoided.

On paper Alice was the most unqualified individual to take down King Leopold's reign of terror. Had she considered her credentials, or written to someone she deemed superior for permission to act, she never would have exposed the injustice. I imagine it took a lot of courage for her to step out alone against such a powerful maniac. This misconception that someone else can knight us into action is as common as it is dangerous, and surely it prevents much good from ever getting started. I still face a lot of velvet ropes, many of which I create for myself. A velvet rope can represent a sense of inadequacy, whether set up by someone else or myself. Here's how I deal with the overwhelming pressure of feeling as if my riot should be handled by a "professional."

I'M A SOUL, MAN

Whenever the imaginary velvet rope in my head makes me feel unqualified, I sing the lyrics to an old Sam and Dave song called "Soul Man" (sung in the voice of a man who grew up as a white, middle-class kid from the suburbs): "I was brought up on a side street, yes ma'am. I learned how to love before I could eat . . . I'm a soul man." This song resets my identity and reminds me that the only permission I need comes from my soul dream, because that is where my purpose lives. Soul dreams are not just what we do; it's who we are. There is no title or position that can stop your soul dream. No one can give us permission to change the world or stop us from fulfilling our purpose. The challenge is to find the courage inside us to believe that. The backstory of the song "Soul Man" came from a similar kind of insecurity.

Detroit in the late 1960s was shifting from the fading embers of the civil rights movement to the beginning of what was to become the Black Power Movement. It was a tinderbox of racial tension. Around 3:00 a.m. on July 23, 1967, police officers raided a popular unlicensed bar called the Blind Pig on Twelfth Avenue. Inside were dozens of African Americans celebrating the return of several soldiers who had fought in the Vietnam War. The police arrested everyone in the bar, resulting in bottles and chairs being thrown by the celebrants. This incident ignited a violent four-day street riot between African Americans and the police. Entire city blocks became war zones. The National Guard had to be called in, and by the end forty-three people were dead, more than one thousand were injured, and thousands of buildings were destroyed by fire.

The cowriter of "Soul Man," Isaac Hayes, lived in Detroit at this time and was walking through his post-riot neighborhood, which had become a virtual demilitarized zone. Stores and residences had been looted and destroyed by fire. He noticed the buildings that were beyond repair were marked for demolition with spray paint. The surviving buildings were labeled with one word: *soul*. Isaac penned the song as a call to rise above your challenges and keep moving. The song is an anthem of self-appointed authority—a reminder that you are here for a reason, you have a purpose, so don't let anyone stop you. Your soul dream, your purpose, is the only authority you need to go around velvet ropes and change the world.

I'm not very enamored with titles or résumés. I've actually never had a résumé. Soul has always been my credentials, and I look for it in others as well. When I'm at events with heads of state and CEOs, my primary qualification isn't my limited accomplishments; it's my soul dream and my riot. I'm on a mission, and I don't need a title to achieve it. On the remix of Kanye West's song "Diamonds from Sierra Leone," Jay Z appears with the declaration, "I'm not a businessman, I'm a business, man." I'm a soul, man. And so are you. Soul is conviction that there is something more. Soul is the hope that what's in you is greater than what's against you. Soul is not strategic or linear, or something you'll find as a third bullet point inside a finely tuned business plan. It's unpredictable and disruptive. Soul isn't necessarily better than getting a degree or working your way up an organizational ladder to a prestigious title, but you can't change the world, or find meaning, without it. Soul gives you confidence to push yourself out into an uncharted world and leads you into circumstances you were not trained for. Just like Alice, we are never truly trained for our riots, but soul is all the permission we need to act. No one told Alice she could take those pictures. She listened to the riot inside of her and acted. This instinctive action, like her willingness to grab that camera, was her soul dream coming out, and it was the purpose of her life.

IDEAS ARE CHEAP

One benefit of doing what I do is that I get to hear some of the best ideas about changing the world. I meet people in my office, at conferences, meetings, universities, concerts, and religious services with fantastic, world-changing ideas. Apps that can find fair-trade coffee shops. A high-speed railroad across Africa. An Uber-like bus app for commuters in Kenya. Women-operated rural banking. Sustainable beekeeping in Madagascar. Some of these ideas make it out of the gate and find traction, but most don't for one reason: they are waiting for permission. Sometimes the people with the ideas want someone to take the first step for them. The first step is always yours to take. Ideas are cheap. Execution is everything.

When the reality of Leopold's reign of terror showed up on the steps of Alice's veranda, she had a choice. She could wait for her husband to return and seek his permission, or she could get her camera and take the first step. She acted on impulse and riot. She acted out of conviction from inside her soul. She didn't stop to count the cost. She didn't think about how many other photos she might take. She didn't wait to consider what the Force Publique or Leopold himself might do if they found out. She didn't wait until she lined up all the other steps needed to get public exposure for the photos. She simply grabbed her camera and took the first step. It's sad that so many good ideas to change the world never get this far.

Talk is cheap, yet expensive. I get invited to dozens of planning sessions every year designed to produce a *working document* that somehow is going to guide someone to act. The term *working document*[3] makes zero sense to me because documents don't work. People do. I'm not against planning or meeting, but I've seen how very powerful and intelligent individuals circle the chairs and talk, and nothing gets done. Why? Because talking about problems makes us feel like we are solving them. Working documents and plans can feel like an accomplishment, but very few people read them, and fewer ever act on them. This is because talk has no risk of failure. Action has risk of failure, which is why we look for someone to give us permission or just plan without acting. I heard someone from the United Nations describe this kind of talking exercise as NATO (No Action Talk Only). Don't talk. Do. Then fail. Then do better. That's how you find meaning and change the world.

Alice trusted her soul. Acting on an idea to change the world never looks wise when stopping to review. If Alice had paused to consider all the possible downfalls that might occur by taking that photograph, she might not have done it. This is why it's so important that you find your own riot and step out toward it. If it's a good idea, then it has probably never been done before. And if it has never been done before, then there is no map to follow, no obvious steps to take. Your first step will be the first step ever taken on your idea. Trusting your impulse and taking a step toward your idea is the smartest first move.

Here is an example. When I set out to make *Call + Response*, it sounded like a good idea to everyone I told. I had managed to confirm some incredible talent for our first film shoot, but my financial and distribution partner backed out at the last minute. All of a sudden I was in uncharted territory and was looking in every direction for someone to tell me what to do. I was looking for someone to take the fear out of the first few steps. I was looking for permission. It was a week away from our shoot date, with confirmed talent, a huge film production, and I had no money. I had worked for two months to get this thing going, with the understanding that the financial and distribution partners I'd lined up would come along for the ride . . . but all of that was gone and the clock was ticking. I remember calling my good friend Brandon Dickerson, who was helping direct some of the performances. I was sitting on my doorstep in Berkeley in a panic telling him my situation. His response was perfect: "You just need a few dollars, a few favors, and a few miracles." Dollars, favors, and miracles only come if you take the first step. I decided to move forward with the filming despite the fact that I didn't have everything I needed. Within days money, favors, and miracles showed up, but only because I stepped out without permission.

Everybody has an idea about how the world should work. Sure, it takes a lot of imagination to come up with a good idea. But it takes several more degrees of courage to take the first steps toward making that idea into a reality. The first step is always yours to take alone. Moving without permission means transitioning between the theoretical and the practical. I meet a lot of theorists with big hearts and excellent modeling strategies. We need more practitioners who are willing to take the first steps on big ideas.

The world needs the veteran who lives in Detroit and learns about the female Yazidi fighters in Syria who need better training to combat ISIS. That guy believes these women could succeed if they could learn what he's experienced. He will take his first step by covertly, and safely, finding an organization on the ground in Syria and then working to set up a private-sector combat coach project made up of veterans. The world needs the university student in Belfast who has an idea to create a SMS texting platform to help farmers in Central Africa get fair market prices. He needs to take the first step by scheduling a twenty-four-hour hackathon at his campus to engineer the first phase of the project. The world needs the young fashion-institute graduate who wants to provide better lives for women in the developing world. She needs to take her first step at designing a web application to connect orders from big apparel brands to women in a sewing co-op in Bangladesh. We need idea-to-step transactions more than we need expensive theories and plans. We need those with ideas to change the world to take those first big steps. The motto at Facebook is: "Move fast and break things." If you don't act on your idea, you will likely never achieve anything.

IN CHAOS, MOVE

I still get stuck inside the torturous merry-go-round of decision making. If a difficult decision is in front of me that either has no viable options, or too many options, I can end up in analysis paralysis, spinning in a feedback loop for hours. A good friend gave me some great advice for situations like this: *in chaos, move.*

My organization gets stuck all the time. We've built something that has never existed before—software to solve slavery. So it's logical that we are going to face chaos, ambiguity, and tough decisions. One time my product team was stuck and was asking me what they should do.

My advice was to just *figure it out*. One of the team members pushed back on me in frustration, saying that just *figuring it out* wasn't a strategy. Changing the world is full of ambiguity, so to do something new, your best strategy will always be to just figure it out—because no one else will.

When trying to act on our riots, we will get stuck looking for that missing tool, person, dollar, partner, validation, or proof to convince us to take a step. I've learned in these situations that I already have whatever is required to take the next step. Alice had a Kodak Brownie camera with a box full of film. That was all she needed to take her first step. She could have talked herself out of acting by telling herself that she didn't have enough training on the camera or that the light wasn't right. She could have convinced herself that she needed something bigger than a camera, like an elephant gun. She wasn't ready for the contents inside Nsala's plantain leaf. She couldn't have predicted that. But in that chaos, she moved. Without waiting for anyone to give her permission, she grabbed what she already had, a camera, and used it.

Whoever finds their riot already has what they need to take the first step. It could be a camera. It could be a job. It could be a relational network or an acquired skill set. My friend Brandon is married to Kirsten, who is an amazing ethical fashion designer. She found her riot in wanting to help women living in extreme poverty. So she started meeting with friends in Los Angeles who are in the fashion business. Together they designed beautiful clothing and jewelry that women suffering a poverty of means could produce. Kirsten's riot became a thriving business called Raven and Lily. We have no excuse not to act on our riots.

When you step out on your own, you will see that you have something to offer the world. Alice offered a few photographs and a PowerPoint-by-candlelight presentation. Kirsten offered some clothes with beautiful beginnings and endings. When you step out, you will find that your voice can speak truth to power, cross velvet ropes, and change the world. And you will discover just how valuable your voice is. We'll learn about the power of your voice next.

CHAPTER 12

HIT YOUR MONEY NOTE

The Eighties
Bay Area, California
My High School

"HI, JUTHIN."

"Hi, Juthin."

"Good morning, Juthin."

Nothing wakes me up faster than the morning salutations from upperclassmen who have deftly identified my speech impediment. This daily walk down the hallway feels like a hazing ritual from a marine boot camp. They sit on the railing with blood in their teeth, confident in their pink Izods and faux surfer pants. They hide in locker rooms, bathrooms, and at the corner table in the cafeteria, waiting to pounce upon a lone underclassman gazelle far from its herd. My suspenders and bow tie do little to mask my inability to enunciate the letter *S*.

I push past them and offer a timid smile that says, "You are higher on the food chain and I reth-pect that." I'm on my way to my favorite and most terrifying period: choir. This class is a hazing unto itself. My fight-or-flight responses heighten before I even enter the choir room. Our choir operates like a college basketball team. There are practices. There are drills. There are games. And there is a coach who throws chairs when he doesn't get what he wants. Oh, and choir is an elective class. So I actually chose this hazing.

I follow the other students into the small room that's connected to the gymnasium. There are forty-three folding chairs in a semicircle surrounding an old upright piano. The sopranos sit in the front left, altos in the back left, basses in back right, and tenors in front right. There are about fifteen soprano singers, fifteen altos, ten bass singers, and three tenors. I am the only rookie in the tenor section; the other two are seniors. My chair is in the front row looking directly at the back of the upright piano. We move like lemmings into our seats, anxious to get settled before the door opens and *he* storms in. His power precedes his entry, and we are all stiff with anticipation in our metal folding chairs. What will he be today—merciful or maniacal?

Five minutes after the period starts, Mr. Thompson bursts into the room carrying a Samsonite leatherette briefcase under armpit sweat marks in the shape of tacos. Without a word he walks over to the piano and sits down, disappearing from our view. The choir room is pin-drop silent but for the opening of the briefcase and the ruffling of papers being placed on the piano. Slowly we see his eyes emerge from behind the piano like Martin Sheen coming out of the water in *Apocalypse Now*. "Helloooo, class," he sings, looking around as if we were new combat recruits. His eyes never blink and remain fixed on us in a dead stare, as his right index finger pounds a staccato C note over and over. We know what this means. Drill practice, otherwise known as scales. His head submerges behind the piano and his left hand emerges, pointing in the direction of the soprano section. At once the girls straighten their backs like the von Trapp Family Singers and sing up and down the musical scale following his notes on the piano—"Mee-nae, mee-nae, mee-nae." The right hand moves an octave down on the keyboard, and the left hand points toward the alto section—"Mee-nae, mee-nae, mee-nae." A few octaves lower and it's the tenor section's turn—"Mee-nae, mee—"

"Stop," he says from behind the piano, without any emotion. He fiercely pounds the last note he played, double time as if trying to break his finger. (*Please let his finger break.*) We know what this means. One of the tenors is singing the scale off-key, and forty-three people in the room know who it is.

Borrowing a page from Joseph Stalin's playbook, he makes each tenor sing the entire scale alone, starting with the two upperclassmen. This is the choral equivalent of a firing squad. I watch, or listen, to each of the seniors next to me sing their scales perfectly, dodging Mr. Thompson's bullets. I know his next bullet will find its mark because now it's my turn. Mr. Thompson's entire head emerges like Ares, the Greek god of war, his eyes wide open this time, pale blue marbles now locked directly on me. He blinks and says in a theatrically sarcastic tone while flittering his eyelids, "Are you ready, my little daisy?" The entire room tries to suppress their laughter, which is exactly what he wants. He loves a show. Every effective drill sergeant is part coach, part entertainer. He is playing the room at my expense. "Yeth," I say, and begin to sing his torture scales, over and over, all by myself, in front of forty-two classmates, until I finally hit the right notes.

Every battalion has its weak link, and for our choir that is me. That means when we go out to battle (to perform publicly), I'm 92 percent sure I'll let everyone down, including Mr. Thompson. We are performing today at a university north of San Francisco. This will be my first performance, and in addition to being a nervous wreck, I'm totally off my rails with excitement. I'm a teenager, so dichotomy of emotions is what I do. Performing live is all I've ever wanted to do. I did a few musical performances at my junior high school and caught the performance bug. I'm pretty much a veteran performer at this point, given my early roles in junior high school as a singing space pilot and an old man who owns an antique store and likes to sing songs with a boy named Corky.[1] Performing for an audience of strangers in a new town is a dream come true for me.

We walk onstage and take our positions in the same formation as the choir room, with me standing front and center. Mr. Thompson then walks onstage to generous applause. He turns to face us with his back toward the audience and offers us a rare smile. Wow. He lifts his hands, signaling he's ready to start, and off we go into the first song. The sopranos sound louder and fuller than they did in our tiny choir room. The guys in the bass section kick in like an 808, full of subsonic goodness. He is directing each of our sections with his hands tucked in front of his stomach so that the audience doesn't see his cues to us. I am in the zone.

The first chorus is coming up, which means it's time for the three tenors to jump in and get this party started. We join the rest of the choir and I instantly feel a warm sense of collective effervescence. I'm singing like Jon Bon Jovi on a motorcycle when I notice Mr. Thompson is looking right at me. He's smiling right at me. Looks like the rookie just became the alpha singer in this here jungle. Mr. Thompson points at me to make sure I see him, which of course I do. I give him a little eye signal that says, "I got thith, Mr. Thompson. I'm gonna sthing this mutha back to Best Buy."

For some reason Mr. Thompson keeps pointing at me. He is using his other hand to mimic a mouth singing. So I give him another nod, telling him I know that it's my singing that's making him so happy. He still gives me the same hand signal, but now his lips are silently mouthing a message for me. I finally begin to decipher what he is saying with his mouth and moving hand gestures, and it's not anything close to what I thought: "Just mouth the words, don't sing . . . don't sing." Forty-two other singers are reading his lips as well, and forty-two other singers will finish singing the concert while one singer will mouth the lyrics in silence.

It's been three months since that fateful concert and I've been practicing like an Olympian. Mr. Thompson hasn't put the invisible muzzle on me for most of the other performances, so I might be getting better. Our choir has been working for months and practicing for the choral competition we're in today. High school choirs have come from all over the Bay Area to compete, which will culminate in a mass choir concert under the direction of legendary choir director Jester Hairston.

Jester is old, a-few-steps-from-death's-door old, and has lived a very full life. He is the grandson of slaves, played a witch doctor in the original *Tarzan* TV show, and composed the popular gospel song "Amen" for a Sidney Poitier film. All the choirs who've come have been practicing old gospel songs like "Swing Low, Sweet Chariot," and Jester is about to lead us all, about five hundred students, in a mass choir rehearsal. I'm no longer a vulnerable single voice in a small section of tenors. Today there are about 150 of us, so I am good.

One of the songs we're performing is called "Keep Your Hand on the Plow." I love singing this song. The aching melody pulls me into the pain from where it originated. The refrain goes: "Keep your hand on the plow, hold on." Our school choir has been practicing this song for months. We learned to sing the refrain as one entire line, without a break between "plow" and "hold on." During rehearsal Jester changes the refrain, and makes us sing it with a break between—but I don't hear him for some reason. So the next time we run through that section of the song, every singer does a hard vocal break right after the word *plow*. As I said, I love this song and feel no apprehension singing it under the cover of 149 other voices, so I sing at the top of my lungs. The words shoot out of my mouth like Jon Bon Jovi popping out of a stage at Wembley Stadium, only my money notes hover above the mass choir like a dove about to be shot because I'm the only person singing in a completely silent, gigantic auditorium. My lone pitchy voice bounces off of the ceiling for what feels like an hour. The auditorium erupts in teenage laughter. All heads turn toward me, and I now wish I were liquid. Jester puts his bony hands in the air and motions for everyone to calm down. He slowly leans into his microphone and says, "Don't laugh at the boy. Pray for him." They must have, because I never stopped singing.

THE MONEY NOTE

The next step in building your plan to change the world is learning to hit your money note. *Money note* is music industry jargon for a particular note a singer sings that enraptures the audience. It's the pinnacle note of a song that lifts the audience out of their seats. When Adele sings, "You could have had it all" during the chorus of the song "Rolling in the Deep," she nails her money note on the word *all*. When I hear that note, I'm transported. It's pure magic. When Freddie Mercury sings, "We Are the Champions," he hits his money note on *we*. That note has made millions of listeners, myself included, feel like a champion. You might have seen audience reactions to money notes if you watch televised singing contests like *The Voice*. *The Voice* judges listen for money notes from unknown singers. A person can be a good singer, but if they don't have that one money note that defines them, it will be hard to stand out.

Just as there are money notes in music, there are money notes in changing the world too. The world-changing money note is a particular achievement of social good that no one else can attain. You've already met people in this book with money notes. Joan Conn's money note was a national singing contest in Haiti. Alice Walker's money note was using photography to bear witness. Common's nonmusical money note is getting kids to believe in their dreams. We all have a money note inside us, but it does require some technique and practice to get it out.

This money note manifests itself when you step out to make the world better. To do this, you need to be sure you are operating in the correct key. In music, a key is a group of music notes that fit together (key of A major, G minor, or C♯ minor, for example). Most singers only have a few different keys that they can comfortably sing in. My keys were G major and A major. Any other key felt unfamiliar to me. There are different keys for changing the world too. The "key" that works best for you to change the world is wherever you are already talented, passionate, and comfortable. If you are a creative person, your key is likely something creative and not something to do with bookkeeping or management. If you are the manager type and love order, then doing something creative to change the world is probably not going to work out well. If you operate in your key, then you have a chance of hitting your money note by leveraging your existing talents into something very powerful that can change the world.

Your money note is an achievement that only you can do. When we are working within our key, we can hit our money notes and doors can open that have always been shut both to us and to the world. Just as Freddie was naturally designed to hit that note, you were designed to hit yours.

Why does this matter? Because we often don't go after our own money notes. We are emulators by nature. We like to do things that have already been done by someone else. Very few of us are pioneers who want to risk everything to try something new. Changing the world means that you are putting something into the world that only you can produce. It requires that you know yourself a little and find comfort and inspiration in what you are already good at. I've seen people try to emulate what someone else does, and I've watched it fail. I've seen individuals try to emulate an organization that breaks into brothels to rescue kids. I've seen university graduates try to get coveted jobs in government and organizations, so they sign themselves up for a master's degree and another $100,000 in debt. I've seen all of these plans fail because they are trying to play in the wrong key and waste their talents. Whatever you are good at right now can be repurposed to change the world right now. That's your key, and that's where you will find your money note.

Here's an example. My friend Dr. Amy Lehman was a thoracic surgeon in Chicago when she started to learn about the absence of healthcare for the twelve million people who live around Lake Tanganyika in Africa. Her key is healthcare. This is what she knows and is good at. Within her key she found a money note, something only she could do. Her money note is a floating medical clinic, a boat hospital that can reach people all around the lake. She has been building toward this money note for years, and I'm convinced she is the only person on earth who can hit this note. She is so committed to her note that she tattooed a map of Lake Tanganyika across her entire back! Looked at another way, if Amy, with her background in health, had decided that she wanted to campaign against illegal fishing in the Atlantic, she would be singing out of key. It would be a waste of her talent, and her tattoo. To better understand how all this comes together, let's learn more about how keys and money notes work.

SONGS IN THE KEY OF LIFE

There is something you can do to change the world that no one else can or will do. It doesn't need to be epic, popular, or even public, but it does need to be authentic to who you are. For Amy, her riot is the lack of health for the people around Lake Tanganyika, and her key is healthcare. My riot is human trafficking, and my key is creativity. My friend Todd Johnson's riot is to see businesses find their double bottom line, and his key is law. He is a corporate attorney at Jones Day with a heart for justice. He uses his skills and passion for law to help fledgling startups get on their feet legally.

You have a key that you work best in. It is simply a mixture of your passions and skills. It may be yoga, civil engineering, software, home design, cycling, eco-care, coffee roasting, panda wrangling, or just about anything for which you have passion and skills. It's important to note that passion alone is not your key. Your key requires some ability. I didn't find my actual musical key until I worked on my singing skills. I've seen many plans to change the world get stifled because someone was all passion and no execution. Well-meaning people have tried to change the world from outside of their skill zone. Your key is likely something you are already good at, and it can be used to produce a money note that will improve someone else's life.

Your money note might not be a film or a floating clinic in Africa. It may be a campaign you start at work to help build homes for the homeless. It may be a blog that promotes fair-trade products. It may be a spinning class you teach where all the proceeds go toward mental health research. Movember, a campaign where men grow mustaches to raise money for testicular cancer research, is a money note. Nuns in Nepal who know kung fu and ride their bikes across the Himalayas to raise awareness about slavery is a money note (yes . . . they exist and they are awesome). A bunch of lifeguards in Spain who quit their jobs to swim out to refugees drowning in the Mediterranean is a money note. Carrying a mattress to a university class to raise awareness about sexual assault is a money note. There have been mobile apps, programs at schools and places of worship, new organizations, social business ventures, blogs, films, book groups, and countless other cultural artifacts launched into the world as money notes. Every note is unique because every note has the maker's fingerprint and key. Every money note requires passion, skill, and perseverance. Every note carries a backstory of successes and disappointments. So don't get distracted with what others have done. You go do you.

Building up to your money note takes work and vulnerability. Adele didn't start off her career with her money note in her back pocket. She had to build to it. Author Simon Sinek, our generation's ambassador of the word *why*, has this to say about the building of Dr. King's money note: "Dr. King gave the 'I have a dream' speech not the 'I have a plan' speech. It's our dreams that change the course of history."[2] Reaching for your money note can be intimidating because it puts you on a precipice with little to hold on to. A great example of this vulnerability is the money note in the United States' national anthem. Maybe it's just because I empathize with singers, but I tense up just before a singer sings the last line of the anthem. When the singer doesn't hit the last note on "o'er the land of the *free*," it's painful, and somewhere a bald eagle is crying. Hitting that note is tough for any singer. You really have to push to reach it. The next time someone performs the national anthem, watch their body language just before that line. That note is a precipice: once you go out on that note, there is nothing else to hold on to. In the same way, it's intimidating to commit to an action that you hope will help others. There are so many ways to fail, but the biggest failure is not trying.

I have found three steps every singer needs to hit their money note. You will need them too. I call them the three *P*s: passion, practice, and people. To hit those high, world-changing money notes, you first need the passion for your riot; otherwise you will never try. But passion alone isn't enough. Professional singers hit money notes night after night because they practice incessantly. Passion gets you started, but practice and effort make it happen. You have to show up and keep showing up. Finally, singers can't hit money notes without an audience to support them. You find strength in the collective effervescence of a tribe of supporters. You will need people around you to give you the courage to step out on the precipice. Let's look at these three *P*s a little more closely.

PASSION: JUST MOUTH THE WORDS

Mr. Thompson's hand gestures at the silence-of-the-lamb concert are seared into my memory. I don't blame him. I'm certain I was terrible. I'm grateful for that feeling of inadequacy that came from being told that I cannot do something I was passionate about. Without passion for your riot, voices like Mr. Thompson's will kill money notes from ever being born. Anytime we begin to reach out to do something we are passionate about, the Mr. Thompson voices in our heads shows up, giving us hand signals to shut it down and just pretend. We are told to pretend we are contributing a verse, when really we are just lip-synching to the passions and talents of others. This is especially true when we begin to act out our passions in hopes of finding meaning and purpose for our lives. Be aware that the Mr. Thompson voice can sound like your own voice, or even the voice of someone in authority or influence. This is another reason why it's so important not to wait for permission to act.

I've had dozens of well-meaning Mr. Thompsons in my life, telling me not to act on my passions. Obstructionist voices like these seldom operate from malice. They often believe they are helping. These voices told me that I don't understand how the game is played, or my organization is too small, or I'm punching outside my intellectual weight class.

They might be right on all accounts, but we are changing the world, not building a rocket ship. Precedent has proven that anyone who sets out to change the world is usually ill-equipped to do so. Steve Jobs, a world changer himself, said, "The people who are crazy enough to think that they can change the world, are the ones who do."[3] We need the room to step out into our passions and see what key they belong in. If your passion is girls' rights, your money note might be a learning exchange program. If your passion is education, your money note might be teaching at an after-school program in your neighborhood. If you are an engineer, your money note might be creating coding curriculum for girls in Nigeria. It helps to remember that the Mr. Thompsons want to keep everything the same, which is the opposite of change. Money notes are about tomorrow, and they often challenge the established and well-guarded rules of today. We don't want to hear another version of Adele's money note. We need new money notes. We don't want what's already been done. We want you. We want what you can do. We want your passion.

There were two reasons why I believe Mr. Thompson was hiding his hand signals from the audience. He wanted to remain professional and didn't want the audience to know he was shutting me down. This is exactly what obstructionist voices do to us. These voices are afraid of what the populace might think, because there's a chance that they might be wrong. How many record executives could have signed Adele to a contract but passed, thinking that she didn't have what it took to be a star? Those executives were operating in the present, judging success by existing data. Obstructionist voices do the same. Stars, just like ideas to change the world, are born because someone has the passion to change the future.

PRACTICE: DON'T LAUGH AT THE BOY. PRAY FOR HIM.

The pitchy note I belted out at the mass choir rehearsal with Jester Hairston wasn't a money note, but it was full of passion. Passion is usually untested, unqualified, and unfit for mass consumption. To mature, passion has to be tested in the crucible of public opinion. Jester's kind response to my teenage nightmare was prophetic. He was telling the other teenagers to give me a chance to improve. I wasn't a natural singer, and I needed a lot of practice. If I hadn't been passionate about music, I would have quit right there, but I kept practicing every day. The crucible of practice is where most world-changing ideas die. Nothing is accomplished without passion and practice. Practice is the unsexy work of showing up and turning your passion into a money note. Many forget this.

When I was in high school, the coolest thing you could do was start a band. Today the coolest thing you can do is start a charity organization or a tech startup. Just like bands, both require passion to get off the ground, then a *lot* of work to make it real. Part of the reason for the mass uptick in startups and new charities is the expectation that success is massive and immediate. The allure of overnight success is foisted upon us ad infinitum, so it's no wonder we think the world should change overnight. Practice. Practice. Practice.

The word *movement* gets used today for activities ranging from ending slavery to vitamin supplement sales. Everything is a movement. We can't help but be drawn to big ideas that lift all humanity. I have always believed that you really don't know if you are in a movement until it's over—if it's ever over. I'm guilty of misusing this word when trying to draw focus to the things Made in a Free World is working on. The reality is that the work we do often feels like we are trying to push water uphill. The resistance we experience to ending slavery is incredible, and it's this resistance that makes us a little better every day. Movements are built with moments—when people show up and practice their craft. Movements last decades, not months, and can only be identified in hindsight, because that's when we get to look back at what was accomplished. We don't find our money notes overnight. We find it when we show up day after day. Practice makes possible.

PEOPLE: KEEP YOUR HAND ON THE PLOW

Once the euphoria of committing to change the world is over and you are left with a bunch of work to do, that's when supporters start to become very important. These are the people who catch you when you literally and metaphorically stage-dive into the sea of change. The more you work on something you care about, the more vulnerable you become. This is why having a tribe of supporters around you is so important.

I had no idea if people would want to watch the film I spent a year and a half to make. I'm a maker and a performer, which means I'm not happy just making a film. I wanted—I needed—people to go see it. I showed early cuts of the film to friends who would not hold back their criticism, to fine-tune the film. It was painful and liberating to have people who care about me drill meteor-sized holes through ideas I thought were brilliant. I also witnessed the incredible generosity of strangers. As mentioned earlier, when you step out to reduce the world's poverty of means, you create a wake of opportunities for others to get behind. People will want to help you.

No one gets to change the world alone. Making something that will make a difference requires having people around you who will speak into your work and support your progress. These people are the opposite of the Mr. Thompsons, who are working off their own agendas. We need people around us who think we are awesome and know we are flawed. These people are critical to helping you build a plan that can change the world. History remembers individuals, but changing the world requires a tribe of supporters. These supporters help you *keep your hand on the plow and hold on.*

It's hard to imagine a world without Adele's and Freddie Mercury's money notes. Those notes have woven themselves into the fabric of our public consciousness. It's hard to imagine a world without the money notes of Alice Walker, Amy Lehman, Paul Hewson, Abel Meeropol, Todd Johnson, Sean Glover, the film crew of *Call + Response*, John

Matejczyk, Alison Friedman, Victoria Ward, Randy Newcomb, Suzanne Sands, Jean Baderschneider, Luis CdeBaca, and a million others. It will be hard to imagine a world without the money note you will produce too. Don't let someone tell you to mouth the words of your money note. All humanity wins when passionate new ideas come in from the periphery, beyond the velvet rope. Finding your money note will figuratively and literally open doors for people. Don't expect to be perfect or to know everything when you start. Let the people who love you help mold your ideas into a money note that gives us goose bumps, reduces a poverty of means, and develops deep purpose and meaning in your life. When you step out, you will fail sometimes. Failing is inevitable. The trick is getting really good at it. We'll learn how to fail next.

CHAPTER 13

WIN AT LOSING

September 20, 2012
Washington DC
National Mall, the Ellipse

THERE SHOULDN'T BE ANY TOURISTS HERE RIGHT NOW. THIS AREA IS SUP-posed to be covered in plywood, generator trucks, security fencing, stage rigging, lights, sound equipment, and thousands of people. It's just grass today, like every other day. Visitors are here to take their pictures in front of the White House and the Washington Monument, throw Frisbees, and picnic with their kids. This is terrible. Today was supposed to be different. I don't know how many laps I've taken around this gigantic oval lawn trying to figure out what just happened, but I'll keep lapping it until I understand what I did wrong. How could I have failed the Emancipation Proclamation?

A commemoration of the 150th anniversary of the Emancipation Proclamation made so much sense. The symbolism is pitch-perfect. We would have used the anniversary as a way to remember the promise we made as a nation, and to reinvest that promise in the forty million people living in slavery today. When I pitched the idea earlier this year to funders, they jumped on it. By March we had a plan to produce a live concert event on the National Mall with top talent, politicians, and some big influential voices. I took the idea to the White House and they quickly became interested too. It was immediately sponsored by

John Brennan, senior advisor to the president who later became director of the CIA. The president has been planning to use his platform
to advance the cause this year. Within just a few weeks, the idea for
a concert event became an agenda item in the White House. Getting
traction on big ideas like this is typically very difficult, like trying to
cut granite with a plastic knife. This idea seemed to find favor right
out of the gate. The mission was simple. Don't let this 150th anniversary go by without looking backward at what we promised as a nation
and then looking forward toward protecting the freedom of those living in slavery today.

I knew the idea had legs early on because I kept getting summoned
to the offices of people I didn't know. Google offices. State Department
offices. USAID offices. Lawyers' offices. Talent agent offices. Secret
Service offices. National Parks offices. Just two months ago I was in New
York City in the middle of a meeting when I got summoned to the White
House for a meeting the next day. When I arrived, I was expecting a few
people in a small room. Instead there were forty people seated around a
long table with an empty chair for me in the middle. As I sat down, the
woman in charge of the meeting informed me that they wanted to be
briefed on every single detail of the event. This went on for two hours.
I was pulling every string I possessed to make this event happen. Little
did I know that other strings were being pulled in opposite directions.

I wanted to find a way to express everything that has, and has not,
happened for African Americans since Lincoln signed the agreement,
so I reached out to a powerful civil rights leader in Washington DC.
She invited me to meet at her home. She was immediately interested in
helping me pull off the event, but wanted to vet me first. She wanted
to see if I truly understood the plight of African Americans. We spent
hours at her house talking about racism, white privilege, slavery, Jim
Crow, exploitation, and injustice. Every other week I flew across the
country to meet with her and other influential members of the civil
rights community, listening to their stories, hopes, and desires that all
the gains they had fought for don't become lost. She introduced me

to amazing people, such as Lonnie Bunch III, the founding director of the Smithsonian National Museum of African American History and Culture on the National Mall, which he was busy building at the time. Each of her guests opened their lives and wounds in a beautiful and heart-wrenching way. After months of these meetings, I was found trustworthy. A great honor. We committed to work together to ensure the commemoration event hit all the right notes, past and present. This alliance was more proof that this event would be incredibly important, but my team and I were starting to see some problems arising elsewhere.

The National Mall is operated by the National Parks Service, the same group who teaches us campfire safety and reminds us to stay on the trails. Every event on the National Mall has to go through them. My team and I had to work very hard to get a permit for our event on the Ellipse, which they assured us would happen, but not before a punishing number of fees, applications, meetings with Secret Service, more fees, permits, hula-hoop time trials, budgets, permits for other permits, and more. We paid all our fees and cleared all the processes needed to put on the event. I had leveraged every relationship I had from the tech, talent, government, and media sectors to pull this off. We were expecting a huge crowd, due to the incredible talent we had booked and the involvement of the White House.

We walked into our last meeting with the National Parks Service to get our permit—the final step in a difficult and expensive journey. Before handing over the permit, they informed us that there was a small snag. It turned out that the Ku Klux Klan had planned an event on the National Mall the same day as our event. They were planning to march around the Mall in protest of the 150th anniversary of the Emancipation Proclamation, and this being America, they were able to obtain a permit to do so. The National Parks Service told us that it had received intelligence that the KKK was aware of our event and was planning to protest it; they were expecting more than two thousand KKK members to be marching that day. With straight faces they told us that we could still have our event, but we would need to dramatically increase our security and pay for additional District police.

If you had told me six months before that the KKK would threaten to protest an event I was producing on the National Mall, I'd have shaken my head in disbelief that: (1) the KKK actually still marched in major cities, and (2) they could somehow impact a commemoration of the Emancipation Proclamation. The officials I spoke with at the White House were also unaware that the KKK was marching that day. With the presidential election just five weeks out from the event, the White House could not risk participating in an event with the potential of KKK involvement. What was supposed to be a celebration of how far we'd come as a country with our first African American president, along with his administration's commitment to fighting modern-day slavery, was now looking as if we had gone backward fifty years. The additional security required from the Park Service pushed costs far beyond our budget. I had spent every hour, dollar, and relationship I had to get us there, and we were sunk. With six weeks to go until the event, I began making calls to the White House, State Department, talent agents, sponsors, funders, distribution partners, senators, artists, and supporters, informing everyone that the event was canceled.

As I flew back home from DC, I stared out the window for five hours straight, bereft with disappointment. I looked at the roads, farms, cities, lakes, mountains, woods, and rivers that connect us into a whole, a country, a people. I rolled over every detail of the event's genesis to find where I had failed. Perhaps I tried to make it too big. Maybe we should have chosen a less symbolic venue than the National Mall. Maybe I spent too much time trying to bring in large partners. Maybe the KKK are more organized than we all thought. I think of all the people I've met across the country that is rolling by thirty thousand feet below me. I hadn't met one person down there who didn't believe modern slavery is wrong. Why, then, were we so afraid? Why is freedom so difficult? How did an event that had so much favor fall apart so quickly? What was I missing? I am not a stranger to failure, but I didn't have a map to deal with this level of public failure.

HOW TO WIN AT LOSING

We start to construct our armor against failure during our early childhood years. We are taught to avoid difficulties, paint within the lines, and not disrupt the status quo in hopes of avoiding failure and loss. We are taught to avoid overextending ourselves. So we put failure-resistant armor on over our time, our riches, our career paths, and our relationships. All the elements that make up what we call *our lives* must be protected. Failure is to be avoided, especially public failure. The more public our failure, the more humiliated and isolated we feel.

I hesitated including this story in this book because I know how uncomfortable stories about failure are. After all, we are a success-driven society, with no time for losers. My failed attempt to produce an event on the National Mall ended in the second act. There was no third act. No resolution. Just public, abject failure compounded by the loss of precious funding, relationships, confidence of people I respected, and eight months of my life. No one likes stories about failures and losing. They are so uncomfortable. I bet you'd think twice before posting pictures of your abject failures. ("Here I am packing up my desk at work. Boss said I don't have what it takes. #losing #pooltime.") But inside the eye of the storm of failure lies a rare opportunity. Anyone who has changed the world has both failed and learned how to win at losing. I'm going to share three lessons on how to win at losing that will help you on your journey toward meaning and changing the world.

LOCUS OF CONTROL

We tend to look at failure from two perspectives: internal control and external control. We believe we are either the cause of the failure or the victim of it. As I was replaying all of these events on the plane, I was engaging in a concept originally researched by psychologist Julian B. Rotter in 1954 called "locus of control."[1] This concept was designed to help us understand how we perceive control in our lives. Those of us with a high internal locus of control believe anything that happens to us, success or failure, is a result of our own efforts. Those of us with a high external locus of control believe our successes or failures are a result of factors outside of our control. So someone with a high internal locus of control believes that the high marks on an exam they received were due to good studying, while someone with a high external locus of control believes the high marks were due to the teacher's skills and the quality of the study materials. Many of the popular self-improvement theories today draw from the locus of control concept.

Fear of failure is healthy. It means we still have most of our sanity intact. Avoidance of any activity that might result in failure, however, is very unhealthy. Avoidance of failure, or ignoring the lessons of failure, is somewhat like dipping a foot in the lake of narcissism. It means we are unhappy unless we have ultimate control over our lives and reject any variable that might conflict with the script we have written for ourselves (rock dreams). It's a small and lonely way to live we have—with some great-looking social media posts paired with bewilderment over why we don't have any real friends. Participation in the bigger narratives of the world means dealing with variables outside of our control. To win at losing, we need a strong internal locus of control.

The failed Emancipation Proclamation event taught me a lot about locus of control. It would be easy for me to say that external forces beyond my control tanked the event, but that would be avoidance of responsibility, and avoiding responsibility would ensure that I don't get better at losing. One of my mistakes was that I tried to do too much. This is a typical mistake for me. I tried to pull off an event with high-profile talent, at a difficult outdoor venue (across from the White House), with a limited budget, and very little time—all while working with large partners, like the State Department, Google, and YouTube. One of the rules we try to follow in our organization is that *enthusiasm does not equal accomplishment*, but here I was letting enthusiasm take over, which meant I lost control of the event. This is a mistake I'm working to correct. I've never had a job, or even a résumé, so for my entire adult life I've only worked for myself. This means I know the street value of an opportunity when it comes along, and this event was a huge opportunity to move the cause forward. I would not have learned the double-edged sword of opportunity if I hadn't run after it and failed, publicly.

Having a strong internal locus of control helps us take responsibility for events surrounding our lives. We tend to eat better, exercise more, be mindful of our actions, and measure our use of time more efficiently and purposefully. We also fail better, because we know we'll be better next time. No matter how much we try to control outcomes, life doesn't play by our rules. When we find our riots and put our money notes into the world, we are entering very unstable territory. No matter how much I obsess over what I could have done differently to avoid failure, the reality was that I couldn't have foreseen variables outside my control—such as the KKK. To change the world you will need a strong internal locus of control paired with a healthy respect of the capricious nature of what you are changing.

It's helpful to remember that failure is metadata for the soul. Metadata is information that defines other data. You win at losing when you let your failure define success. Every great victory for human rights was only possible because of previous failed attempts to do the same. The civil rights movement in America failed several times, but it learned and improved each time, along with every other movement. You can't find your soul dream, your purpose, without experiencing failure. Failure is how we learn.

Failure is a popular topic. A gaggle of books exists about dealing with failure. This can include failures in career, personal life, health, business deals, finance, or anything we do on a daily basis. Most of these are failures that you don't get to choose. The failures I'm talking about here have a different nature and power because they are elective. Failing for the benefit of others is the greatest refinement a soul can obtain. Failure at something we choose to do (like ending slavery) as opposed to something we have to do (like making money) has a different sting to it. When you fail at trying to help, the natural response is to question why we allowed ourselves to be vulnerable to helping others in the first place. I've seen amazing people achieve early success at changing the world, but as soon as failure comes along, they question why they ever tried to help. There is a better way.

THE DIFFICULT WE DO TODAY

How we respond to failure at changing the world shapes how we think about ourselves, our loved ones, and those we are trying to help. We are not the first ones to take on something difficult to benefit others, only to have sand kicked in our faces. A few years ago Ambassador Andrew Young, who worked with Dr. Martin Luther King Jr., recorded a message for a few leaders of the modern slavery effort. He was encouraging us to learn how to win at losing. Ambassador Young worked alongside Dr. King and was with him when he died. He told us a story about one particular disappointment Dr. King and he faced when trying to get the Voting Rights Act passed. They had just met with President Johnson, whom they felt was not moving fast enough with Congress. Johnson claimed he had all the responsibility to run the country but none of the power. Ambassador Young recalled walking out of the West Wing with Dr. King, dejected and silent. Without looking up, Dr. King calmly said they needed to get that man some power. The result of that statement was the march in Selma.

Ambassador Young was teaching us that obstacles and failures are chances for us to get better at our game. Giving up says more about us than it does about our obstacles. Ending problems as vile and entrenched as racism, hunger, genocide, dirty water, disease, sexism, or lack of access to education will be difficult. Seeing obstacles as opportunities is key. I hope you will have the right perspective when something obstructs your soul dream. Winning at losing requires a stillness inside of you that no matter what happens, you are still in control of your soul dream. Ambassador Young shared with us a mantra that he and King used to share with each other: *The difficult we do today; the impossible just takes time.*

BITTER OR BETTER

I have one more story about how to win at losing, a difficult lesson lived out by a guy named Matt. I didn't know Matt very well, but I could always count on seeing him whenever my band played a local show. He was easy to spot in the crowd because he always stood in the same place, directly in front of the booming speaker mains on the right side of the stage. He practically hugged that speaker, and I was sure he would lose his hearing one day. Matt was a live music photographer whose work I had come to respect. Live music photography is highly instinctual. In order to get a great shot, you must anticipate what the artist is about to do. Some of this instinct develops from photographing the same artist night after night, which Matt did. The shots he took of us were fantastic. He understood our energy, songs, and personalities. Matt was easy to spot in the crowd for another reason as well. One of his eyes was protruding almost an inch out of its socket, severely disfiguring him and rendering him blind in that eye.

I met Matt backstage one night and learned more about his talent, his story, and his challenges. He had struggled with tumors riddling his head for years. As we were talking, I noticed more tumors pushing out of his skull, along with several scars where others had been removed. Despite his disfigurement, Matt was confident and curious, asking me questions about my music and influences. I learned that Matt's love for music and photography started when he was young. It wasn't until he reached his early teen years that the tumors began to appear. His speech was severely limited, which I assumed was due to the tumors, so I had to lean in to understand him. That's when he told me through squeaks and long vowels that he is completely deaf. Over the last few years the tumors had slowly robbed him of sound, separating him from the thing he loved most—as if a current was slowly pulling him away from shore. These tumors made Matt a deaf, one-eyed live music photographer. And he was great at it.

Here's how he did it. He would lean against the speakers to feel the subwoofers pushing out vibrations. If you have ever looked at a speaker cabinet, the lower, larger speaker that moves in and out is called a subwoofer. Subwoofers produce the low-pitched audio frequencies. Even small desktop subwoofers turned up loud can make things near them shake. Now picture several twenty-five-inch subwoofers at close range, and you can imagine the vibrations they were putting out. Matt would time his photos based on the vibrations of the subwoofers. In most songs, whenever something new or big is about to happen, like a chorus or a solo, the drums and bass will do a little rhythmic prelude, like a drum fill. These turnarounds in the music also tend to happen when musicians move and gesture, like lifting their arms or shooting fire out of the headstock of their Fender Stratocaster. Matt learned to feel these rhythmic preludes and would time his shots accordingly. Boom. Boom. Boom. Snap the picture. He was literally using sonar to photograph live music, and it worked. In complete silence, without auditory cues, he could feel the subs and hit his money note, without hearing a note. Every time.

We decided to have Matt get up and speak at one of our concerts. The audience was dead silent as they listened to Matt tell his story through squeaks and moans. He told them that when he started to get tumors he was sad for himself. When he started to lose his hearing, he became mad. He faced a simple sobering choice. He could either be bitter or better. Choosing to be bitter would forfeit his internal locus of control, allowing the illness to become the dominant story of his life. Instead he chose his internal locus of control and focused on *being better*. Despite losing his hearing. Despite losing sight in one eye. Despite his face becoming disfigured. Despite constant surgeries. He became better than his circumstances. He found his key and his money note. He became a live music photographer.

Matt is a world champion at losing. His life choices challenge me to this day. The choice to be better, instead of bitter, is my choice as well. When we step out to change the world and build meaning, adversity shows up. The natural response is bitterness because it doesn't seem fair. The failure of the Emancipation event certainly didn't seem fair. The world doesn't give us a pass just because we are choosing to make it better. I wanted to be bitter when I failed to pull off the Emancipation Proclamation event. To win at losing, and keep pushing to change the world, I needed to become better and let the failure teach me. I am better because of it. The failure will always remain, but only as a form of very expensive equity. This equity in failure is valuable because it teaches you that failure can't kill your riot.

I eventually lost touch with Matt. He seemed to be showing up less and less at our shows, and my band was constantly on the road. Years later I learned that Matt had passed away. His tumors increased and the doctors couldn't remove them fast enough. I wish we could have had one more conversation. I wish I could have told him how much he taught me, so, as a tribute, I wrote what I imagined our conversation would've been into a song called "Can You Feel It Now?" I imagine that he can finally hear music again.

> *You used to stand off to the right of me*
> *I'd look in your direction we'd agree*
> *I used to sing to you subsonic blues*
> *You had a faraway look in your eye*
> *Your soul was strutting in its earth disguise*
> *My music moved in you*
> *Boom Boom Boom*
> *And at the perfect moment you would*
>   *go and light up the room*
> *Can you feel it now?*[2]

CHAPTER 14

PRACTICE THE ART
OF CHANGE

SEPTEMBER 28, 2015
NEW YORK CITY
HIGHLINE BALLROOM

BILLIE HOLIDAY LOOKS DOWN FROM ON HIGH, ABOVE THE TURNTABLES spinning Michael Jackson's "Billie Jean," into Wham!'s "Everything She Wants," followed by the Weeknd. Her eyes look gracefully over the sea of freedom lovers on the dance floor getting down to the hardest-working DJ, drummer, author, producer, teacher, designer, musicologist, and television music director in the business—Ahmir Khalib Thompson, otherwise known as Questlove. They are dancing out of the palms of his hands, while Billie Holiday—projected on the giant LED wall behind him—once again surveys a nightclub full of patrons looking for something bigger than themselves. Questlove's DJ booth brandishes the letters FRDM, short for freedom, the theme of this evening. We are here to announce a new partnership, a success, that our organization has labored over for years. The club is jumpin'. The speeches are soaring. The red carpet is flashing. The celebrities are mixing. And the cause of freedom is pumping like an 808. Success in a room like this can look like it happened overnight, but this labor of love has been four years in the making. Tonight art and commerce will collide in the most perfect way.

Rock in a Free World is an idea I've had for a while to combine everything my organization does into one event. We've reached more than thirty million consumers worldwide with Slavery Footprint. We've established projects around the world to get kids out of slavery and into school. We've built a community of businesses, consumers, and organization partners who work together to leverage the power of the marketplace to end slavery. It's a crazy idea, to be sure, but I am betting on capitalism to catalyze the end of slavery.

We are a long way from ending slavery tonight, but we needed a moment to celebrate success and publicly demonstrate that freedom is something we can all get behind. Our biggest reason to celebrate tonight is the partnership we've made with one of the largest business software companies in the world, SAP Ariba. That's not a company that most people have heard of, but it's nearly impossible for you to go throughout your day without being impacted by their technology. SAP makes cloud-based software for companies to run all of their activities, including financials, human resources, sales, manufacturing, and procurement. Over 70 percent of the world's transaction revenue touches SAP technology. The partnership we are celebrating tonight has the potential to shift the global marketplace in the direction of freedom. We are forging together something that has never been done before. For the first time in history, businesses around the world will have the opportunity to learn about the risk of slavery in their supply chains and act on it.

Every success has a long backstory, and this one goes back several years to a gigantic dome in Atlanta. A movement of college students called Passion hosts a conference every January at the Georgia Dome in Atlanta, drawing tens of thousands of college students and many more online. Students gather to sing, pray, and learn. Passion is also active in making an impact in the world around issues of justice and mercy. In 2012 they chose to focus on modern-day slavery. They invited a few antislavery leaders to speak briefly on their massive stage, and I was honored to participate. Slavery Footprint had recently been released, so I shared Made in a Free World's vision of a connected world using the power of our purchases to protect freedom. It's safe to say that few of the students in the dome had ever thought about their slavery footprints, or how their purchases affect the lives of men, women, and children around the world. Over the course of the conference, these students gave over $3 million out of their own pockets to fight slavery. The issue officially became a priority for millennials.

The Passion conference only allows entrance to university-aged individuals along with any older chaperones. There was a man (an older chaperone) in the audience who sat up in attention when I mentioned how supply chains are the best way to ensure freedom in the world. Somehow he figured out that he knew my brother in Chicago and texted him to confirm. My brother gave him my info, and as I walked out of the Dome, I received a text. He told me his name was Kelly Miller and he worked for one of the largest supply-chain software companies in the world, SAP Ariba. He thought there might be a way for his company to help with my efforts. We agreed to meet the next time he came to California.

I had never thought about supply chains before I worked on Slavery Footprint. Like most people, I knew that most of the products I bought were manufactured overseas, but I had little understanding beyond that. Rapid globalization over the last thirty years has made supply chains longer and more complex. In America we often hear about sending jobs overseas, but we seldom hear about how many countries a product hits before it ends up in our stores. The integration between companies and governments of different nations has made our world more connected and flatter, according to Pulitzer Prize–winning journalist Thomas Friedman. In his book about globalization, *The World Is Flat*, he recounts a conversation he had with his daughters:

> Girls, when I was growing up, my parents used to say to me, "Tom, finish your dinner—people in China and India are starving." My advice to you is: Girls, finish your homework—people in China and India are starving for your jobs. And in a flat world, they can have

them, because in a flat world there is no such thing as an American job. There is just a job, and in more cases than ever before it will go to the best, smartest, most productive, or cheapest worker—wherever he or she resides.[1]

Globalization promised to lift some countries out of poverty by opening up markets to them—which it has, for some. We consumers reap the benefits of these open markets every day. One of the downsides of globalization is the race toward cheaper and faster manufacturing. Just as a root searches for water, supply chains have pushed further and further, fragmenting into multiple arms in search of the lowest prices and "just in time" manufacturing. One of the unintended consequences of globalization is the sub-economy it's created for individuals and agencies to exploit the labor of vulnerable people groups, children in particular. These individuals, some of whom we've met in this book already, are able to work behind the veil of complex supply chains, often undetected by the public-facing and publicly traded companies. These labor brokers have been able to exploit with impunity, which has created challenges for companies and consumers.

When my organization launched Slavery Footprint, we asked consumers if they wanted to know about slavery in their products by counting the number of slaves it takes to produce their lifestyle. We chose to look at our own consumer footprints before we started talking about corporate footprints. This was intentional. When anyone first learns about something as horrific as slavery, the natural response is catharsis. We want someone to blame so that we don't have to feel the weight of it anymore. The purpose of Slavery Footprint is to prove that we all have a role to play in ending slavery because our lives directly benefit from slave labor. It's uncomfortable, but true. Once a consumer answers several questions on Slavery Footprint about the types of generic products they use, they see a number of how many slaves are required to produce all those products. When we initially launched it, people were shocked. Then they shared it—a lot. We set a target of reaching 150,000 people with Slavery Footprint within the first year. We achieved that goal in the first week.

The response to our question of "How many slaves work for you?" was large, but it wasn't all positive. We were asking people to tell us what they buy, and how much of it. We received frequent hate emails from people we upset because, for instance—and this is true—we didn't account for the fact that one visitor only used a single recycled bra. It's amazing how much information people share. Then there were the attacks in the newspapers, magazines, and journals from people questioning our motives and calculations. I was on national television in Australia on one of their primetime news shows, where the producer asked me to bring along any typical products made with slavery. So I brought cosmetics and doughnuts. I'm not used to having to defend our efforts to reduce slavery, but this news anchor made a great show of explaining how audacious it was to believe companies would care about slavery in supply chains. To add even more spectacle to his news show, his coanchor looked straight at the camera and ate the doughnut I brought as a visual punctuation of their point.

There were some positive responses too. The primary question we would get from consumers who used Slavery Footprint was "Who can I buy from?" That was a great question with no clear answer at the time.

That's when my team and I started working on our supply chain footprint tool called FRDM. We researched all of the goods, services, and commodities a business might purchase, from steel to lightbulbs, apricot jam to industrial refrigerators, and palm oil to Wi-Fi routers. We built an algorithm that can determine the risk of slavery in almost any product, down to raw materials, such as cotton and petroleum. For instance, when FRDM analyzes a generic kitchen blender, it doesn't just look at the factory where it was assembled. It looks for risk of slavery where the metal for the blade is made. It looks for risk in the copper wiring on the inside. It looks for risk in the rubber components. We designed the tool to help businesses see what they might be missing. This may sound like we geeked out too far on blenders, but this kind of data empowers companies to be the heroes by working with their suppliers to protect the freedom of their workers. We had no idea if companies would want this knowledge, but we knew that no one in the world had created a tool like this. And we knew the world desperately needed it.

I eventually met with Kelly Miller at his company's headquarters in Cupertino, California. His company, SAP Ariba, is a procurement software company, which means they help companies buy and sell things. When a large company wants to make a large purchase, like office furniture or tons of steel, they can perform their transactions on the SAP Ariba platform from a network of millions of different suppliers, kind of like eBay for supply chains. This network of buyers and sellers is one of the largest commerce networks in the world. Together, we decided on a plan. We would find a way to integrate our FRDM tool into their platform, empowering millions of companies to protect freedom in their supply chains.

The hero in this story is Kelly. All he did was ask, "How can I help?" and use his money note (sales) to change the world. He was leveraging his position as one of the top sales agents in the company to drive this partnership. This was no small sacrifice on his part. He took a lot of chances and spent a lot of his relational capital. He knew that this had the potential to change the global marketplace because it would empower companies to be informed when they purchase. Our mission was clear. If we can wield the power of the global marketplace, we can change the world at scale.

Kelly worked every angle he had inside his company. Launching new ideas in the corporate world is a lot like performing in a nineteenth-century circus: you have to jump through flaming hoops of bureaucracy, box with kangaroo courts of lawyers, and fly on trapezes of managerial approvals, knowing that you can fall to your career death at any moment. This idea moved fast and achieved buy-in quickly, no doubt due to Kelly's passion and commitment. The leadership was quickly convinced that partnering with us was a good move for the company.

Soon we were hosting stakeholder meetings with some of the biggest companies in the world. It was clear that most companies had no idea how people were being treated deep within their supply chains. They had no tool to deal with it, and no safe way of talking about it publicly.

Many people forget that slavery is a behavior. It's not a war. It's not a germ. It's not a carbon emission. It's one person making the conscious choice to exploit another person. Anyone who has had kids can attest that behavior is hard to track. You can't be everywhere on the playground, monitoring every child's behavior, yet when consumers learn about slavery in supply chains, they expect their favorite brands to be able to police their entire supply chain 24-7. It's not possible. It's not even reasonable. It's easy to point at what's wrong, but it's another thing to build a solution—especially a solution that doesn't require donations year after year to implement. We knew we had to build a new way for humans to be humans. Instead of boycotting companies for what they aren't doing, we decided to build a network of *buy-cotters* who buy better. We committed to applauding efforts that led to transparency, rather than requiring impossible perfection. So we committed to work alongside companies who commit to that journey. But ideas are cheap. Execution is everything.

Launching a new idea is like making a cocktail. It's all about the mixture of ingredients, of which there are three (everything is in threes in this book). The first is the idea itself. Is it strong enough to stand on its own in the chaos of the world? The second is the execution of the idea. Can this group of people deliver the new idea? The third is timing. When is the world ready to accept a new idea? The first two ingredients you have control over, but the third is a wild card.

For the last three years I have spoken at no fewer than a hundred events, participated in dozens of television appearances and interviews, and had more meetings than I care to remember trying to convince consumers, businesses, governments, and anyone who will listen to my idea that the way to fix slavery is with commerce. Slavery is a highly profitable business with few risks. If you can increase the risks for bad guys, they will run away like cockroaches. We had to prove the business benefit and the social benefit without one diluting the other. Simply put, there was no example or precedent we could pull from. We were certain that our idea could change the world, but the world had to want it. We had to create the idea, execute the idea, and hope the timing was right— which it wasn't, at first. Many of the companies we were meeting with were telling us that though the issue of freedom is important, it wasn't a business priority for them. We had a huge challenge ahead of us.

During this period of time the Obama administration issued Executive Order 13627 requiring companies that do business with the United States to increase their efforts to remove slavery from their supply chains. The White House highlighted Made in a Free World as the organization that can assist businesses in this process. This was a huge endorsement for us. The United States is the largest purchaser in the world, which means that this executive order has the power to protect millions of people.

Soon after, the United Kingdom passed the Modern Slavery Act, requiring businesses to produce proof that they were looking for slavery in their supply chains. Other laws were being passed as well, and companies were beginning to be prosecuted in court for slavery in their supply chains, some cases reaching as high as the Supreme Court. Journalists were uncovering slavery in seafood, even discovering a remote island in Indonesia where slaves were being kept in cages. The world was quickly changing its view on slavery in supply chains, moving it from a remote problem to a high priority for businesses. It took more than three years, but it looked as if the timing for our solution was improving.

No one here in this club tonight knows that it's taken four years of hustle and jive to get here. Tonight the Highline Ballroom is an oasis on a thousand-mile journey. Tonight friends like Natasha Bedingfield, Estelle, and Kimbra are lifting up their voices for the invisible. Tonight Questlove is spinning the best set of freedom songs since the ones Harriet Tubman sang with the runaway slaves along the Underground Railroad. Tonight we are telling the millions of people trapped in slavery that we see them and that we are doing our best to protect them. Tonight we are proving that you can protect people in your supply chain while also protecting your company's profitability. None of this was possible three years ago. It's all about hustle and timing and believing in something that doesn't yet exist.

As I walk through this jubilant ballroom, I'm reminded of a timeless fact: change isn't a science, it's an art. The world doesn't know what it wants until it sees it. We didn't know we wanted automobiles, televisions, X-ray machines, Snuggies, seat belts, lavender lattes, and the Internet until someone put them in front of us. Fifteen years ago, two of the sketchiest activities we could engage in were using the Internet and getting in cars with strangers. Now we use the Internet to get into cars with strangers. Fifteen years ago slavery was something we learned about in school, but now it's something we learn about in corporate conference rooms. Watching these young movers and shakers moving and shaking to Questlove's freedom mix from his FRDM DJ booth confirms to me that change isn't science; it's art.

THE ART OF CHANGE

Even though change is an art form, we still tend to treat it like a science. Science explains what already exists. Art creates what has never existed. Science is a process of hypotheses, predictions, tests, theories, and observations. It looks for patterns, systems, connection points, and causalities. There is no doubt that we've relied on science to fix some of the world's most vexing problems. We wouldn't have antiretroviral drugs or climate change research without science, but it first took a herculean effort to prioritize spending for drug and climate research. Long before we started using science to produce those antiretroviral drugs, there were individuals operating like artists to show the world that HIV and melting glaciers are major problems facing humanity. Before something becomes normal to society, like recycling, the world has to change, and that's where the art of change comes in handy.

Art requires just as much work as science, but the process is more fluid and the results less planned. Art leaves room for variables to influence it, turning obstacles into progress. An artist allows their environment to influence their work, as opposed to the scientific approach of trying to control an environment. The artist finds a riot inside, then works and works to express the riot to the world. Without asking for permission, the artist puts their riot into the world where it did not exist before. Art enriches humanity and creates new norms. Change operates exactly the same way, and you will benefit from understanding the similarities. Women's suffrage was art. The civil rights movement was (is) art. Girls' education is art. The reduction in extreme poverty is art. The people who worked to elevate humanity were all operating as artists. The net result of all art is to open up the depths of our humanity. And opening the depths of our humanity is exactly how we change the world and find meaning.

Practicing the art of change will help you negotiate the pitfalls and obstacles that come with changing the world. You don't have to be a professional artist. Practicing the art of change is just that, a practice. There are three practices that can guide you, ensuring that the world sees and reacts to your riot. The practices are simple: vulnerability, creation over critique, and letting action be your promotion.

VULNERABILITY

Vulnerability is an invitation to participate. There is a reason we love to support people who make themselves vulnerable to something bigger. When I watch the film *Once*, I see vulnerability at several levels and I'm drawn to the characters in the story who are artists. The story is about a thirtysomething Irish musician who is trying to make a living by busking for money on Grafton Street in Dublin, all while trying to build a career as a big recording artist. He meets a girl and has to decide between her or the career. *Once* is a classic story of vulnerability, but when you learn that Glen Hansard, the actor who plays the musician, was a previously not-so-famous musician in real life, and that the director, Jim Carney, is a former bandmate of Glen's who made the film for about $160,000 (a fraction of typical film budgets), you can see how their real-life vulnerabilities were captured on film. It's a film about risk and the vulnerabilities associated with risks. This film's story on- and offscreen was so vulnerable that I just wanted everyone to win—the characters, the filmmakers, and the actors. And they did. The film won multiple awards and later opened as a musical on Broadway.

I don't believe we're the ones who take risks. I believe we let risks take from us. As we've learned, risk is intimate and personal. It can be used as a tool to change the world, or as concrete shoes to drown you in the river. Risk also affects the ones you love because you are giving away nonreturnable time, energy, and financial resources instead of using those resources to improve your life. You won't ever get those resources back. The more we risk our time, energy, and resources, the more vulnerable we make ourselves. This is the vulnerability that every legitimate artist faces. The painter must stay with his canvas, willing it into existence day after day, without any certainty of success, knowing that his time and talent could be spent on another work of art but choosing to stay with this canvas until it comes to life. Such is the vulnerability one must face when trying to change the world.

The problem with vulnerability is that it looks great on others, but is terrifying to wear yourself. We are vulnerable when we rip open our chests and let our hearts out. All of the people I've talked about in this book opened up their chests and exposed their hearts, and let out their riots, some at great risk. Just as the painter feels vulnerable while looking at a blank canvas, or the screenwriter feels inept while looking at a blank page, so too did these individuals look at the challenges in the world and open up their hearts by asking, "How can I help?" Alice walking into the jungle with a camera was vulnerable, just as a young Kayne West was vulnerable rapping for Jay Z the first time. Amy Lehman campaigning to build a floating clinic on Lake Tanganyika was vulnerable, as the performance artist Marina Abramović was when she performed her piece *The Artist Is Present* at the Museum of Modern Art in New York City, where she sat totally still, in silence, directly across from museum visitors, for 750 hours. An exposed heart is a vulnerable soul. Changing the world will cost you your vulnerability, but the returns are immeasurable and infinite.

Everyone loves the idea of change, but few are willing to be vulnerable to it. As I've already noted, changing the world is not about being a hero; it's about being a helper. Self-proclaimed heroes who are more focused on marketing than on making an impact in the world are holding back their hearts. They have not yet allowed themselves to become vulnerable.

Joseph Campbell was a literary scholar who wrote about narrative structures and is famous for coining the idea of the "hero's journey," which many writers use today. He laid out three stages, or acts, in typical narrative, which we have already discussed somewhat earlier in this book. Act 1: the hero leaves their world. Act 2: the hero is tested in another world. Act 3: the hero returns with new power to their original world. There are subsections in each of these acts, but most relevant to us are the subsections at the end of act 1 and beginning of act 2. In act 1 the hero is called to adventure, but refuses the call for some reason. Reluctantly the hero sets out to face tests in act 2, but first will meet a helper. This helper offers some wisdom or assistance to help the hero on their journey. One of the most famous helpers of our time—or a long, long time ago—is Yoda. Yoda taught Luke Skywalker, the hero, about the Force. When heroes set out to change the world, their vulnerability inspires the help of others.

As you set out to change the world, the level of your vulnerability will determine the level of help that will come your way. The amazing individuals who work at Made in a Free World don't consider themselves heroes, but we receive calls every week from people wanting to help us in some way. They see how large the task of ending slavery is, and they want to offer us some form of useful assistance. Don't be afraid to step out further than you are comfortable. For example, if you are working to change racial injustice in your city, don't be afraid to put together a few more public rallies and events than you are comfortable with. If you are trying to reduce the number of child marriages in Virginia, don't be afraid to spend some of your own money to go to DC and sit in your senator's office until his or her chief of staff will meet with you (bring a sandwich).

Don't be afraid to show your heart and push your risk tolerance. Your riot will require you to open up your chest and be vulnerable. When you feel vulnerable, when you risk like an artist, that's when you know you are in the company of Dr. King, who would agree that you are bending the long moral arc of the universe a few more degrees toward justice.

CREATION OVER CRITIQUE

We're a society that's heavy on opinions and light on creators. We live in a loud world with endless voices who bloviate on social media that "doth protest too much, methinks."[2] There is a common misperception that simply having an opinion is equivalent to actually doing something, but I disagree. Opinions, especially unsolicited opinions, tend to operate as distractions from real change. Having an opinion about how the world should change doesn't accomplish anything. Art and change are acts of creation. They speak cosmos to the chaos. Creation is the opposite of critique. The artist takes common raw materials, like musical notes or paint, and constructs them into something the world has never seen before. It's the same with creating change. Changemakers take broken pieces of our world and reconstruct them into something new and beautiful. Sounds easy, right? The reality is our natural default is to critique and copy, not create. I'll give you a personal example.

I used to write songs wherever I could: the backstage of a club, in the studio, in a field, in the back of a van, and in the bedroom of our bungalow in Oakland. Anyone who has met my wife knows that she tells it like it is. If she likes or dislikes something, you will know about it.

I would be writing a song in the bedroom and she would walk by without even looking at me and say, "Sounds like Coldplay." With just three little words, my precious sonic gift to the world would be melted into an ashen heap of Coldplay chords. She was right. She's always right. I was being derivative and couldn't hear it. This is easy to do when making art and changing the world. So, to protect myself from writing derivative songs, I would change up my writing system. Whenever I was in a focused period of songwriting, I would avoid listening to songs I'd typically listen to in order to push me outside my comfort zone. Instead of Radiohead, I'd listen to Carole King and Fleetwood Mac. Instead of Ryan Adams, I'd listen to Muddy Waters. You have to work against your own defaults to create something novel for the world, whether it's a pop song or justice.

The world doesn't need another Coldplay song because it's got Coldplay for that. Similarly, the world doesn't need another plan to change the world that's already been tried. It needs yours. Emulation is a fast track to mediocrity and failure. It's easy to get stuck trying to do something that already worked for someone else. The lives of those we want to help deserve better from us.

For instance, sending auditors to foreign factories was once the primary tool businesses used to protect human rights in supply chains. But some factory owners who were using child labor would hide the children or send them away the day the auditor came to the factory. Auditing was not very effective, but it was still considered the only way to address slavery in supply chains. This became evident in 2013 when an eight-story commercial building in Bangladesh that housed an apparel shop supplying products for major international brands collapsed, killing 1,130 garment factory workers. The owners had been warned about the safety of the building but ignored it. The controversy was that auditors from major brands had performed multiple safety audits, and still the tragedy occurred.

The world needed a new idea. That's why my team and I decided to create something novel to empower companies to better protect the people in their supply chains with our FRDM software. Consider the $80 trillion in the global marketplace. We knew that the world needed better intelligence, a digital truth teller, to help it spend those dollars ethically. No one had created anything like FRDM before, which meant that we faced years of vulnerability and scarcity to build it. It's hard to convince people of new ideas, especially when they are so invested in other concepts. There were many months when we were close to shutting down. Established thinking in both the charity and business circles was telling us that audits were the only thing that worked. Why not build something new that works better? Just when we thought we would have to shut down, a few companies started knocking on our door, asking for the software. Within very little time our FRDM platform was directing hundreds of billions of dollars in the marketplace to "buy better" and protect freedom. Creating something new is as risky as it is thrilling.

Makers make, and talkers talk. My friends who do venture investing in San Francisco say their number-one challenge with entrepreneurs is separating hype from substance. The best ideas come from hard work, not luck or attention. If we spend our time telling people about our ideas without entering into the vulnerable act of doing them, then we are only interested in attention, not change. Steve Jobs is credited for saying to his team, "Real artists ship," meaning that you must execute your idea and launch it into the world.

Focus on your riot and be sure you do something with it. Talking about what's wrong with the world doesn't accomplish much. Create something to help those in a poverty of means in a way that no one else has done. Bonus points if you do something for someone else and don't seek the credit for it. Then maybe you too will be blessed with someone's critique. That's when you know you are a maker, not a talker.

YOUR SUCCESS IS ITS OWN PROMOTION

My favorite performers are surprised by applause. They are so focused on their work that they forget people are watching and appreciating.

True artists focus their time and energy on improving their craft, not talking about it. Society has an inflated and deflated view of artists—an artist is either a demigod of spectacle and success or an almost-homeless bard living on the fringes. The role of an artist is to help us remember to be human. Artists reintroduce us to ourselves through their creations. When artists look up from their work in need of affirmation, their work suffers.

When it comes to changing the world, attention doesn't equal impact. I've seen groups and individuals who want to change the world work harder on their image than their impact. Brand and image are important, but never at the cost of impact. We want your substance, not hype. We are hungry for authenticity and vulnerability. Don't seek our affirmation by sharing your ideas to change the world; impress us with the execution of your idea. Charity organizations are as eager to tell you about their success as artists are. There is a fear that if you don't promote your accomplishments above the noise, then no one will hear you. This is not true. Your success will promote itself, which is a much more powerful way to gain attention. Try to develop a healthy sense of *success amnesia*, which allows you to see success for what it is: a goal reached, allowing you to move on to the next amazing thing you will accomplish. Approach your riot like an artist who wants to project what's inside of them out into the world.

PRACTICING THE ART OF CHANGE

There's an old quip about writing that authors love: "It is easy to write. Just sit in front of your typewriter [computer] and bleed." That is a cavalier and telling perspective on the agony and ecstasy of creating something new. If you want to change the world, you will have to open a vein. You will give something away that you will never get back. Injustice and poverty thrive because they are deeply entrenched in our history and present. Changing what is broken requires us to open a vein of vulnerability, to open up our chests and let our hearts come out.

This kind of sacrifice cannot be masked with self-promotion. When you open yourself up to risk, you open yourself up to the reward of purpose and meaning. These simple practices can help you stay on your path to reducing the two poverties in the world.

CHAPTER 15

SOLUTIONISTS OF THE WORLD UNITE

I've been saving the story in this chapter for the end of the book, which I will get to shortly. In Theodore Roosevelt's autobiography, he quotes a man named Bill Widener, who said: "Do what you can, with what you've got, where you are."[1] This advice couldn't be more timely. Humanity is at a tipping point. The systems we once counted on to govern, protect, and guide our world have become too large, myopic, and ineffectual. We can no longer subcontract the world's poverty of means to governments, large charity organizations, and philanthropic corporations. We need a revolution from the periphery, the populace. We need open-source change, where those with a poverty of meaning can leverage their power to reduce the poverty of means. We need individuals who design and execute their own plans to change the world. This revolution is focused on going upriver and changing the way the world works. This new era will be built on not just awareness and actions, but solutions. The era of the activist is fading. A new era is emerging from the embers. The era of the solutionist is on us.

Anyone who pursues their riot, enters the chaos of others, and selflessly projects their money note into the world is by definition a solutionist. Solutionists are born out of their own backstories and refined in their practices. They listen to the riot inside of them and act on it without asking for permission. The solutionist brings novel ideas and actions to broken systems of injustice and neglect. The solutionist never gives up and keeps finding ways to pivot around entrenched thinking and systems. Solutionists build a new world that everyone can benefit from.

This new era of solutionists will build a new democracy, the democracy of participation. We are the first generation who sees everything, everywhere, all the time. We watch live feeds from fashion shows in Milan, and a live feed from the car of a man in Minnesota who has just been shot by a police officer. Twenty years ago refugees in Greece, melting glaciers in the Arctic, slaves in Haiti, and live footage of shootings were essentially invisible to us. We have been handed the challenges of our world at such a time as this, a time where we are more informed and connected than ever before. Twenty years ago people could not share images of their cats from their phones with someone halfway around the world. Twenty years ago a plane ticket was a huge expense. Twenty years ago we would never summon a stranger's car or rent a bedroom using a phone that fits in our pockets. Twenty years ago large charities and activist organizations handled most of the poverty of means. The world operates much differently now. The sharing economy permeates arenas far beyond hotel rooms and taxis. We all share in the economy of change and we all benefit when both poverties are alleviated. Participation in the reduction of the world's poverty of means has been democratized. These challenges are not only ours to be concerned about but also ours to participate in.

In this new era we might see a student in Michigan come up with a health tracker for the homeless population in his city. A corporate attorney at a law firm in San Francisco will host a town hall conversation with a recently retired police officer and black urban youth from Oakland. A software engineer in Brazil will create a coding academy for young girls from the favelas in Rio. World-changing activities like these will integrate into our everyday lives, becoming part of our lives' narrative rather than something we just do to "give back." This new era is not just about *giving back*; it's about *giving in*. It's an era of people who share and leverage their talents, time, and relationships to reduce the poverty of means. In the ways that hotels and taxis have been disrupted, so too has the world-changing sector of society been disrupted.

Success in this new era is defined by achievements, not amplitude. Success isn't overnight, but over a lifetime. There is no act too small in this new era because deep down we are hungry for substance, not hype. We want to see someone step out into the chaos with their own money notes of change and create a small wake for us to follow in. We are hungry for bravery, sacrifice, humility, service, innovation, and grace. Above all things, grace. Those who suffer from a poverty of means, and those of us suffering a poverty of meaning, are desperate for heroes who will fearlessly walk out their riot.

Our plans to change the world are ultimately about changing ourselves. If we genuinely pursue improving the lives of others, the quality of our lives will improve. This is a universal axiom that's never been proven wrong. We were made to experience resistance and to participate in a bigger story. Your backstory, along with its disappointments, is what makes your offering to the world so unique. Things that bother you about the world bother you for a reason. Listen to that, and don't let it sit idle and atrophy. That's your soul dream, and it wants to live. No one will give you permission to change the world. Only you can do that. Don't default to the obvious, but bring a novel change that challenges the status quo. If your riot sounds crazy, it's probably right. Bring something new into the world, and we will support you—because we love to come around vulnerable people. If you do all of this, you have truly built a plan that will change the world, and change yourself, for the better.

I have one final story and one more tip I'd like to offer you.

ONE FINAL STORY

DECEMBER 5, 2013
NEW DELHI, INDIA
UNDISCLOSED LOCATION

We know they are in there, maybe twelve to fourteen of them. We get the signal and move quickly from our cars toward the dilapidated building that looks abandoned. The police tell us we need to move off the street and into the building. It can get rough out here quickly. Our team rushes through broken fences and alleys toward a stairwell in the back of our targeted building. While police cover the front of the building, we run up the back to the third floor. The police burst through a large door at the end of a hallway, and we rush in. Nothing prepares you for a scene like this.

Inside the small room we find about a dozen young Nepalese boys, ranging from eight to twelve years old, sitting around big tables, stitching embroidery. Their big brown eyes (it's always the eyes) look up at us with indifference, as if we are just another bunch of illicit fabric brokers coming to inspect the textiles. There is no sign of emotion on their faces. There are no arms being lifted up to their First World rescuers. They just stare at us the way most kids their ages do when a visitor comes to their classroom or, in this case, prison cell. The boys kneel at these tables for sixteen hours every day, then sleep underneath them at night. After a few inquisitive glances at the group of adults folding into their small room, some of whom are very white, the boys turn back to their work and keep stitching. They have no idea of what's about to happen.

Yesterday my team and I were doing reconnaissance not too far from here. We were driving around a neighborhood outside New Delhi in a small car, looking for our fixer in the crowded urban streets full of vendors, elephants, shop owners, and the frantic efforts of those building a life in a poverty of means. No one from the outside comes here.

So no one would ever look here. My film team had to be split up in two cars because our fixer demanded we "spread out the whiteness." We pulled up to our other fixer, but he waved us on to keep going because it wasn't safe to get out yet. He then called our driver on his mobile phone to tell him where the next drop-off would be. A few minutes later we found him a few blocks away, and this time his head nodded as a signal to stop and get out quickly.

We followed our fixer through alleys and stairwells reminiscent of a scene from a Jason Bourne film. Within a few minutes I'd completely lost our way back and realized our fixer was our only ticket out. Waves of eyes came out from doors and windows as we moved through tight ravines of peeling stucco and open sewage with overpopulated floors of humanity stacked upon humanity. After what seemed like an obstacle course of stairs and hallways, we came to our target destination: a small textile factory with an eager owner waiting to meet me. But not me, actually. He was there to meet Justin Dillon, textile buyer from Santa Monica, California, interested in new textiles for his import/export business. That was my cover. What the owner didn't know was that my colleagues and I had hidden cameras on us. We were investigating his textile factory for child laborers.

He welcomed us inside, proudly draping one of his prized textiles across his arms, inviting me to draw my fingers across the detailed beading and stitching. I played along and chatted him up, doing my best acting while trying not to react to the children all around, bent over a stitching table. Next to the table were a few piles of torn rags for the children to sleep on at night. I thanked the vendor and walked out as my partner gave me a look that confirmed that we'd captured the evidence needed for our raid the next day.

The recon from yesterday is what led us here. The kids are still in work mode, so we are helping them to stand up and quickly walking them out of their prison. There are no tears of joy. No hands in the air. Just the sad compliance of children trained to do what we ask because that's all they've ever known. We remove them from the building, lead them into vans, and start driving them to a safe house. As our car is driving behind their van, one child looks back at us and gives us a thumbs-up. That's the first sign of freedom we've seen all day.

Once at the safe house, I sit down with the kids to ask them questions and play with them a little. They are as filthy as chimney sweeps, hungry, and wearing tattered clothing. We bring them some food and watch as remnants of smiles return to their faces. The safe house has given each of the kids a number, which is safety-pinned to their shirts in order to identify them temporarily. Number nine bears a slight grin and the same type of shy mannerisms I often see on my own boy. I ask him his name through an interpreter. His name is John and he is about ten. He was kidnapped from Nepal three years earlier, and his parents had no means or rights to retrieve him. I ask him some more questions. "Do you want to see your mommy and daddy?" He nods. "Have you ever been to school?" He shakes his head no. "Would you like to go to school?" He nods his head with a look of guarded optimism. Throughout our exchange John keeps mentioning to me that he is a professional at what he does, a line taught to him by his master. I ask John one last question. It's similar to the question Common asked the restavek girl in Haiti. It's the one question that most kids I've met have an answer for. It's the question that gets at their rock dreams and soul dreams. "Is there anything you would like to be when you grow up?" John puts his head down to think for a minute, draws a half circle in the dirt with his bare foot, then looks up at me with his big, brown eyes and says, "I want to do what you do."

THE PERMANENCE OF CHANGE

John understands more about the power of change at ten years old than I ever will in a lifetime. Within the first hour of John's newfound freedom, he already wanted to free others. Change is kinetic. The change we make in ourselves and in the world will move into and onto others, just like the airborne riot virus I caught at the Oakland Coliseum. Our selfish plans to change the world are not static, but kinetic, constantly moving. When we reach out to reduce the poverty of means for another, we increase that individual's ability to do the same for someone else. We are not the saviors. We are solutionists investing ourselves in the permanence of change.

Change in the twenty-first century, both internally in our souls and externally in the world, will operate more like a platform and less like isolated events. Most of the disruptive changes and advancements we are seeing in the early twenty-first century are all being built on platforms. Facebook, Google, Amazon, Uber, and Airbnb are just a few examples of platforms whose value is due to the input of their users. The social connections on Facebook, the knowledge on Google, the products on Amazon, the rides on Uber, and the rooms on Airbnb all come from outside contributors who offer their relationships, knowledge, products, cars, and rooms to others on the platform. The era of the platform represents a complete disruption from the one-to-many commerce and connection model of the twentieth century. I believe we are seeing a similar platform model emerge in the *world-changer* sector. The access of people with a poverty of meaning (us) to participate in the reduction of the poverty of means is wide-open. Changing the world is now open-source and not closed off to a one-to-one model where our only option is a donor-to-charity exchange. We no longer need to feel qualified or granted access to participate in some of the world's greatest challenges. We are still in the early days of this platform, but the examples of the social change hackers mentioned in this book, along with the steps I have laid out, will give you access to this incredibly fast-growing network of change.

I hope this self-help-others manual has helped to reveal a larger narrative in your life. I hope you understand how very important your rock dreams and soul dreams are to the rest of us. I hope you know that you were born for your life and there are still many more stories yet to be written. I hope you have begun to understand just how much the world needs you. You have everything you need to find big purpose in your life by changing the world; even your own personal challenges can become an asset in this pursuit.

Alchemy was a tradition from the Middle Ages that tried to turn base metals into gold. There is an alchemy at work in our lives when we allow our base and banal events to heat up in the crucible of changing the world. We can make gold for others out of our failures and spin our disappointments into meaning.

I want you to live. You were made to live a life much bigger than your rock dreams. You were made for your soul dreams and made to find out what the world needs from you. You now have what you need to start acting on your plan to change the world. I wonder what you will do. I wonder how many lives you will impact. I wonder what new idea you will come up with. I wonder what problem you will solve. We are ready for you. You were born for this. Now go find your riot.

ACKNOWLEDGMENTS

I want to thank my wife, Danelle, for loving me through all the chaos and wonder. You are truly the better half. My son, Valentine, for showing me how to be brave, how to play, and how to look at life one minute at a time. My mother, for grace under pressure. My father, for turning hustling into beauty for others. My brother, Jarrett, for being a constant encouragement. My sister, Robin, for being a second mom. My brother, Bob, for protecting me. My brother, Scott, for being on my side.

Elbert Paul, for being the most distilled version of peace on earth I've ever met. Stephen Beck, for pragmatic love and friendship. Scott and Kelli Walchek, for being our champions. My friend and constant comaker, Shadd Williams, for producing my life. My brother, Sean Glover, for being a self-hidden tower of justice.

My staff and leadership at Made in a Free World, for believing and working toward the impossible. Mrs. Phyllis Goady, for teaching me how to diagram sentences.

My agent, Roger Freet, for convincing me to write this. My editor, Webster Younce, and the entire team at Thomas Nelson. Dr. Cornel West, for declaring me an official bluesman.

Suzanne Sands, for pushing water uphill with me for over a decade. Victoria Ward, for your faithfulness to justice. Alison Kiehl Friedman, for your indefatigable passion for justice. Dr. Jean Baderschneider, for your leadership. Randy Newcomb, for your support. Amy Lucia, for your encouragement. Amy Nyquist, for your patience. Erik Lokkesmoe, for your friendship. Jennifer Benthin, for reading my very early draft.

For every manager, agent, advocate, friend, and colleague who tolerated my nonlinear ways and gave me the courage to keep running. I love you all.

ABOUT THE AUTHOR

A professional musician turned filmmaker and social entrepreneur, Justin Dillon is founder and CEO of Made in a Free World, an award-winning platform that brings together consumers, organizations, and businesses to disrupt the $150 billion business of human trafficking. Justin's leadership as a "practitioner of change" has awakened a global movement of more than 30 million, improved laws, and freed thousands of slaves. He has advised the United Nations, the US State Department, the White House, the Vatican, Fortune 500 companies, and more on issues of innovation and social justice. He is the director of influential films—with voices such as Cornel West, Questlove, Amber Valetta, and Nicholas Kristof—including *Call+Response* and *Common Dreams* for CNN. Justin has been featured by the *New York Times, Washington Post, Wall Street Journal, Forbes, USA Today, Fast Company, Vogue, Huffington Post*, CNN, CBS, FOX, MSNBC, NPR, *Cosmopolitan, Glamour, Rolling Stone*, and more. His work has received many high-profile accolades including a Cannes Lion Award and a SXSW Interactive Innovation Award.

NOTES

CHAPTER 1: FIND YOUR RIOT

1. Whenever one is using sound gear once graced by Led Zeppelin, one must sing the obligatory "We come from the land of the ice and snow."
2. Paul Klee, *Creative Confession and Other Writings* (Mustang, OK: Tate, 2013), Kindle edition.

CHAPTER 2: I HAVE A SOUL DREAM

1. Luis Buñuel, *My Last Sigh: The Autobiography of Luis Buñuel*, trans. Abigail Israel (New York: Vintage, 2013), 92.
2. I never wore a sequined unitard, and I deeply regret that I never released any doves.
3. Barack Obama, "Remarks by the President to the Clinton Global Initiative" (lecture, Sheraton New York Hotel and Towers, New York, NY, September 25, 2012), https://www.whitehouse.gov/the-press-office/2012/09/25/remarks-president-clinton-global-initiative.
4. More than thirty million people have used it to understand their direct connection to slavery and to adjust their buying habits.
5. Madeleine L'Engle, *Walking on Water: Reflections on Faith and Art* (New York: Convergent, 2001).
6. He did look into it. See Apple's Supplier Responsibility 2014 Progress Report, http://images.apple.com/supplier-responsibility/pdf/Apple_SR_2014_Progress_Report.pdf.
7. Rev. Dr. Martin Luther King Jr., "Remaining Awake Through a Great Revolution: Commencement Address for Oberlin College" (Oberlin, OH, June 1965).

A POVERTY OF MEANS

.d today consistently ranks as one of the most violent and
.expensive cities in America.

ford English Dictionary, s.v. "means."

'Overview (Poverty)," WorldBank.org, October 2, 2016, http://www
.worldbank.org/en/topic/poverty/overview.

4. "Drinking-Water" (Fact Sheet), World Health Organization,
November 2016, http://www.who.int/mediacentre/factsheets/fs391/en.

CHAPTER 4: DON'T TRY TO SAVE THE WORLD

1. "Forced Labour, Human Trafficking and Slavery," International
Labour Organization, 2016, http://www.ilo.org/global/topics/forced
-labour/lang--en/index.htm.

2. Martin Luther King Jr., "Letter from a Birmingham Jail," Martin
Luther King, Jr. Research and Education Institute—Stanford
University, April 16, 1963, http://okra.stanford.edu/transcription
/document_images/undecided/630416--019.pdf.

CHAPTER 5: A POVERTY OF MEANING

1. Walt Whitman, "O Me! O Life!" from *Leaves of Grass* (1892), Poetry
Foundation, https://www.poetryfoundation.org/poems-and-poets
/poems/detail/51568.

2. Carl G. Jung, *Modern Man in Search of a Soul*, trans. W. S. Dell and
Cary E. Barnes (New York: Harcourt Brace, 1933), 66.

3. Viktor E. Frankl, *Man's Search for Meaning* (Boston: Beacon Press,
2006), 76–77.

4. See also Roy F. Baumeister, et al, "Some Key Differences Between a
Happy Life and a Meaningful Life," in *Positive Psychology in Search
for Meaning*, ed. Dmitry A. Leontiev (New York: Routledge, 2015),
59. The study has been reprinted here in its entirety.

CHAPTER 6: YOUR NEEDS? WHAT ABOUT MY NEEDS?

1. Séverine Autesserre, "Dangerous Tales: Dominant Narratives on the
Congo and Their Unintended Consequences," *African Affairs* 111,
no. 443 (2012): 202–22.

2. Students of Maslow's hierarchy of needs, not Maslow himself, created
the pyramid structure.

3. Jennifer Robison, "Happiness Is Love—and $75,000," Gallup,

November 17, 2011, http://www.gallup.com/businessjournal/150671
/happiness-is-love-and-75k.aspx.

4. "The Economic and Social Cost of Illiteracy," World Literacy
Foundation, August 24, 2015, https://worldliteracyfoundation.org
//wp-content/uploads/2015/02/WLF-FINAL-ECONOMIC-REPORT
.pdf.

CHAPTER 7: BREAD AND CIRCUSES

1. Juvenal, "Satire X—The Vanity of Human Wishes," trans. A. S. Kline,
Poetry in Translation, http://www.poetryintranslation.com/PITBR
/Latin/JuvenalSatires10.htm.

2. Hungry + angry = hangry.

3. Juvenal, "Satire X."

4. Kevin McSpadden, "You Now Have a Shorter Attention Span Than a
Goldfish," *Time.com*, May 14, 2015, http://time.com/3858309
/attention-spans-goldfish.

5. Ben Cosgrove, "The Invention of Teenagers: LIFE and the Triumph
of Youth Culture," *Time.com*, September 28, 2013, http://time
.com/3639041/the-invention-of-teenagers-life-and-the-triumph
-of-youth-culture.

6. Yuval Atsmon, Vinay Dixit, and Cathy Wu, "Tapping China's
Luxury-Goods Market," McKinsey.com, April 2011, http://www
.mckinsey.com/business-functions/marketing-and-sales/our
-insights/tapping-chinas-luxury-goods-market.

7. Richard Verrier, "China Is on Track to Surpass U.S. as World's
Biggest Movie Market by 2017," *Los Angeles Times*, November 5,
2015, http://www.latimes.com/entertainment/envelope/cotown/la-et
-ct-china-growth-20151105-story.html.

8. See Jean M. Twenge and W. Keith Campbell, *The Narcissism
Epidemic: Living in the Age of Entitlement* (New York: Atria, 2009).

CHAPTER 8: ALTRUISM (AND OTHER LIES WE TELL OURSELVES)

1. Almudena Toral, "History of Violence: Struggling with the Legacy of
Rape in Liberia," *Time.com*, April 30, 2012, http://world.time.com
/2012/04/30/history-of-violence-struggling-with-the-legacy-of
-rape-in-liberia.

2. Please don't come up to me and say, "I finished half of your book."

3. Jordana Cepelewicz, "What's Your Real Motive for Being Altruistic?"

American, March 3, 2016, http://www.scientificamerican
   .rticle/what-s-your-real-motive-for-being-altruistic.
   R. Rogers, "Reinhold Niebuhr's *The Self and the Dramas of
   .story*: A Criticism," *Pastoral Psychology* 9 (1958): 15–17.
   Lori Kozlowski, "Impact Investing: The Power of Two Bottom Lines,"
   Forbes.com, October 2, 2012, http://www.forbes.com/sites
   /lorikozlowski/2012/10/02/
   impact-investing-the-power-of-two-bottom-lines/#67bdd2c82a47.

6. "ILO Says Forced Labour Generates Annual Profits of US$ 150
   billion," International Labour Organization, May 20, 2014, http://
   www.ilo.org/global/about-the-ilo/newsroom/news/WCMS_243201
   /lang--de/index.htm.

7. Aristotle, "Book II," *Nicomachean Ethics*, trans. W. D. Ross, MIT.
   edu, http://classics.mit.edu/Aristotle/nicomachaen.2.ii.html.

8. Kate Vinton, "Seat of Power: Inside Michael Milken's Pine-Paneled
   Office," *Forbes.com*, April 20, 2016, http://www.forbes.com/sites
   /katevinton/2016/04/20/seat-of-power-inside-michael-milkens
   -pine-paradise/#9291fe47300a.

9. Banksy, Twitter post, October 22, 2016, https://twitter.com
   /therealbanksy.

CHAPTER 9: A SPOONFUL OF FICTION

1. "Worst Forms of Child Labour [as defined by Article 3 of ILO
   Convention No. 182]," International Labour Organization, http:
   //www.ilo.org/ipec/facts/WorstFormsofChildLabour/lang--en/index
   .htm.

2. Robert McKee, *Story: Style, Structure, Substance, and the Principles
   of Screenwriting* (New York: HarperCollins, 1997), 13.

3. William Blake, "The Chimney Sweeper: when my mother died, I was
   very young," Poetry Foundation, https://www.poetryfoundation.org
   /poems-and-poets/poems/detail/43654.

4. William Blake, "The Chimney Sweeper: A little black thing among
   the snow," Poetry Foundation, https://www.poetryfoundation.org
   /poems-and-poets/poems/detail/43653.

CHAPTER 10: YOU WERE BORN FOR THIS

1. "Strange Fruit" written by Lewis Allen.

2. https://www.bls.gov/news.release/nlsoy.nr0.htm.

CHAPTER 11: DON'T WAIT FOR PERMISSION

1. Mark Dummett, "King Leopold's Legacy of DR Congo Violence," February 24, 2004, BBC.org, http://news.bbc.co.uk/2/hi/africa /3516965.stm.
2. Magic lanterns were the PowerPoint of the early twentieth century. They looked like steampunk slide projectors.
3. A *working document* is a type of technical report that is a work in progress, a preliminary form of a possible future document. Does that sound productive?

CHAPTER 12: HIT YOUR MONEY NOTE

1. Corky was actually Shadd, who went on to help write and produce *Call + Response* and just about every other film project I did. Clearly Corky and I made a soul connection at a young age.
2. Simon Sinek, Twitter post, August 28, 2013, https://twitter.com /simonsinek.
3. "Steve Jobs: 20 Best Quotes," ABCNews.com, October 6, 2011, http:// abcnews.go.com/Technology/steve-jobs-death-20-best-quotes/story ?id=14681795.

CHAPTER 13: WIN AT LOSING

1. J. B. Rotter, "Generalized Expectancies for Internal Versus External Control of Reinforcement," *Psychological Monographs: General and Applied* 80, no. 1 (1966): 1–28.
2. Five Before Midnight Publishing, ASCAP 2005.

CHAPTER 14: PRACTICE THE ART OF CHANGE

1. Thomas L. Friedman, *The World Is Flat* (New York: Picador, 2007), 279.
2. William Shakespeare, *Hamlet*, act 3, scene 2, lines 222–30.

CHAPTER 15: SOLUTIONISTS OF THE WORLD UNITE

1. Theodore Roosevelt, *Theodore Roosevelt: An Autobiography* (New York: Da Capo, 1985), 350.